Spir

Journal of a Medium

Lynn Quigley

First Published and Printed in the UK

Spirits In The Sky

Journal of a Medium

Lynn Quigley

Published by
J & L Quigley
P.O Box 122
Penmaenmawr
LL30 9AJ
UK

Copyright © 2008 by: Lynn Quigley

First Edition, 2008
ISBN 978-0-9534946-4-4

Published and Printed in the UK

Dedication

I dedicate this book to you the reader.

It is my celebration of the continuing Life -
Teachings – Guidance – and – Unconditional Love
Of my Spirit Guides

SILVER CLOUD.   **WHITE CLOUD.**

BUFFALO.   **WOLF.**

Epigraph

"Death itself is a return Home – but as we grow – our Home changes – the distance changes – we have to keep going further, further Home.

We do not know where our next Home will be. The passage of time takes us to our next Home."

Kato
(extract from Chapter Four)

"The power of the individuals – is in the uniting of the individuals. One thought – one hope – one plea.."

Silver Cloud
(extract from Chapter Eight)

"Those of us outside your Universe, wish you to know that we are there to help and assist, and that the visual aids that we have – show us that the planet Earth is indeed, in need of help and assistance. This is why we come – to aid the planet Earth, so that it can continue its' path within it's own solar system, which, in turn, aids the path of other planets in similar solar systems."

Peter
(extract from Chapter Eleven)

Contents

Acknowledgements

I wish to thank all those readers of "More Friends Than You Know" who have taken the time and trouble – to contact me. You have all been so generous in your comments, telling me how much you "got out of it" - how you have "enjoyed it" and how - by reading it – you have found "answers".

I am humbled by your responses.

Your responses, together with the never-ending pile of notebooks, have spurred me on to now complete "Spirits In the Sky."

I thank all those in Spirit who have channelled through me and given me the contents of my notebooks.
The greatest gift I can give to you – is to share your communication.

Finally – I thank my husband John.
Once again, you have supported, encouraged, edited and published this book.
Without you, your never- ending patience – and your ever-growing computer skills – there would be no "Spirits In The Sky".

Love you lots.
Lynn.

Foreword

Spirits in the Sky is a book absolutely full of communication from Spirit. It's one of a number of books written by Lynn Quigley, who over the years has become well known as, the "Mediums, Medium" – her link with Spirit being so clear and precise that other mediums and healing channels worldwide, seek her out for the clarity and guidance, of her channelled advice.

In writing it, Lynn honours a contract she has with Spirit to deliver their message in as direct a way as possible, to those who are ready to hear it, and their message goes far beyond proof of continuance of life after death.

Picking up quite literally the day after the previous book ended, the range, spectrum and depth of communication within "Spirits In The Sky" is at times simply, mind blowing. From the four-year-old child telling us, one minute about growing up in the Spirit world, and then asking us the most profound questions about children dying here in the physical world - to the deepest philosophical communication about the nature of our very being and place within the universe – punctuated at times by a visiting Inca Spirit with a grudge against God for "betraying" his people. The range of communication is truly remarkable – the messages, many and varied.

In her first book of the series, "More Friends Than You Know", Lynn wrote about the development of her natural communication skills with the world of Spirit.

The result was a down to earth, inspirational, moving and frequently humorous story of Lynn the developing medium. The story of a young girl growing up into adulthood with all the joy, happiness, heartache and pain that physical life brought - interspersed within the book was a story of early Spiritual awareness and a totally honest account of the method Spirit used in training Lynn to work the way she does, with her channelling, spirit release/rescue, healing and "day to day" mediumship.

"More Friends..." was so well received by readers in many countries, the comments and feedback so positive that there is a waiting list for "Spirits In The Sky"

As one reader said;
"The mix of Joy, tears and wonderment makes this book a must for your bookshelf..."

And echoed by many others;
"...it's as if Lynn is sat opposite me and talking to me personally..."

In continuing to share her story, her journey, and the techniques and communication given by Spirit, Lynn has devoted a year of her life to extracting and compiling information from the transcripts of many hundreds of hours of sittings and direct Spirit communication, and, with her own special style of writing created this brilliant book "Spirits In The Sky".

In writing this book for you, Lynn re-visited all of the experiences – happy, sad, painful and joyful - as she travelled back through a lifetime of personal memories and some four years of notebooks from the 1990's.

As with her other books Lynn writes as she lives her life – "Spirits In The Sky" is a book, not only written from the Heart but written from the Soul too.

It is Soul level communication she shares with you in her usual open, refreshingly honest and down to earth manner – she tells it, "as it is" with, compassion, integrity and lots of humour.

No matter how much I personally understand the workings of Spirit, Lynn's communication skills still amaze me. Every day that goes by, her insight, guidance, love and understanding help me personally, and many others move forward through this life, and I consider it a privilege as well as a pleasure that we travel this path together – Lynn, as well as her work, is truly a gift from Spirit.

John Quigley

Preface

May 2007.

Hello.

As you join me in this part of my story, the date is the 18th October 1994.
I have met my new doorkeeper (my protector and the protector of visiting Spirits) whose name is Buffalo, and my new guide – Silver Cloud – both Native American Indians. I have been working and training with them for 3 months.

During those 3 months, Buffalo and Silver Cloud have urged and encouraged me, to raise my inner vibrations, in order to make the communication clear and precise.
The continuous practice of raising my vibrations, had led me to a "room" in which I met with Buffalo and Silver Cloud.

I will be referring to this work place, as "my place", throughout this book. I will also be making references to – "raised vibrations" and "returned to my chair".

These phrases have been explained in my first book "More Friends than you Know" – but for those who have not read it – I will now use the same text in order to explain.

To those of you who have read it before – you may be glad for the reminder.

My Place;

In order to speak with, and hear Silver Cloud, I found that it took longer for me to tune in to him and I noticed that whilst we had been communicating, we seemed to be in a room – a space that was very brightly lit.

The next day – pushing my vibrations upwards, I found myself in this same room. Silver Cloud was standing in front of me, with Buffalo in his usual place – in front and to my left. Silver Cloud looked towards a door, which I hadn't noticed. The door was placed in front of me and to my right, in the back wall of the room.

*"Buffalo will open the door. They (*visiting Spirit) *will come and stand by me and speak – this is for as long as the three of us are together"*.

I thought that this was brilliant – a room where we could all meet, a room where we were protected, a room that was so bright, it made me squint, even with my eyes shut. A place where, energetically, we would all meet, and a place towards which, I could aim my vibrations. I knew that having merged with its vibrational energy once, my body would remember the frequency, enabling me to visit again.

I felt very fortunate, to have Buffalo and Silver Cloud as my teachers. Their attention to detail – along with clear instruction was very welcome and reassuring. I have always responded to clear and precise language, never being one to enjoy, as others do, flowery language as found in some poetry – such words just go "over the top of my head".

I have never understood why some people use twelve
words – when three would suffice!
(More Friends Than You Know. P175/176)

Raised vibrations;
The act of raising vibrations is a disciplined task which
entails;
Sitting and calming myself – clearing or ignoring those
everyday – often mundane - thoughts that run through
my mind. Grounding – feeling my connection with the
earth energies. (I was still using the root visualization).
Asking for protection from my doorkeeper – and NOT
proceeding until I see, feel, or sense my doorkeepers'
presence, agreement and readiness.
(More Friends Than You Know. P201)

By now, the daily evening sessions began at 11pm; this
allotted time allowed for distant healing to be done at
10pm, plus the all-important cup of tea afterwards.
These sessions, depending on my ability and the
number of "visitors" combined with the length of the
communication – could last for up to 4hrs.
To this day, my preference is to work in the early hours
of the morning.

I must point out here that in order to receive his
communication, it took me a few minutes to align
myself with his vibrations. Each individual Spirit
energy vibrated slightly differently than another;
feeling to me, as though they were either very close, or
further away from me. Also; the personality of each
individual shone through their vibrations. The length of
time it took me to communicate with them, depended
on my physical reaction to that personality; just as in
the physical world, there are some people I judge it, to
be easy in their company, and some, I do not.
(More Friends Than You Know. P205/206.)

Returned to my chair: means.
Thanking Spirit for their protection, guidance and communication. Lowering my vibrations by closing down my chakras and grounding the energy.
Grounding until I know that I am re-connected to the earth – this can take more than one attempt.

During the narrative, I will use these phrases, almost like a "post script", as if they are unimportant – that could not be further from the truth.
(More Friends Than You Know. P201)

Returning to my chair allowed me to relax and clear the energy of the last communication, it allowed John and I to discuss the communication if we wanted to, and, it was a further opportunity to have another cup of tea and a cigarette for me. Clearing the energy is a very important exercise for me, as this allows me, to not only clear my energy field, but my mind – ready to give total concentration to the next Spirit.
(More Friends Than You Know. P220.)

Grounding.
My first grounding experience, had been assisted by a healer, who had instructed me to sit in a chair with my feet flat on the floor, and imagine tree roots coming up from the ground and into my feet.
(More Friends Than You Know. Ch 6).

This simple technique was still my way of grounding myself, at this time. The necessity to ground myself was a daily occurrence, which enabled me to practice raising my vibrations.
Silver Cloud had also grounded me, by laying his hands on my feet, as indeed, my guide William, who preceded Silver Cloud, had done.

Grounding is so important! We must take responsibility for it! If someone were to open their charkas and raise their vibrations without the discipline of grounding – then they would soon feel the ill effects, which can be numerous.

So I hope that I have set the scene. I am to be found grounding myself. Asking for Buffalos' protection – and not "going" until I receive it.

Raising my vibrations.

Going to my place.

Receiving communication.

And returning to my chair.

These sessions took place every night – starting at 11pm (after my husband and I had completed our distant healing sessions) - and they could last up to four hours. John was always present for the evening sessions. All these sessions were taped.

There is one item that musn't go unmentioned, and that is a feather. This feather was given to me by Silver Cloud, and it is kept on the red sand floor of "my place".

My husband John, who at that time, was working in our own photography business, was also a practicing spiritual healer. Work he continues to do, as well as working as a counselor, dowser and hypnotherapist - tutoring in those subjects.

Another love of my life, is music. I grew up in a household in which music was played and singing was "in the blood". Both my parents had sung in a choir – I had sung in the school and Methodist Church choir (as my sister does to this day), and both my sister and I had

had piano lessons. My Uncle Armon – who had died during the 2nd world war – had played the Church organ and as I was growing up – and attending Church 3 times on a Sunday – I had had the opportunity to sit next to the Church organist, whilst she practiced on the pipe organ, in preparation for that evenings service.

So music is a very important part of my life. I love many types of music, from classical to rock and roll.

Music has also played it's part in my Spiritual development – aiding me to "raise my vibrations". Spirit have also used music to communicate with me.

I have always become "hooked" onto one piece of music, or song – and will play it repeatedly – until I have "finished" with it – finished working with it's energy or until it's message/vibration has reached me.

During those 3 months, working with Silver Cloud, I had begun to channel, not just for myself and John – but for two other people. One person was a healer and the other was a dowser.

All these guides were introduced to the reader in "More Friends Than You Know" and it is my wish to begin "Spirits In The Sky", as a continuence of that book.

With that in mind, and not wanting to interrupt the flow of the narrative too much, with lengthy explanations of who these guides are - I have decided to list the names of these guides now. I will of course, expand on detail where necessary

I hope that you find this a simple solution to those "whos who" questions.

To those of you who have a copy of "More Friends Than You Know", I have inserted the relevant chapters in italics.

Silver Cloud *(ch 11)* My guide.

Silver Cloud is a Native American Indian Chief of the Cheyene race.

He appears, to me, as an elderly man, (although I have seen and worked with him – when he chose to appear as the younger Silver Cloud). He is dressed in white skin, fringed - trousers and top – and always wears a full headdress. Silver Cloud is – generally speaking – very calm and ALWAYS - very precise in his communication.

He has been teaching me to work as a medium – using clear, step by step, instructions. He knows me far better than I could possibly know myself – and his encouragement and directions are invaluable, and will remain so – for as long as I continue in this work.
Having said all that – the one thing that I value most highly – is to sit with him - neither of us speaking – but just BEING together. It is during those times – that I understand just what PEACE is.

Over the years – he has shown tremendous compassion and care – not only for me – but for people that I have come into contact with.

Using his carefully chosen words – his wit – and his sense of fun – he has gently walked with me, as I move forward in my life.

———

Buffalo (*ch 11*). My doorkeeper.

Buffalo is a Native American Brave of the Sioux race.

Buffalo appears to me, as a man between the ages of 40yrs – 50yrs. He wears brown skin trousers and he is bare chested but wears a waistcoat. He has a few feathers attached to a band, that hang down the right side of his head, and a couple of feathers, which stick up, at the back of his head. His face is dark – with a square chin – and he has a long nose. Buffalo is a strong, forthright character – who assisted me as I was learning to "raise my vibrations" – literally pulling me upwards into the realm of the Spirit world.

He described our relationship, during the early days of our meeting, – with the following words:
"We shall be like the sparks from the same fire."

Buffalo is much more than my protector – Buffalo engages me in conversation, thus teaching me to communicate. He instills discipline into my work – via that communication, and the manner in which it is delivered. Buffalo is a very big "spark" in my life.

––––––

White Cloud (*ch's 12&14*) Silver Clouds' guide.

White Cloud is a Native American Indian Chief of the Iowa race.

Silver Cloud introduced White Cloud to me, as "his guide". Silver Cloud further explained, that White Cloud had been his (Silver Clouds) guide, both in the physical realm, and now, within the Spirit realm.

White Cloud has shown an interest in my progress and initially – Silver Cloud has channeled White Clouds words – to me.

As my vibrations are becoming finer, higher and quicker – I have increasingly, been able to channel the words of White Cloud, myself. White Cloud always has a large glowing aura around him.

_____

Mr Shush (*ch's 11&13*) My guide.

Shush is not his proper name - I didn't catch all of his name the first time I heard it - consequently – and with his permission – I have always called him Mr Shush.

Mr Shush, is an elderly, white haired gentleman – who I initially met, during my dreams. We would spend time talking about all sorts of things.

Now, he visits "my place" and advises me on the use of tissue salts and is a kindly, wise and guiding light.

_____

Katamoro (Kato*) (ch13)* Johns' guide

Katamoro's arrival was for me, quite scary.

Katamoro had been a Japanese Samurai Warrior and the first time I met him, he was dressed in the full, black uniform and holding a VERY big sword.

The combination of - not knowing who he was – being unable to see his face, and seeing that sword – meant that I hastily – "returned to my chair".

However, when I returned to "my place", Katamoro was dressed in - what can only be described as a white judo suit – and this time, I could see his smiling face.

Katamoro is a healing guide.

He is gentle, caring and wise.

He is an "Ancient" Spirit - who said that he wanted to be known as Kato.

———

Mr White (*ch 13*) Johns' guide

Mr White is a gentleman who works within the Spirit world as a receiver of those who pass over - and - in particular – receives those, who pass over as a result of a sudden trauma. This is work that he and John – do at night – when John is asleep.
Mr White had been a general practitioner.
Mr White is a true, old fashioned - gentleman.

———

Mr Bennet (*ch 12*) Johns' guide.

Mr Bennet is a healing guide who bounced into our lives, on the evening of 19th September 1994.
His first words were:

"Good Evening. I am Harold Bennet – Eminent physician."

He is of strong character - always very smartly dressed in a tailed suit – circa – late 1800s – early 1900s, complete with a starched collar that stands upright.
Mr Bennet has strong views, he is passionate about his work, and is emphatic – to the point of rudeness – in what he says.
Mr Bennet is a wonderful man – his energy is invigorating – his communication is direct. He has a softer side to his nature and it is then that you find – he has a dry sense of humour.
He also has a great love of jazz music – which he and John share - in the car.

Laura (*ch's 10 &13*) Works with John
Laura had been introduced to John and I - by William. William had been my first "working" guide.

At the time of introduction, Laura, then a child of 8yrs had come to say "hello" - and having greeted us – she then left. That introduction had taken place in June 1994 and during a communication from Mr White, on the 23rd of September that same year – Mr White referred to Laura, as being a helper – "a scout" – for those people who were passing over - as a result of a sudden trauma. The next time that I saw Laura (which was not long after Mr Whites' communication) – she had transformed into a young woman – in her 20s.
Laura is a gentle, caring healer.

———

Angela (*ch12*)

Angela is a little girl who came to deliver a message for her mother. She wanted her mother to know that she was safe and well, in the Spirit world. Angela is about 4yrs old, a pretty child with blonde hair. During that first meeting – she was shy, coy and quietly spoken.

———

Kylifa (*ch10*) An Egyptian guide of a dowser friend

CHAPTER ONE

SILVER LININGS AND BLACK CLOUDS

18TH October 1994. Afternoon

18TH October 1994. Afternoon

John and I were at the home of Stan – our dowser friend – he had asked me if I would communicate with his guide – Kylifah - as he had some questions that he wanted to ask. All previous communication had taken place at our house.
My notes from that day show that I had difficulty in finding "my place" and I had obviously been unsure as to whether I had the permission of Buffalo and Silver Cloud to continue in my effort to raise my vibrations.

My hesitation and uncertainty was a culmination of a variety of things:
I was not in my own surroundings were I felt safe – nor did I have the security of my favourite chair.
It was obvious that Stan expected his guide would be there – he was poised, ready and waiting, with a notebook and pen. I didn't know whether Kylifah would be there or not?
My nerves – and trying to remember all that Buffalo and Silver Cloud had taught – and expected – from me – obviously caused some delay.
All the pressure came from myself; there was certainly none from Stan nor John.

However – I did settle down and saw Silver Cloud.
He was standing with his arms folded across his body – and - was it just me, or, was he really tapping his foot up and down impatiently on the floor!

Silver Cloud said:

"I've been stood here waiting for you to come and visit. You are a child – you have a lot to learn."

Kylifah was waiting to speak to Stan and during the communication with him, Kylifah (who is Egyptian) expressed his wish - as he had done before - to continue to work with Stan, through his dowsing.
Kylifah also asked that Stan continue in his efforts to communicate directly with him, adding:

"If you listen – you will be amazed at the knowledge that comes through."

Adding:

"In many respects, the earth is in a far more dangerous place – than it has ever been before

At each turn – there are improvements to be made – great benefits to be had – through the knowledge

She (me) *can go now."*

As I saw and felt Kylifah leave – Silver Cloud said:

"You can go now"

I returned to my chair.

18th October 1994. Evening.
John and I were together for the usual evening communication session.

I knew that during the afternoon session, I had dithered and fidgeted, the session had – initially – not been as smooth and easy, as it should have. Having said that, I knew that once the communication had begun – it had flowed well.

I also knew that my hesitation, had meant that "they" had been kept waiting.

With these thoughts in my head, the first thing I asked Silver Cloud that evening, was:

"Can I ask for someone in particular, to come and communicate?"

Silver Cloud replied:

"It is all perfectly clear from where I am standing

You are in a position, where you can ask for help for someone."

Being a pernickety, annoying, type of person – I said:

"So, I can ask for someone to come?"

The reply:

"How many times do you want to be told!"

Throughout this exchange, my vibrations continued to lift. As had happened before, I realised that White Cloud – Silver Clouds' guide – was now speaking to me. I was still seeing Silver Cloud, and watching, as the words came out of his mouth – but the communication was from White Cloud.

This channelling – through my own guide – enabled White Cloud to communicate with me directly – my own vibrations – not being fine enough – at this moment in time.

White Cloud said:

"Silver Cloud is impatient – he knows he must be more patient – and wait.

Each time you devote yourself to Spirit – we will be able to work with you.
We will work with the time that is allotted.
You must find as much time as you can."

At this point, the communication reverted from White Cloud – to Silver Cloud.
Silver Cloud continued:

"White Cloud is a very wise man, and although he has been in the Spirit world for a long, long time – he has more empathy with the physical stresses.

White Cloud – approves of your nature."

The familiarity of combining my vibrations, with those of Silver Cloud, had given me the freedom to raise my vibration to a higher level, and, still channelling through Silver Cloud – White Cloud communicated once more.

"There is so much work that Kylifah sees that needs to be done – and can be done – and it is important that this work is done.
The chemical reactions and the radiation coming from the Earth – and then returning – they are returning, more powerful, than when they leave – concentrated – as they come back – doing a lot of damage."

"Dowsers have got to get into industry – they have got to make the industrialists listen, because their poisons and toxins are going into the atmosphere – and they are returning – concentrated. They must be stopped.

This is one of the major works, that Kylifah wants to do. He wants to go into industry – the waste chemical companies. This is why he wants to work with a respected dowser - but - the dowser must listen and acknowledge.

These industrialists will eventually accept that Spirit is providing the knowledge of what is happening – and the knowledge of how to amend the situation. It is only through them knowing the existence of other worlds – can they take any responsibility, in a major way – the responsibility of keeping their own world clean.

It is imperative that they know that other worlds exist – this is the key to them taking on the responsibility for the Universe.

They suppose that when their lifetime is over – they are out of it. They are not – there is another world – and so it goes on. They do not leave it behind. They take it with them – it is still their problem – still their responsibility. They cannot wash their hands.

You must pass this message on to Stanley so that he can know the magnitude of the work to be done – and the reason, as to why Kylifah is so keen to work through Stanley.

Please pass the message.
I have enjoyed the communication.
I shall leave you in the capable hands of my Brother."

Silver Cloud said:

"White Cloud needs no introduction – we are as one.
You speak to me – you hear his words.
You speak to him – my thoughts are there.

Take a break."

I returned to my chair.

Raising my vibrations once more, I saw Buffalo. He was waving to me.
As I approached him, I saw a large square package, wrapped in gift-wrap, a large ribbon had been placed around it, and that had been tied into a bow.

Silver Cloud spoke:

"I want to work with your potential. I don't want the physical part of you – but I realise that you come as a package."

As he spoke these words, I saw the ribbon un-tie and free itself, allowing the paper to fall away – revealing an ordinary cardboard box that had been hidden under it's wrapping.

"We have to unwrap the package and discard the wrapping. We have opened the package.
I was not an impatient man, in my physical life. My impatience has arisen from your spiritual development – your keenness to learn.

In my last physical life, I was of an even character and now that I am here and I know the great works that we can do – I am impatient."

6

"Through working with you, my evolvement has done a backward flip. I have found the fire of life in the physical term and I have to say – that I am enjoying it.

I am enjoying the physical contact – after many years of Spiritual learning.

I am - of course - highly evolved! I have great knowledge – but I am enjoying the physical contact, and so we will continue in this mould.

We three are a team. And now, be off and come again tomorrow – and don't be late! We will be waiting."

Although I heard Silver Cloud dismiss me, I felt as though another Spirit was waiting to speak. I was also beginning to realise that Silver Cloud had a sense of humour – most of which was at my expense and although I trusted him implicitly – I was learning that – it was always safer to wait and check again – just in case we hadn't finished the session.

I raised my vibrations again and heard:

"Fooled you. 10/10."

I was feeling really pleased with my little self. Not only had I read the situation correctly – but this was the first time I had ever scored 10/10 for anything!

Standing, waiting to speak, was Laura.

When John and I had first been introduced to Laura, she had appeared as a child and we had been surprised, when, during another of our nightly sessions – she had returned as a young woman – to say that she would be working with John.

Laura came to tell John that he would be working with children not only as a spiritual healer, but also that:

"The healing that you will be doing is on a mental level – providing guidance for children and parents, and assistance, should a passing occur."

(John is indeed – working within this field – at this moment in time).

John took the opportunity to ask questions of Laura and one of his questions was about a patient's cat that he had given healing to.

John:
"Was it you that gave the healing to the cat?"

Laura:
"The poor animal has had a traumatic life – it has lost two of its' nine lives. It is now feeling more secure.
The eczema will disappear.
I shall see the cat again – if it is not there, when you are there, don't worry – I shall find it."
As Laura left, Mr Bennet, an *"eminent physician"* (his own words) and guide of John's, came to communicate.

Mr Bennet:
"Good evening.
I would just like to say that we have much healing to do. In the meantime, we must continue on our course and we must offer our services to as many people who may require it. I felt as though I should have my chance to communicate!"

"The future is the future – we are now – and so let us remain focussed on the now. Good Evening."

As Mr Bennet said, "Good Evening" in his usual brusque manner – he turned and swiftly left "my place."

The next person to communicate that evening was Kato – John's guide.

Kato.
"I am pleased to have the opportunity of speaking with you. I would ask that you continue your efforts to communicate with me because I feel that this would be of great value. Take note of what you receive.
Laura has explained where your future lies.
This is a decision that was made a long time ago.

You will become a counsellor as well as a healer. There are many that say that one goes with the other and this is so – but – you will be given guidance in counselling – this guidance will come from Spirit – which is why I am asking you to continue your efforts to communicate now – and heighten your awareness. This is work for the future, but we need to start now. You will be a mediator between my world and your world.

I shall endeavour to aid in the communication myself.
Keep up the good work.
I am pleased to communicate.
I thank the channel.
I thank Silver Cloud.
Farewell."

Silver Cloud:
"Well, I think that went very well."

I asked if there was anyone else who wanted to communicate.

"Not at this moment in time, you may go."

John and I both said "Goodnight" to Silver Cloud, who replied:

"Ah – who can tell?"

19th October 1994. Afternoon.

When I arrived at "my place" I saw Silver Cloud, who had a black dog with him.
Although I was surprised and curious about the dog, experience had taught me that I must ignore it and concentrate on the reason that had brought me to seek Silver Clouds' advice.
I knew that John wanted to ask for guidance about a patient who had lung cancer and so I had come to ask on his behalf. This patient had undergone major surgery, which did not include the removal of the lung.

Silver Cloud.
" The lung has been stuck to the ribs – this has created an air pocket."

There is some function and recovery – but not enough.
A tiny piece has been activated by the healing.
The doctors are going to take her back into hospital.

You need a detailed explanation which can't be given now.

This dog is for you."

I asked the dogs' name.

"Dog of more sensible appearance – functional."

(This last line was Silver Clouds' humorous reference to conversations' he and I had had, about our much loved and missed Old English Sheepdog – Trampas.)

I thanked Silver Cloud for his communication and said that I would return that same evening.

Looking in my notebook, I see that there was some reason why John and I would be a little later than the usual time of 11pm and I see that I told Silver Cloud that I might be a bit late.

"I have to put up with these things! You will come as soon as you are able.
I am off – and I shall take this animal with me."

Buffalo:
"The dog is a companion, but not all the time.
He was a much loved pet in the physical – but no animal is a stray here."

Little did I know it – but those words from Buffalo would – in time – become very significant – and I would like to tell you the story now.

Some 8 or 9 months later – during the summer of 1995 – I decided, one Sunday morning – that I would creosote the fence panels that ran the length of one side of our garden. You probably know the type of fencing that I'm talking about – fence panels that slot down in between concrete posts.

Fence panels, that seem like a brilliant solution - at the time of purchase. Fence panels - that are not such a good idea when you are struggling to dig holes for the "heavier than they look" concrete posts - and all you find are stones and "half" bricks.

Fence panels – whose colour fades very quickly in the summer sun! and I'm not even going to mention the frustration of using a spirit level whilst attempting to support a wobbling concrete post!

Anyway – back to that Sunday morning.

Having decided to creosote the fence and not having any creosote, I told John that I would just "nip out" to our nearest DIY store to buy some.

I couldn't believe it! They didn't have the colour that I wanted and I presumed that I was not the only person to be galvanised into creosoting, that day.

Now, once I am on a mission – I carry on with it - and so I drove to the next town, which had TWO DIY stores.

I found the creosote that I wanted and having carefully wedged it upright in the boot of the car – I set off home.

By now, I knew that John would be wondering where I was, (mobile phones were not the norm then). Having said that – the phrase "nipping out" – covered an unspecified length of time, and this was not the first time that one of my missions had taken longer than expected.

I chose to drive home a different way than I had come, (something my Dad always preferred to do). The road - a long straight roman road - would take me through the country side that I had grown up in, and would give me a view of the church spire – alongside which, I had lived – and eventually past the school – in its' own grounds – in which I had spent 6 years.

Suddenly I heard the sound of the creosote container falling over and I looked for a convenient place to stop the car. I spied a small area at the side of the road where I could safely pull in.

I jumped out of the car and went to "rescue" the container not to mention the carpet in the boot.
Satisfied that I had firmly wedged the container again – I shut the rear door of the car (it was a 4x4) and it was as I did so – that I heard the sound of a dog barking.

I stood still, listening for the dog to bark again. The barking began, this time, it seemed to carry a more urgent note – and I knew it was very close to me. Following the direction of the sound, I crossed over the road to where there was a gate in the hedgerow. The dog barked again. I looked over the gate, and down to my right and saw a medium size, black, mongrel dog in the field, it was tied, close into the hedge, with a piece of rope.
I looked across the open field expecting to see someone – the owner - but no one was there.
I went back across the road and peered through the hedge on that side – but there wasn't anyone around.
It began to dawn on me, that this dog could have been abandoned.
I climbed over the gate and the dog greeted me excitedly. Its' brown eyes smiling at me, tongue lolling out of the side if it's mouth, it's tail wagging.
I untied the rope. The dog shook itself – as if it were glad to have some freedom and looked up at me, as if to say; "right – where shall we go now?"

That was just what I was thinking!

I looked again around the field, and shouted "hello".
Having satisfied myself that no other person was about,
I put the dog through a gap in the gate, and climbed
back onto the roadside.

I was left with no other option than to put the dog in the
back of the car, and go home.
When I got home, John was busy in the back garden.
As I approached he had his back turned towards me and
didn't seem to hear me arrive.

"I'm back" I called.
John turned - to see me standing there – a container of
creosote in one hand – and a dog on a rope, in the other.
Showing no surprise, and as cool as ever, he said;
"I wondered what had taken so long."

I quickly explained what had happened, then took the
dog indoors, to give it a drink.
There was no way of knowing how long the dog had
been in the field, but it was a hot day, and the dog was
obviously very thirsty.

Taking the dog back into the garden, our good friend
and neighbour, popped her head over the long forgotten
panel fence.

"Have you got a new dog?" she asked.

I told her the story and said that I was about to ring the
police.

"Have you got any dog food to give it? – I'll go and
fetch you two tins of mine."

My plan was to ring the police and then take the dog (at their request) to the police station. However, my neighbour was obviously more in tune with the actual response that I would receive from the police.

The policeman, having taken my, and the dog's details, and the details of where I had found it - was – unlike myself – not interested.
"Can you keep it?" he asked "We will get in touch with you if anybody asks about the dog."
And that was that.

I took the rope off the dog's collar, which had no identity disc attached to it, and he (I forgot to say that it was a "he") walked round the garden and then went back in the house and sat himself down on the hearthrug.

It was really strange to have a dog in the house again after nearly 3 years without one – but this chap made himself right at home.
He looked in good condition, if a little thin. His jet black coat was shiny and well groomed, his teeth very clean and white.
Someone had obviously loved and cared for this dog, who, in turn, was very affectionate and calm.

I wondered if maybe, the dog had belonged to an elderly lady who had died, and her family had not known what to do with him.
I wondered if someone had left him – only to return later – expecting to find him.
I wondered what, or who, would have happened, had the creosote not fallen over just as I was approaching the place where he had been left.

I wondered if Spirit had shown me the dog that I was beginning to find room in my heart for, after our last dog had been put down.
I wondered when the police would ring and how long it would be, before this dog went home.

That evening, which was phone call free – John, I and the black dog, sat and relaxed in our living room – it was as though we had lived together for years.
I began to wonder all over again and went to bed wondering what it would be like to keep the dog.

The next morning as I came downstairs I looked at the happy dog and panic began to build inside me.
My one thought was, "This dog has got to go."
I couldn't explain my change of heart, the panic and the fear – I just knew that I had to get the dog out of the house – and soon.

I explained to John, as much as I had an explanation to give – and he suggested that I rang a friend of ours who had got a "rescue" dog from a local kennel.

I rang her and as I was explaining how I had come across this dog, I could hear the panic rising in my voice. "I've got to have this dog out of the house today." I screeched at her.

"OK" she said, "I'll give the kennels a ring and get back to you."

Not long after, and true to her word, she rang to say that she would come and pick the dog up as the kennel had agreed to take him.

I had very mixed feelings as I watched the happy dog climb into yet another car. I felt as though I had let him down – he had done nothing but show affection.

I felt relief that he had gone. I felt guilty and pathetic.

About four days later, our friend rang to say that, as was their normal practice, the people who ran the kennels, had asked their vet to check the dog over. The examination and blood tests had revealed that the dog had cancer, which he must have had for some time, as it had progressed quite far.

On the vets advice, the dog had been put to sleep.

Our friend was upset and I felt guilty about getting her involved. I was sorry for, but very grateful to, the people at the kennels - sorry for getting them involved.

I was glad, yet angry, that I had been involved.

I was glad that the dog had not been left undiscovered and tied to that hedge – maybe to die a slow death.

I was angry to think that someone could have left this dog to its unknown fate.

I was glad, in a selfish way, that I had been guided to pass this dog on to someone else. The questionable manner in which I did it – is purely my responsibility.

I quickly realised that had I kept the dog – it would have inevitably died quite soon. That, would have been very upsetting and would have pushed those thoughts that I was having - those of - being ready to have a puppy again – to the back of my mind, and this last 3 years had been the longest time I had ever lived without a dog.

But overwhelmingly – I was grateful for those words of Buffalo:

"No animal is a stray here."

CHAPTER TWO

REFLECTIONS ON HEALING

I will begin this chapter with a lengthy communication from Kato – John's healing guide.
The communication refers to a patient of John's, whom I will refer to as "Mary."
If you remember – in chapter 1 – I had asked Silver Cloud about a patient of John's, (in his absence) and Silver Cloud, although giving a short answer, had said that a more detailed explanation would be given.

The following passages are the direct communication that John and I received, that same evening.

All guides are individual – just as we are –
All guides have their own opinion – just as we do –

Here follows Kato's reflections on the healing progress – thus far – for "Mary."

19th October 1994. Evening.

Kato.
"The healing on "Mary" has worked better than anticipated – she has responded well.
There is a small part of lung wall that has responded to healing. Unfortunately, the lung is in such a position – it will not function as a lung.
There is a small part where the air is coming through – air is seeping out through this healed piece. Because of what the surgeon's have done – this lung cannot inflate."

John:
"What can be done?"

Kato:
"This small piece will continue to let the air through – if it is left. It isn't harming "Mary", but it is uncomfortable."

John:
"My concern is that the doctors will put it down to deterioration and want to operate."

Kato:
"My concern also"

John:
"Is there nothing I can do or say?"

Kato:
"No. I have to say, that this shows the power of the healing energy – but obviously, the surgery that has gone on before does not allow any room for improvement."

John:
"If the healing energy has had that effect on a severely damaged lung – then it will have improved the lung that wasn't so severely damaged?"

Kato:
"Correct. She is now functioning adequately on the one – given the unfortunate circumstances."

John:
"Many people do live on just the one lung, don't they?"

Kato:

"Correct. The sensation that she is feeling can be likened to a scan healing – when before – it hurt – and now it itches. The sensation is the tiniest function of the lung – the air coming through. A thing that has been alien."

John:

"It's trying desperately hard to work – but it is restricted?"

Kato:

"Such a tiny…. If the surgery had not taken place – more recovery would have been seen. This sensation is not life threatening. This is not damaging. This is uncomfortable and I would say that, if the surgeons opt to remove this piece – then we have to accept that – we are not the one that is feeling the effect. I would suggest that we do not direct healing to that spot."

John:

"Is it alright for me to continue distant healing?"

Kato:

"Yes, we know that the problem has arisen – it is not a problem to us. The healing has been doing it's work – the effect of the healing is causing the problem now.
We did not foresee this problem and perhaps we have been remiss – but our intention with healing – is to heal those parts that are ill – diseased.
We learn as we go along.

This would normally be a time for rejoicing – unfortunately – the unfamiliar feeling, which is obviously pinpointed…"

John:
"Because the spot is so small?"

Kato:
"...has caused alarm – but without the healing received – this patient would not be in the acceptable condition that she is."

John:
"I understand that."

Kato:
"This patient would have been in hospital, with little future. We must continue, when allowed – with the healing – because the benefit received – is life.

Any more questions?"

John:
"Do I need to avoid that area?"

Kato:
"Yes. The responsibility for the condition now – of this lung – lays at the doctors feet – the surgeon.
The healing has been effective – unfortunately, we cannot discuss this with the surgeon and we feel that we must allow the surgeon to act as he thinks necessary – therefore we shall not interfere with that process.

The patient is not in danger – merely – unusual sensations.
The patient may have the strength to refuse any operation that may be offered.

This has been a difficult case – had we met the patient, prior to surgery – there would have been a great improvement on both lungs – a substantial improvement on both lungs"

John:
"There is a lesson there?"

Kato:
"Indeed – but we can only do, what we can do – given the circumstances.

The surgeons knew that this area – all be it small – was not as badly damaged as the rest – unfortunately the whole, has affected the small area. The whole has determined the future of this area, and indeed, without the surgery, we would not be having this conversation.

So, our advice is to continue with the healing – avoid the area. The healing on the functioning lung has avoided surgery and so we have that to be thankful for. I have been with her this evening – if you require – I shall spend more time absently – but I ask you – to ask.

I hope this has been of some comfort.

Good Evening."

Silver Cloud:
"Kato was eager to come to answer your questions.

There is no one else for communication. I will see you tomorrow – and do not be late."

At this point – I could feel another – unfamiliar energy about – a draught, wafting around.

Buffalo:
"We are attracting attention – nothing to fear – close down."

I "returned to my chair."

20th October 1994. Afternoon.

When I went to "my place" I saw Silver Cloud.
He was sitting in a deck chair, and, as the floor of "my place" was always covered in red sand – he looked as though he was sitting on a beach.

"I'm glad I'm here – and not there he said
I think that we could have a photograph – a likeness – in The Book."

(This was a reference to a book that Spirit had mentioned to me a couple of times – a book that I would write – a book that I ignored for 12yrs – and the book that is now, "More Friends Than You Know.")

These references to the book, really used to "wind me up." I would cringe as - what was to me - the daunting task of writing it - enveloped me - and of course, Silver Cloud was showing just what a good "wind up merchant" he could be.

"There is nothing for you to do.
Thankyou for visiting – I shall go and speak to my friends – Buffalo is busy – we shall speak later.

Off you go."

20th October. Evening.

When I arrived at "my place", Silver Cloud had a broom in his hand – the type of broom, which had twigs, attached to a thin branch.
He was busy sweeping the floor. He looked up at me, whilst still sweeping and said:

"If we are going to have visitors – we want to be spick and span.
Remember the training. We are all here."

I waited to see what would happen next, and, as I waited - I began to feel a new energy enter from the rear of "my place."
As the energy moved closer, I began to see the Spirit – it was my Uncle Arthur – one of my mothers' brothers.
Silver Cloud stopped sweeping, just as I was telling Arthur how great it was to see him and thanking him for popping in to visit me.

Silver Cloud's words came back to me:
"Remember the training."

I stood still and looked towards Silver Cloud – hopefully - showing him that I had remembered his words – and I waited – just as I respectfully waited - when a guide came to communicate.

Uncle Arthur gave, what seemed to me, to be a rather insignificant message for his daughter, my cousin.
And he ended his communication with:
*"I have seen Dinah (*my mother*), it is like old times – we are all back together again.*
I've got to go now – it's been lovely to see you – Cheerio."

I went into panic mode – my cousin knew nothing about my mediumship – what was I going to do?

Silver Cloud.
"Can you pass that message on?
Will you pass that message on?
Go and wait."

I "returned to my chair" looked towards John and said:

"I can't believe they've asked me to do this.
What am I going to say to her – how do I explain."

"Well," he replied, "You'll just have to ring her."

John has this happy knack of remaining calm in any situation – and as far as I was concerned – panic was more applicable!

I "returned to my place" to see a sign which I had seen before, the sign read:

"Closed. Gone to lunch."

You see – I was very happy to be receiving communication from Spirit – I was thrilled to have the contact with Spirit – I was glad to be able to pass the communication to those "like minded" people – where no scepticism existed. BUT – to have to explain to my cousin, who I only met at weddings and funerals – was a different matter entirely.

However, the next day, I rang my cousin - who seemed to be as surprised as I was, to hear my voice on the other end of her phone - to ask if John and I could go and visit, and we arranged to go that same evening.

On the way over to her house, I kept saying to myself:
"Well if she thinks I'm crazy – then I can't help that – I
just hope that I don't upset her."

On arrival, we were shown into the living room and
with a welcome cup of tea in front of us, my cousin, her
husband, and John and I, sat down.
I realised that my cousin was feeling "edgy", which
didn't help my own nerves, when suddenly she asked:

"Have you two come to tell us that you're emigrating?"

"Nooooh" I replied "No, we're not emigrating –
whatever made you think that?"

"Well" she said "We haven't seen each other since your
Dad's funeral three years ago - I worked it out, after
you rang – so I was surprised when I answered the
phone and asked if you could visit."
She added: "I'm glad you're not emigrating – there's
only me and my brother and you and your sister left - of
the family now."

I immediately relaxed – passing on a message from
Spirit seemed so easy - when compared to the
horrendous idea of emigrating!

I simply told her that since we had last met, I had been
learning to be a medium, and that I had come to see her
because her dad had given me a message for her – then
I gave her the message – and waited for her reaction.

Her reaction was one of relief – she explained that she
had been worrying about something and now she felt as
though she didn't have to.

This was the first time that I had had to explain my mediumship to anyone and I was relieved that the explanation and subsequent message, hadn't upset my cousin - in fact she appeared to be quite interested, and asked both John and I some questions about what we had been doing.

Spirit had tested my resolve and I realised I needed to trust "them" and their guidance, even more than I believed I did - thus far.

Also – I acknowledged the ease, with which Silver Cloud had introduced, what was - for me- a momentous occasion – without "batting an eyelid."

I vowed that the next time I saw him performing some mundane task or sitting relaxing, looking innocently at me – I would be on my guard! – Silly me!

Two days later, and still flushed with the success of passing the message onto my cousin – I was asked to do a reading by a friend of John and myself – I agreed – and went to ask Silver Cloud if it was alright to do the reading, (by which I actually meant – "will someone come and pass communication for him?") Silver Cloud answered:

"We will do it when the time is right."

I arranged with our friend, that he and his sister would come on the evening of the 30th October – in 7 days time – I was nervous and excited – but in the meantime – there was more communication to receive.

27th October 1994. Evening.

As I was raising my vibrations, to get to "my place" I saw a man, whose face had been badly damaged, and now had deep scars across it.

I wanted to communicate with him, even though Silver Cloud had not introduced him, but nonetheless – I felt that I must communicate if I could.

Because the communication was spasmodic – I asked John to dowse to confirm the communication and, although I had asked for protection from Buffalo – I also wanted John to check for any negative energy - which he was already doing.

John knows when I am happy during my communications, and he can "read", very quickly, when something strange is happening or senses that a negative energy may be about and is always ready to assist – if needed.

The gentleman in question, told me that his name was Flight Lieutenant George Anderson and explained that he had been burnt, whilst in a aeroplane – which had crashed, He was agitated and distressed and said that he was surprised that I could see him. Then he became more agitated and I too, could feel his emotions.

George Anderson then said, loudly:

"No, I can't do it."

I hurriedly asked for Buffalo and Silver Cloud to help.

I saw Silver Cloud standing in front of me and felt the energy of George Anderson, go away.

Silver Cloud said:

"They have taken him away.
Not everyone here is at peace.
He has been dragged back." (to the physical world)

Silver Cloud then explained that a woman (in the physical world) had been thinking of George, and those thought forms had brought him back into the physical world – in the same form that he had been in, when he left it. He further explained, that the woman still loved George and although she had never seen his injuries – she had imagined them after hearing of his death in a plane, that had been set alight – the injuries that George received, had been very real – and whilst he was free of his physical body now – the thought forms (including the perceived injuries) – and the love that George had for the woman – held them both within this circle of despair.

Silver Cloud added:

"This link has got to be broken – you will meet her."

To date, I have not knowingly, met, or helped, this lady – but my hope is - that she has met someone else who has helped her and George.

John and a friend – had been asked by a man who knew that they were both healers – if they could possibly help with the many ailments, from which he suffered.
Earlier that day, they had both been to visit him, in his home.

The communication that follows – is the reflections of healing, (in regards to this man) of Mr Bennet, – who, in his unique manner - expressed his views – not only on that same evening, but some 6 days later.

I have chosen to combine the two communications, as I believe they illustrate the passion, and commitment, within which Mr Bennet works.

Silver Cloud:
"Mr Bennet would be interested in taking this case on, because he has been studying the illness."

John:
"What is the illness?"

Mr Bennet:
"This is the effect of stress - on certain organs and glands.

This is absolute proof, that stress can cause these ailments. It is in the mind with him and he is causing his symptoms himself. Absolute proof!

I did research on this (when he was in his physical life) *and NOBODY believed me. We must get into the mind of this gentleman – and that is why I have been saying that You should see him and not the other.*
He (the patient) *is absolute proof of my research."*

Me:
"Mr Bennet is adamant that you see this person"

Mr Bennet:
"It is a very interesting case.
The gentleman is producing a chemical, which is being produced in his mind – not in the organs."

John:
"The endocrine system?"

Mr Bennet:

"Yes – a classic case, absolute proof that it comes from the mind – a great experiment. We will completely reverse everything by changing his mind – an absolute classic case.

Well that is my opinion. I feel that it would be very exciting to take this patient on and it would prove my point.

The other healer does not yet understand the connection of the mind with the body and he is wanting to treat the body – but it will not succeed because it is in the mind. I would be delighted to help you."

John:
"Have you been with the other healers guide?"

Mr Bennet:
"I have indeed."

John:
"So you have been in discussion with the other healing guide?"

Mr Bennet:
"It is a classic case – I have written much on the subject.

I shall withdraw. Excuse my haste.
I have been put in my place – but – it is so exciting – an absolute classic case. Good day."

Silver Cloud:
"Oh dear – Oh dear – he is so excitable.
Anyway – be off – be off."

Neither John nor the other healer had been to visit the patient yet, and on the evening of the 3rd November 1994 – during our usual evening of communication – Mr Bennet returned:

Mr Bennet:
"Good evening.
I am quite exasperated! This is an absolute classic case. Although – yes – I can work distantly – in your terms (a reference to the distant healing that John did*) – with this patient – I would love to work directly through you. There seems to be some confusion over responsibility for this client and I have made my wishes known!*

The other guide, is in the most part – in agreement, but understandably – must also honour the wishes of his channel.
I have asked him to make it known to his channel, that in the best interests of this patient – he should be handed over to my channel – but – if this is not to be – I would still like to visit distantly – but the request must come from you – I cannot go on my own free will.

This must be requested.

I did think, that we had all decided on this matter and I am in the position of not being able to assist – unless requested.

I feel that the other channel would greatly benefit from communication – direct from his guide – as the communication being received, or thought to be being received – is being mis-interpreted."

"I have realised, over the past few weeks – how important communication is – I am talking of direct communication – as this speeds up the work to be done.

I must admit, at first, I had to be persuaded – but – having communicated that first time – it is a tremendous asset to the healer – and – in my opinion – the other channel should receive, said communication.

I am told that we now need more patients and I would ask you to endeavour to acquire some. Idle hands!

I hope that this can be achieved soon in your busy schedule.

The other matter, will, I'm sure – reach a satisfactory conclusion.

I shall continue in my efforts with the other guide.
I can say no more.
I bid you farewell."

Me:
"He hasn't gone."

Mr Bennet:
"It is a classic case. I well documented - similar cases.
I feel the frustrations of the physical body returning."

Unlike healers in the physical world, who belong to professional bodies with a strict code of conduct – guides are not restricted in what they say.
The other guide, did come to communicate with his channel – through me, and his arrival was memorable, because one evening, I arrived in "my place" – to find

this particular guide – surrounded by Natives, who were drumming on large, skin covered drums.

I couldn't hear myself think – because of the noise, and energy of the drums was overpowering.

After a few seconds, the drumming ceased and the guide stepped forward. He said:

"I come with these drummers – by way of a celebration – as a gesture to Silver Cloud, Buffalo and you – it is a greeting.

I have been observing and have decided to communicate through you. I realise that you are a novice – but in a short space of time – you will be adept. I have not been persuaded to come – I come of my own free will – this is an honour for you.

I have much communication to pass and would like to feel free to communicate when necessary as indeed Kato has the same honour.

This will be discussed with Silver Cloud.

I will leave now.

I thank Silver Cloud.

I thank the channel.

I shall return."

Silver Cloud:

"He is a most respected and honourable guide and I shall discuss with others – his request.

I am pleased that he has chosen my channel.

Go – but return."

When I returned to "my place" Silver Cloud said:

"You will be a dual channel – working both with those who merely need communication from loved ones – and guidance – and those who are working with guides – their own personal guides – but who also need guidance.

The guides will use the same channel – if satisfactory – and you WILL, be satisfactory.

I feel, that when we are dealing with those people who are receiving "survival" evidence – that I should speak directly – to assist where I can. I shall enjoy my role – speaking through you.

When guides communicate – I shall stand back and only speak as required. The message, thoughts and philosophy that a guide has to pass to their channel is not necessarily my way of speaking – but it is not my place, to do anything, other than allow those guides to use my channel.
It is not your place to question – merely to pass.

On the other hand, we must help those loved ones who come through to your sitters, as they get flustered and in exactly the same way, as when they were in their physical life – they leave, saying – 'I wish I had said...'
So – I will assist them, and Buffalo will assist – as he has been up-graded.

Buffalo will discuss with the loved ones, what they will be saying – what messages they have to pass on – and Buffalo will guide them to pass their messages in such a way, as you can understand."

"Buffalo understands your way of thinking and we take that as a measure – all be it approximately – of the way in which a message can be received.
Buffalo will not only be the door keeper – Buffalo will be door keeper and guide – working with the loved ones. This will be good experience for Buffalo, who will move on himself – to be a guide."

I was very grateful to receive this detailed explanation from Silver Cloud, He knew, that generally, I was a person who preferred to know – to coin a phrase – "where I stood" rather than being someone who "went with the flow", although, in truth, during this period of training - I increasingly found myself swinging between both those places.

However, I was dismayed to hear him say that Buffalo would move on. I had only been working with Buffalo for just over 2 months and during our initial meetings – Buffalo had displayed feelings of exasperation, humour, care and assistance, and unfailing protection.

It saddened me – to think that I would lose all those things, and yet – how fortunate his new channel would be – to be in his care.

Nonetheless I had already experienced a guide leaving, and believe me when I say – it hurts. Buffalos' leaving would be painful - and experience also told me, that this could happen – today – next week – or in a few months time – with or without any further warning.

Following the successful visit to my cousin and her ease in response to the message I was reasonably calm on the afternoon of 30th October 1994 when our friend and his sister came to our house for their reading.

For the purposes of this narrative – I shall refer to them as "Joe" and "Sarah."

John was also present, and as they all settled into their chairs - I prepared to "raise my vibrations".

All the communication was taped.

My notebook tells me, that although I felt that the communication was disjointed, both parents came through for them and gave sufficient evidence that convinced "Joe" and "Sarah" that it was indeed their parents that I was seeing and talking to. And I noted that, "most of the communication meant something to them."

They seemed to be pleased and I felt as though I had done all that I had been asked to do – from both worlds.

Three days later, on the morning of 3rd November, John and I received a phone call from "Sarah" to say that "Joe" had been rushed into hospital – it was a shock.

"Joe" had suffered for a number of years, from ill health – most of which had been severe, serious and "on going." – but he always bounced back – continuing with his work in a very cheery, up beat manner.

John arranged to take "Sarah" to the hospital later that morning – visiting was anytime – the illness being severe. I went out to do some shopping and whilst I was out – Silver Cloud told me, that "Joe" would die.

I had to turn my energy towards the reading I was going to do later that afternoon, for our dowser friend and as I prepared to "raise my vibrations" for that sitting –I found myself transported into "Joe's" hospital room.

"Joe" was in the bed, and "Sarah" and John were sitting either side of it. As I stood and looked on, Silver Cloud quietly came and stood by my side.

Feeling as if I must stay in the room – I turned to ask Silver Cloud if I should cancel the dowsers sitting. Silver Cloud replied:

"You have finished your work with "Joe" – Go home."

I "returned to my chair" and began preparations for the sitting again. That reading took place as planned.

Later that same afternoon, after John and "Sarah" had returned from visiting "Joe" – "Sarah rang again, to say that the hospital had asked her to go back in.

John rushed round to pick her up and take her   – unfortunately – "Joe" died before they arrived.

During the early evening, John told me that when he had gone to visit "Joe" – the day after the reading – Joe had said, that because of the reading, (and presumably his conviction that his mum and dad were alive and well) that he wasn't afraid to die any more. John then told me that, as he and "Sarah"left the hospital that morning, "Joe" had told "Sarah" – that she was to look after her own life, adding, that if he died in the afternoon – she was not to go and see him – but to go and see me.

You know – I still can't totally express what I was feeling about "Joe's" death.

I was in shock – "Joe had always recovered from his illnesses, always shrugged them off and continued with his life. I felt humbled by "Joe's" words, yet I felt unable to acknowledge that I may have helped – and it scarred me to know that he had died, just 3 days after a sitting with me. I remember thinking – "if I hadn't done the sitting – then he would still be alive."

That last thought remained with me for several days.

At 11 o'clock that evening – John and I sat - as usual - for that night's communication:

When I arrived at "my place" I was surprised to find myself standing by a river. On the river, and sitting in a rowing boat, was Silver Cloud. He explained that he was relaxing and added, *"Water is very therapeutic."*

As he spoke those words, the boat drifted towards the river bank – that, I realised, I was standing on – and he climbed out.

We were now back "in my place" – with it's sandy floor and Silver Cloud began his communication.

"It has been somewhat of a trying day for you and John – but – for spirit – it has been a joyous occasion.
Another member has returned to the fold. Let me assure you that he is tired – but happy – and after a period of rest – will begin his tour of life in the Spirit world.

His loved ones, thank John – as through the healing channel – they have been able to move closer – culminating in the communication"

Silver Cloud directed these next words to John.
"You were unaware of the two-fold task which were undertaking. This is rightly so, as you cannot be privy to all the mechanics of the Spirit world. In steadfastly visiting and opening as a healing channel – you have allowed the loved ones to gather and have aided a speedy passing – which has brought much relief."

"This is an occasion for celebration and thanks.

Understandably – those left behind must travel through their personal grief and your assistance is again required – to aid the travel.

The loved ones have recognised the compassion that you have shown and are very grateful in the knowledge, that you will continue - to aid, where you can – particularly in these first days – on a practical level.

So – we must carry on – it is a joyous occasion and we would like to express our gratitude."

The communication continued – but on a different subject.

Six days later, John and I attended "Joe's" funeral.
It was a lovely, but sad, traditional service, attended by family, friends and colleagues.

As the coffin came into the church, I noticed that "Joe" and "Sarah " had quite a large family – although John and I had only met "Sarah."

As we all walked towards the burial plot, I realised that it was just a few feet away from that of my maternal grandparents – a grave that also bore the name, but not the body - of my uncle Armon.
Armon, whom, although not knowing him in my physical life – I knew - as the guiding, fun, playmate of my childhood – (although I never learnt to play the piano as well as he had) and now - as a guiding light, a helper of those "trapped earth bound" spirits, and someone that I am thrilled to see – thrilled - when I hear his words of greeting: "Hi ya kid."

But - standing near that open grave, my thoughts returned to "Joe" and his family – this was their day.

A wake had been organised, to which John and I had been invited. And it was with that thought in my head - "if I hadn't done the sitting, "Joe" would not have died so soon" - I walked into the room in which the wake took place.

"We don't need to stay too long, do we?" I whispered to John. "Well we should stay for a while" he replied.

A short time into the gathering – I began to notice that one or two relatives were glancing in my direction and as they saw me notice them – they would hurriedly look away. I began to feel very uncomfortable. Then, to my horror, "Sarah" went over to speak to them and, in unison – they all looked in my direction.
I smiled weakly at them, thinking – "Oh no – they think "its" my fault as well!"

Hurriedly, I turned to John and said: "I think we should go now", and as we turned to move, two of the relatives, a man and a woman, began to walk towards us.

We had no alternative, other than to stand still, and I well remember how the palms of my hand began to sweat.

They both smiled as they approached:

"Sarah" has let us listen to the tape that you gave them" the man said - I noticed that he had tears in his eyes – and we just wanted to thank you – the tape gave "Joe" peace."

And then they turned to John, and thanked him for the healing that he had given "Joe."

I was almost speechless, but managed to mumble a "Thankyou."

I noticed the rest of the family group, standing looking on, smiling and seeming to nod as if agreement.

I will never forget, what I consider to be, my first real reading for loved ones.
The healing and reading had impacted so many lives, and had enabled one - joyous return home – it had eased some of the pain that grief brings.

The impact that these events made on me – have stayed with me.

I learnt that – no matter how seemingly insignificant I judged a message to be – I was wrong to make that judgement. I am the messenger - the recipient and giver of the message, are the significant ones in the exchange. I learnt that – the Spirit world has plans – of which – I will be un-aware.

I was thankful – that I had been un-aware.
I learnt that – I needed to Trust in that process.
I discovered – that the word – Thankyou – when said sincerely – has a healing power of it's own.

The love and compassion – that is the Spirit world – is a truly awesome thing.

CHAPTER THREE

WOLF AT THE DOOR.

There was so much happening in my life – so much to learn, and to understand.

I was very comfortable – and happy - to be learning with Silver Cloud and Buffalo, but the thought that Buffalo would be leaving – felt like a dark cloud looming in the distance.

William – my previous guide – had left suddenly - one evening. I was totally unprepared for that "happening" – I thought that he (William was my first "working guide") and I would work together - for always, and then one night, I had been told by Armon – my uncle in spirit – to "*say goodbye*" to William.
The pain and emotion, that I had felt that night – could still reduce me to tears – if I re visited the event.

On the 30th October, Silver Cloud mentioned the subject of Buffalo's impending departure, again.

"We are a team, but Buffalo will move on – as is his right, but in the meantime, he will gain experience as a guide. I – on the other hand – will remain – as our work has only just begun – this will be a partnership. You may go."

I "returned to my chair."

I told John – during this brief intermission of communication – that I felt secure and safe with Buffalo – and didn't want Buffalo to go.

John tried to reassure me that I would like working with my next doorkeeper – but I wasn't convinced. I loved and enjoyed being with Buffalo. I loved the way he had told me off, during those early days when we were getting to know one another. I trusted him.

And - I knew he cared about me.

The communication continued when I returned to "my place."

"Buffalo is training the doorkeeper – and one day – Buffalo will introduce him – himself – before he takes his leave, but he is not ready to go yet – he thinks that being a guide is easy – even after watching our relationship growing.

He has a lot to learn and you must help to teach him.

Just wait until he has a cluster of loved ones – and he is trying to sort them into order – he will realise that the work of a guide is a thankless job – but I jest."

At this point – Silver Cloud turned to Buffalo – and asked him to stand in front of me. Turning to Buffalo – Silver Cloud said.

"Promise me, that you will introduce your brother – when the time is right – and we will have a celebration of Buffalo moving on."

Buffalo:
"I am not going yet."

Silver Cloud:
"We three have a lot of work to do – we are a team – and the new member – when he comes – will be the team. This concludes today's business – we will speak tomorrow.

Time to go. Goodbye."

I was enjoying being on this journey - on my - "spiritual path" - to coin a well worn, but misunderstood, phrase. Life was exciting and new – and the "path" allowed a certain freedom – which my "physical path" at this moment in time – did not.

It didn't really occur to me – that these two things were one and the same. I felt as though I lived in two different worlds – stepping out of one and into the other.

My "physical path" - which was a world of the self employed and an employer – was becoming an increasingly uncomfortable and difficult path to tread.

John and I had our own photographic and picture framing business, which we had built up together - after John had worked for years - as a press photographer. We were successful and respected in our field. However, a related business opportunity had come along, which we both thought would be a very good venture to be involved in.

The venture appealed to us because it was a joint venture with two friends – one of whom we had previously worked with.

It was new and exciting and potentially – very profitable. Also, we felt that very soon, John's 7 day working week could be a thing of the past. (When you are self employed – 7 day working weeks – are normal). So we made an investment, both of time and money - we took out two loans, using the house as collateral for one of them.

We had closed our picture framing business, which freed that part of one of our commercial premises up, for the new venture to move into. We moved our studio into a huge double garage, which we bought, and had placed at the bottom of our garden. I manned the phone calls for the photographic business from home and found lots of time on my hands, to devote to Spirit – I was very happy.

However, this new business had begun to struggle – alongside which – we lost a very lucrative contract we had with a business that had just been taken over by a new management. The details of the contract, I won't bore you with – suffice to say – that unfortunately - it is a reality - that – when a person – (who has fought, at all costs, for his power) - buys his way into a new business - he feels that he has no alternative, but to wield that power, and this person wielded his power in our direction. Ending in the loss of our contract.

That person admitted that he could think of no reason to remove our contract, he acknowledged that we had done good work, and provided an excellent service. In fact he said that his planned alternative to us, would cost him more money. But remove it he did.

Over time, John and I found ourselves on the "slippery slope" – the downward spiral of our finances. We lost another contract but found other work to replace it.
Finding work was never an issue with us – chasing payment for that work became a constant hassle.
I've heard all the excuses!
"The cheque is in the post".
"We haven't received the invoice – can you send another one?"
"The person who deals with invoices is off sick/on holiday".
 "The person who deals with invoices, only works on a Thursday afternoon – you will have to ring back next week."
"There is a problem with our new computer system".

I took on the challenge of chasing money with gusto – calling on the abilities I had – those abilities of persistence, consistency and generally being a right pain in the neck. I learnt – not to ring an accounts department on a Friday afternoon – they are just not interested in helping you. Far better to ring on a Monday morning. Listen to their promises of payment – and then (if necessary) you have at least, another three days to chase them – if the cheque doesn't arrive!

Despite all my efforts, and with John, still working 7days a week - cash flow problems began to mount. The bills kept coming in and interest rates kept going up. John and I weren't the only people to find ourselves in this position - the boon of the late 80s and early 90s was declining for many self employed and small business people.

It was, therefore, with reluctance, that John and I had put our house up for sale.
We knew that this would keep the banks' happy and we expected that our downward spiral would soon reverse itself. We neither wanted, nor thought, that we would sell the house.

I reflected those feelings onto all those (and there were many) perspective buyers. I had no interest, initially, in selling the house, and absolutely no interest in showing people around it. I lost count of the times when I stood in the kitchen and heard myself saying, "This is the kitchen" – followed by my silence, and I'm not going to allow myself to mention the nosy woman who started to open my kitchen cupboard doors and peer inside them!
Nor will I mention the couple who, after they began to ask questions about my ornaments, pictures and hi-fi system – were shown the door!

Neither will I speak about the CHILDREN who were under the misapprehension that they were visiting an adventure playground!
But I suspect, that if I had mentioned these things – many of you would recall similar experiences!

I had moaned to Silver Cloud about the situation, I had occasionally asked his advice on how to improve the cash flow and he had always answered me – suggesting that PATIENCE and TRUST, were the key to unlocking the spiral that I found myself in.
Trust – I believed I had – but my moaning showed that I hadn't.
PATIENCE – was a quality I knew I did not possess.
The word PATIENCE and the name Lynn Quigley, nee: Jenkins - did not belong in the same sentence!

31st October 1994. (extract from notebook)

Did vibrations – found myself walking into a house – a double fronted cottage. I was being shown round.
Silver Cloud said:
"I thought we should have somewhere nice to live."

The house is in the country somewhere.
When I asked when I would live in the cottage – I was told – March 1995. When I looked out of the back window – the garden was a bit un-kempt – winter time. There is an archway with dead flowers on it.

1st November 1994.

I had been to a meeting run by a book company and I was considering going into the business of selling books.

Extract from notebook:

Did vibrations. Silver Cloud and Buffalo are sitting at a table – there are four chairs around it. The table and chairs are on a patio, at the house that I saw before.
It is a summer day and the birds are singing.

Silver Cloud says:
"Come and join us."

I sat with them and asked Silver Cloud if he thought it would be a good idea for me to sell the books.

"They are lovely books – they are very informative – it is important that they are seen by people – they are very useful."

I told him that I didn't know what to do. He replied:
"Come and walk with me."

We walked down to the bottom of the garden, where we both leant against a wooded fence.
Silver Cloud turned to me and asked:

"What do you want to do?"

I told him I wanted to be a full time medium but in order to do that – I would need to charge a fee and I wasn't comfortable with that thought.
Silver Cloud advised me to sell the books as a part time occupation – adding, that in time – I would be a full time medium. He also said that selling the house was a good start – to future financial stability.

Silver Cloud and I returned to Buffalo who was still sitting at the table.

Silver Cloud and Buffalo left.
I "returned to my chair."

As I was "raising my vibrations" on the 3rd November
1994 – I was aware of the familiar vibrations of Buffalo
and Silver Cloud – and detected the presence of
someone else – but I did not see who it was. I said to
myself "Oh, there is someone else in my place."
The evenings' session began with communication
surrounding the death of "Joe". (As mentioned in the
previous chapter) and then Silver Cloud who was
sitting in a boat, said:

*"Buffalo has not been surprised – that you have noticed
the stranger in our midst – I did advise that this would
be the case. It is important that you accept this stranger
– as he is known to you, at this moment in time. As he is
the one who will replace Buffalo. You will not be
formally introduced – not yet. But I believe that you
have already seen him. The stranger in our midst will
continue to adjust his vibrations – and will gradually
take over the work of doorkeeper.*

*I understand your apprehension – feeling one so close –
but I ask that you be patient and assist us to do our
work. Your senses have heightened over the last few
months – so you must bear with us – as everything we
do is necessary.*

*I say again – that it is a time of rejoicing (referring to
Joe's death) – the return of a member, to the fold – It is
an indication of the work that is being done by channels
in the physical world.*
I shall return to my boat."

Buffalo continued the communication with:

"As Silver Cloud explained – the introduction of the new doorkeeper must progress through a set pattern. I myself, was introduced in this manner – but you were not aware."

Me: "Will the new doorkeeper communicate?"

Buffalo:
"You will find that when my brother finds his voice – he will communicate to the level – as we do. He has not yet found his voice – there is no need for him to speak.
We will continue in our efforts.
We will speak again."

The evening session continued with the return of Silver Cloud, Mr Bennet and Kato. (Both, healing guides of John). Then I began to feel an interference – another energy – which was blocking the communication – or rather, my ability to receive the communication. Whilst Kato was speaking – Silver Cloud interrupted the proceedings by standing in front of Kato – Silver Cloud told me to close down.
I "returned to my chair."

The next day, I asked Silver Cloud who the interference had come from, and he said *"Marauding Bandits."* As explanations go – that was enough information for me!

That evening (4th November) I "raised my vibrations" in preparation for the session. I realised that White Cloud was near – I recognised his vibrations. Feeling that I had the permission of Buffalo and Silver Cloud – I continued to raise my own vibrations in order to receive direct communication from White Cloud.

Whenever I practised raising my vibrations to a higher level than I had obtained before – feelings of dizziness and/or sickness would try to overwhelm me. But I knew that I had to work though these feelings – using grounding myself - as well as pushing and releasing, my vibrations upwards.

Experience had also taught me, that as long as I tried my best – Spirit would wait for me.

Buzzing from head to toe, and sitting in my chair within a tingling energy – I saw White Cloud. He was standing in a line, with approximately, eight other people. A phrase came into my head – as I stood still in front of them – "The Council of Guides".

Silver Cloud was now standing beside me and he said:
"*You must lower your vibrations.*"

My vibrations began to lower and I felt as though I was slipping down.

Silver Cloud:
"*I am here. The Council of Guides are interested in your progress. You are correct in thinking that these guides are your guides.*"

This last sentence, was in answer to the question – "Are these guides – my guides?" that I had silently asked myself, as I was standing before them.

Silver Cloud continued:
"*But, we must turn to our daily work. Let us not leave our heads' in the clouds.*"

I asked Silver Cloud if he had any more information about the interruption that had occurred on the previous night.

Silver Cloud:
*"The interference was not interference from this level –
but on your level.* (the earth plane)
*There was much communication and many bright lights
and I felt – as a precaution – the communication should
cease. Buffalo has given extra protection – but
nonetheless – I felt that in everyone's interest – the
communication should cease."*

If you remember, the previous nights interruption had
occurred during communication from Kato. Kato had
been talking to John about a visit John was going to
make – to a patient's house.
So it was – that during this evening session – Kato
returned, to continue his communication.
I will now share the end and beginning, of those two
separate communications – as I feel that it gives an
insight into the continuance and fluidity of a Spirit
guides' communication. Time, events and our own
physical tasks that we have to do every day – are no
barrier or diversion – within the world of Spirit guides.

3rd November 1994.

Kato.
*"Good evening.
If you take this case on – I would suggest that before
you proceed with any healing – even talking – you
dowse. The premises need cleansing. Do not open as a
healing channel until this has been done.
We as guides, cannot….."*

Silver Cloud stepped in front of Kato at this point – and
told me to close down.
However – the next evening – Kato continued his
communication on the subject of healing.

4th November 1994.

Kato.
"Good evening.
Before you open as a healing channel – even to sit and
talk – you must dowse – as the house needs cleansing.
This is a major concern for the other guide (the guide
of another healer) as he knows his channel can not do
this and does not understand – therefore, the other
channel could be affected by certain elements."

During this session, John had the opportunity to ask
Kato about a patient of his – his question was more of a
statement really – it was:

John:
"I feel that he doesn't want to get better – but he still
needs the contact with me."

Kato:
"Correct.
This is a long term healing session. He has much to sort
and come to terms with – in his mind. The healing he is
receiving is affording great benefit, in certain areas –
but he is not willing to let go – and until he lets go – the
healing will only have minimal effect.

I would suggest that the contact be more on a friend to
friend basis, as the healing energy, which is entering –
is being diffused by a very strong negative energy –
which he, himself, is creating in his mind. He wants to
continue the friendship.

This is a matter for yourself to consider. I feel that you
will continue – but you will have the choice."

"More patients will be guided to you.

That is all I have come to say. I felt we were cut short and so I have returned to complete our conversation.

I thank Silver Cloud for the opportunity to continue our conversation.
I thank the channel.
I take my leave."

Silver Cloud. To me.
"You understand the communication between the guides and the channels and you understand how important this work is. The guides are realising the benefits of communication, and the word will spread – you will be meeting so many interesting people – it is indeed a privilege.
It is rare to have two channels together – to give help and understanding to one another.
Well – that's all folks.
I thank the channel" (said in a sarcastic manner, but with a smile on his face.)
"Goodnight."

On the 6th November 1994 I was feeling down when I went to see Silver Cloud and Buffalo. My notebook doesn't reveal the reason for this, but it was probably the ongoing money hassles.

Silver Cloud said:
"*You have a physical problem – money.*
We will do what we can to smooth things – but you must have patience and faith."

"Oh no", I thought – "not the dreaded P word again!"

White Cloud was there and he asked me to approach him. As I stood in front of him, he said:

"You must have faith."

Even though I was standing within their energy – the energy that exudes love, peace and wisdom – the energy that is tangible and awesome – my little brain was saying: "It's more money that I need! You don't understand. You don't need it."

And as for the word patience – well – really!

Recovering my composure and remembering that I had a job of work to do – I calmed myself – cleared my mind of my frustration – and "raised my vibrations" ready to work.

My vibrations were lifting and lifting and I heard the name Joseph. I felt very cold down the left side of my body, then the cold moved away and went to the right side of my body. It moved again – settling on the back of my neck. Silver Cloud said that Joseph would pass philosophy for channels.

I don't recall meeting Joseph again until some five or maybe six years later. (It is in my notebooks but for the purposes of this story – I have not checked the exact date - sorry.) One day, in the late nineties, I was walking Jack and Jill in a wood near our house. Joseph was standing on the narrow pathway that led through the wood. He told me to look to the ground – and there I saw – just to my left - a staff.
A staff to *"Aid me on my journey."*
Joseph is a wise and caring man and when John and I find the resources and building for our "Centre of

Light" – which is our intent – Joseph, is and will be – the "Father of the House." Joseph wants – at his request – to be involved in the work that will be carried out there. Joseph already inhabits this centre and I visit it regularly – in the etheric realm.

Afternoon of the 7th November 1994.

When I went to my place, I found Silver Cloud, sitting on the ground by an open fire – he was toasting crumpets.
"I just wanted to know what it would be like – to retire." he said.
He stood up and taking me by the hand added: "*You need to "chill"."*
With that, he began to stride around in a circle – dragging me behind him.

"Take things in your stride – things will work out."
And we continued to stride around the room.

I was reminded of that phrase used to describe a strange day - "It's just another ordinary day at the office!"
Nevertheless – as I strided – I repeated to myself, "things will work out."

After we had stopped striding, I noticed Buffalo had appeared – and so I asked him, "How the stranger (the new doorkeeper) was?" Buffalo just shrugged his shoulders and said nothing.

I supposed that this was one of those occasions when words were not necessary!
Buffalo moved away.

Silver Cloud spoke.

"When I was a little boy, I used to sit with the other children and with the Great fathers. They would tell us of stories of long past. Not stories of heroes – but stories of ordinary people. These stories gave us hope that, one day, each one of us could rise to greatness – greatness, as seen in the eyes of someone else – not greatness as in power and wealth.

A simple person can be great without knowing. Greatness is in other peoples eyes – another's' vision.
Endeavour to be true – to give – the most important gift you can give, is of yourself.
Recognise the needs and wants of others and play your part. I grew to be a leader, not through choice but through the greatness in other peoples eyes – the greatness that they saw.
This was a heavy responsibility – one which I was forced into, by circumstance and the want of my people.
I look back on these times with some sadness, I had to lead my people into war. Many were slaughtered – I myself was spared – only to continue to lead, but the sadness must be balanced in the knowledge that the decisions I made – were made with guidance. Had those decisions not been acted on – many more would have been slaughtered.

I tell you this story to show that the path is hard. Your path will not be as hard as mine.
Your decisions and choices – not life threatening. But nonetheless – when we lead with knowledge – we can become uncomfortable.

Our reward? – when we return home."

This final piece of communication with it's reference to death – is a reference to past communication in respect of "Joe's" death.

"You will not be leading people to war.
You will both be leading people to death.
It is the same – although the death will not be at your hand. You will see flames flicker and disappear from your world. This is part of your path – but rejoice in the knowledge that you are leading people to a better world. A world in which they can function and BE.
You will both light up and distinguish.
You will need strength and guidance.
We shall endeavour to keep the path bright – there will be comic moments, but the path that you are now embarking on – is a solid, flat, straight road.
We shall all do this together – all the guides that are known to you both - and yourselves – are now on this road. Together we shall light many lives, and even in death – the flame will relight, You have knowledge of this, which is your strength to continue."

Immediately – Kato entered – and said:

"I have come to give my blessing to the words of Silver Cloud. He speaks for those who are known to you – I think it is called – team work. We have a strong team – we are united in our efforts – we go in the same direction. We have many of your years ahead of us – to light those lives.
Thankyou."

Silver Cloud:
"Go now and don't worry so much."

I "returned to my chair."

Just as on that evening - the power of this revealing insight into the thoughts and feelings of Silver Cloud, combined with his fluent communication - still leaves me feeling very humble and speechless.

7th November 1994. Evening session.

As I was raising my vibrations, I could feel the energy of a spirit, very close to me. The energy was buzzing around - very close to my body.

Feeling the presence of Silver Cloud, through the buzzing energy – I hastily asked for more protection from Buffalo. As I arrived in "my place" I saw an adult Indian Brave standing with a young Indian boy.

Silver Cloud stepped forward his arm outstretched towards the Indian Brave:

"You know Buffalo – this is our Brother Wolf.
The boy is Little Beaver. Little Beaver is visiting.
Wolf will be your doorkeeper – but not yet.
He is a novice and he is getting too close – he does not need to be THAT close!

I felt that it was time you knew his name, as this will help you to work with him. Wolf has not yet found his voice."

Silver Cloud then proceeded to clap his hands towards them – just as one might do in order to send a small child out into the garden to play and to remove them from "under your feet".

Wolf and Little Beaver left.

Silver Cloud:
"We all meet together......... PUT THAT MACHINE ON!"

I had forgotten to turn the audio tape machine on and with Silver Clouds words ringing in our ears, John and I both dived for towards the record button.

Quite rightly, Silver Cloud does not expect – or enjoy - being kept waiting. He has, in the past, given me very stern "advice" on the subject. He expects and demands a high level of professionalism from his channel! Unfortunately – I didn't always deliver!!

With the machine now switched on – Silver Cloud continued:

"We all meet together – those who are available at this time – to consolidate the union.
It is a meeting of energies to consolidate the bond.
It is a moment of reflection and of uniting our energies.
We can use this time together..." (there was a pause of several seconds – during which, John and I felt and attuned with the energy that had filled the room)
"... as we have just done – to link together and unite our efforts.

Those on high – the Council of Guides – will use the opportunity to speak – using the waves of positive energy from the two channels.

Let the other channel (John) *know that his input is valuable – although the communication will come through my channel.*
You are acorns – the tree will grow.

Although these words are spoken through me – they are the words of White Cloud."

*"The delay in speech is like that of a satellite delay.
White Cloud channels through two channels.*
*It is not possible or necessary for White Cloud to lower
his vibrations to this level, each time he speaks.*
*It is possible to channel up and up – we are all
channels. White Cloud thanks you for your attention.
He will visit in person at a later date.*

*You have heard much today of the work you are about
to undertake. We feel that it is necessary that you have
the understanding."*

Kato:

*"Again I give my blessing to the words of White Cloud
and Silver Cloud. Where possible, we will unite – all be
it....*
I am receiving communication from on high.
*I have been asked to pass my gratitude to my channel
on behalf of the Ultimate. That is the end of the
message. We will use these times to unite in our efforts
– to solidify the union of us all.*
Thankyou."

Silver Cloud:

"I will say no more.
*Buffalo and Wolf have much work to do and I ask that
you have patience and allow the work to carry on.*
Now I am being called.
I must go.
Say Goodnight."

John and I:

"Goodnight Silver Cloud."

CHAPTER FOUR

TWO FEATHERS AND A BUTTERFLY

It was the evening of "Jim's" funeral and when I went to "my place" Buffalo and Silver Cloud were both sitting down on the floor. Remaining seated – Silver Cloud said:

"Churches are strange buildings. Why would you want to confine your energy – to reach the heavens – in a building? When we – the tribe, wanted to contact the Spirits, we walked to a place in the open – to reach the Spirits. This is a strange tradition of encasing – in a building, where negative energy remains.
Your ceremonies should be outside. What a strange way of thinking.

These buildings are placed upon other buildings – on sites where misguided rituals have been performed – and nobody checks – nobody cleanses.

The basics of what is achievable – the aim of what is achievable, is to reach into the Spirit world.
These buildings, on sites of past misdemeanours – are not good, and the negative energy is in the building itself. You are fighting with the negative energy.

We shall speak later. Poor Buffalo is tired – we shall get Buffalo onto his feet and speak later."

It was usual for me to "return to my chair" for a short space of time – to wait for the call to return to "my place". These intervals could last anything, from two minutes, up to half an hour – and very often – as I would "return to my chair" – I would be told exactly how long to wait, before returning. The call would usually come, by means of descending Spirit vibrations – in simple language – I would start to feel a buzzing sensation around my head. I was never told how long an evening session would be – my job was to make myself available.

When I "returned to my place", Silver Cloud and Buffalo were standing – Silver Cloud told me that we were expecting a special guest. I stood and waited for someone to appear through the doorway at the rear of "my place" – instead – I heard the words;

"I have come from on high, to welcome you."

Silver Cloud moved to stand in front of me and said:

"This is Sitting Bull."

The voice continued:

"I am the Spirit known as Sitting Bull.
I welcome you both as new channels.
I have come as a member of the Spirit of Guides.
We are as One. We are as One – One body – One body of men. We are the collection of One Spirit – the offspring of many nationalities – spread far across your world. We return as One – yet individual. A nucleus – yet separate – of One being. We are the lives of One – sent at different times and yet – at the same time – a thought dispersal.

You do not understand the dispersal of one seed.
It is not within your realm to comprehend.
We gather Home as the offspring of One.

We are together now – the nine.
Our differing experiences – coming Home to the One.
The knowledge returns to the One."

At this point in the communication – I could see Sitting Bull – dressed in the finery of an Indian Chief.
Sitting Bull continued:

"I am but the Spirit of Sitting Bull.
The Spirit of – long past – Sitting Bull – not the man.
I came as the man – in order to communicate – my fasard – but We are from the One.

We are not alone – there are many sets of nine – returning to the One.
We are the set of nine who belong to you – through your guides.

Sets of nine.

The Spirit of Sitting Bull from long years past – is not able to communicate any more – remember the set of nine – returning Home to the One."

Sitting Bull, disappeared from my place and Silver Cloud said:
"Relax your vibrations."

I "returned to my chair" and looked to John for an explanation of all that we had just heard – it seemed to make sense to him – but I was having difficulty getting my head around it – although – when I was channelling Sitting Bull – I understood everything he said – and why he was saying it.
Very often - after channelling – I would ask John to tell me what I had channelled – I didn't always recall what had been said.

This was why it was so important to tape everything – and spend, however long it took – to transcribe the tapes the next day - word for word. What I did feel – after reading his words, the next day – was – I felt small. Small minded. I had believed that it was my "open mindedness" which enabled me to work with Spirit. I had believed that I understood the physical world in which I lived.

I believe that those two worlds help one another.

I simply - believed in those things.

But Sitting Bulls' words were telling me that there was a far far bigger world than I had ever imagined, a world in which we all play our part – whether we choose to believe in that greater world – or not.

A world where everyone is connected to each other – yet they are separate – yet remain connected, and - not just connected to one thing – but to a group of nine.

I like the idea of all those connections – I like to think that I am part of a bigger picture – but – I also like being in my small world – it gives me a sense of security.

When I "returned to my place" Silver Cloud said:

"The Council of Guides are, our true parent. Our heritage. Our Homeland. It is where we truly belong and where we will return."

As Silver Cloud was speaking, I noticed that there was a second feather on the floor of "my place."

If you remember, in the Introduction, I mentioned that Silver Cloud had already given me a feather, which was always kept in "my place."

Silver Cloud saw me looking at this second feather, and before I could ask anything – he told me that Sitting Bull had left it as a gift for me. I was thrilled to receive it and asked Silver Cloud to thank Sitting Bull, when he next saw him.

The communication continued with Kato.

Kato:
"I am nearer Home than I have ever been, and with your progression – I take a step nearer Home.
I am enjoying the communication.
I take steps further Home.

The heart is the true beginning. Our Home changes through our passage in life – and in death.
Death itself is a return Home – but as we grow – our Home changes – the distance changes – we have to keep going further, further Home.

We do not know where our next Home will be.
The passage of time takes us to our next Home.
We cannot presume where our next Home will be.
We can only carry on through our life's work – as I am doing – and we find ourselves in our next Home.

Sometimes, along the way – we have to turn back because we have left something undone – and hence we start again from where we left – to continue to reach our destination.
We may not reach our final destination in our present form. This is meant to be, because the form we are – we create, and with the passage of time – the form crumbles and recreates – and so it goes on."

Kato then introduced Mezulah, who came to pass communication for John and after that communication, Kato said:

"I thank Silver Cloud.
I thank Buffalo for his protection – as without his protection – the Council would not communicate – would not come near – would not speak.
Thankyou."

Silver Cloud then began to speak, but suddenly stopped mid sentence, to inform us that; *"The bright light has attracted attention. Close down."*

"I returned to my chair."

Kato was obviously talking about Home with a capital H. Home, in the sense of the, "bigger picture of our creation", but his words were – to me – twofold.
Here I was living in the home that John and I had created and worked for – and now, with increasing money pressures – was up for sale.
I wondered whether we would have to sell it.
I wondered where we would move to if we did.
I wondered if we would move to the cottage that Silver Cloud had shown me.
I heard his words – *"Home changes"* – *"We cannot presume where our next Home will be"* – *"We may not reach our final destination in our present form."*
I wondered just what my future would be.

10th November 1994.

Whilst John and I were sitting, waiting for the clock to reach 11pm – we were discussing what to do with the communication we received. Some of that communication was about John's patients - some was for a particular channel, from their guide - and that posed no problem. But we were now receiving communication that we thought was not just for our ears but should be shared with other people – but the question we both had was, "Should we pass the communication on?"

As I "raised my vibrations" I began to get very hot.

Silver Cloud:
"I have been listening to your conversation. We feel that we can put our trust in you, to be selective with the messages and the philosophy that you pass.
We appreciate that you have in mind our protection.
We would not pass information that we felt would be misused – there is a element of trust on both sides.

Sitting Bull would be happy for his communication to be passed onto the Dowser. Please accredit the communication to the correct transmitter. I know you take care with this.
I hope this has answered you question."

I asked Silver Cloud if there would be anyone else coming to communicate tonight.

Silver Cloud.
"I don't think we are expecting anyone – although you never know who will drop in."

Me:
"Should I go away and come back again?"

Silver Cloud:
"You may return.
Why do you have to plan everything!?"

Me:
"I'm not planning it!"

I "returned to my chair" a little disgruntled. He knew that I just liked to know where I stood – he knew that I liked order - as he did.
I was only asking!! Some people can be so, "touchy".

When I "returned to my place" Silver Cloud had a black dog with him – I asked what the dog's name was.

Silver Cloud:
"He has no name – he is dog.
He is the great great grandfather of something.
Look into his face – the eyes "run in the family"."

I felt as though Silver Cloud was really trying to "wind me up" and he was succeeding. Why did he keep bringing this dog? What was the point? I was beginning to think that Silver Cloud was more obsessed with dogs, than I was. In order to explain that last sentence, I must tell you that: - It had now been three years since our last dog – Muppet - a Bearded Collie, had been put to sleep. This had been the only time throughout my life – that I had lived without a dog. In fact I had always lived with at least two.
The death of Muppet, had hit me very hard, as it had quickly followed the deaths of both my mother and father. These deaths, along with finding extra time on my hands' - had led me to begin my journey of mediumship, and during the first twelve months, after these three deaths – I wouldn't even visit anyone who owned a dog - if I could avoid it.
But after three years of living without a dog – my thoughts had begun to turn to the possibility of owning

another one. I had begun to ask myself – "Can I commit myself to at least 12yrs of caring for a dog?"
John and I had discussed the possibility of having another dog. But they were only thoughts!
I even had a dream in which I saw a black dog, lying in some straw, with her puppies. So I knew that the subject of dogs' was never very far away from my thoughts - but Silver Cloud was beginning to irritate me with the presence of his black dog.

When, "I returned to my place" Silver Cloud called Buffalo to come and stand by him. Buffalo wasn't speaking and I asked Silver Cloud why this was.

Ignoring my question - Silver Cloud spoke to Buffalo:

"How is your apprentice doing?"

Still Buffalo did not speak – and I kept looking at him – and wondering why he was silent.

Silver Cloud:
"The work has begun. Listen to me!
You must focus on me – I am the guide."

Me:
"But Buffalo does such a lot to help me and I don't like it - I don't like that I can't speak to him – and he can't reply!"

Silver Cloud:
"Buffalo is saving his communication energy for when he is a guide. I can speak for both of us. It has to be.
He still knows how much you think of him – even though he does not respond."

"We have much work to do. We are going to be very busy. You need to focus your attention on me – to channel your energies.
Buffalo understands this and does not take offence."

I was not happy – Buffalo was my constant companion - we went everywhere together. We loved to listen to Pan Pipe music together. I felt that he was a part of me – and now he was drawing away – I could feel his energy moving away from me. Just like I had felt the energy of our Old English sheepdog – being dragged out of me – even though I wasn't present at the very moment that he had been put to sleep. Just like I had felt the energy of William, my first guide, leaving my body – as I said "Goodbye" and he had walked away.
Moments - like the deaths of my parents – that leave huge holes inside you.

Looking for some selfish consolation in all of this – I asked Silver Cloud:

"Why has Wolf not found his voice?"

Silver Cloud:
"Wolf will take over when Buffalo leaves. He has but a tiny voice. We would not want Wolf to strain his tiny voice. You must work with the guide.
I know you have been working with talking doorkeepers, but now you will talk to me.
Acknowledge the doorkeeper – but talk to me."

Silver Cloud then sent Buffalo to the rear of "my place" and I was near to tears as I saw him walk away.

Silver Cloud said, in a jolly fashion:

"Well – I shall take this dog – this grandfather – he is a lovely dog – don't you think? (I ignored this question) *I have people to see – we will speak tomorrow."*

My vibrations lowered very quickly that night as I "returned to my chair".

I began to recall memories of our time together.

Like the time when Buffalo - after my constant questioning – had shouted - *"ENOUGH you must wait!"* followed by *"We shall be like sparks from the same fire."* I remember thinking how great I felt – to be part of his fire!

I recalled how his hand had suddenly appeared out from a cloud - reaching out for me as I struggled to raise my vibrations to a new level, and I recalled how warm and secure that grip had felt as I clung on to him.

I recalled how grateful I was, when I reached my new "place" – for without his help – I would not have achieved it. That was the moment when - I KNEW that I TRUSTED Buffalo, and I KNEW - that without his protection – Spirit would not have been able to come to pass their communication.

I KNEW that I owed a great deal to Buffalo.

I didn't know how I could ever repay him.

I still didn't know when Buffalo would leave for good – which only prolonged the agony.

11th November 1994.

As I "raised my vibrations" that evening – I asked for the familiar protective light, the rainbow colours, that Buffalo had instructed me to ask for.

I realised that Wolf was providing the protection. The protection had a different vibration.

When I arrived at "my place" I saw Buffalo standing, not in his usual place, which was by the entrance, but at the rear – where Silver Cloud had sent him the previous evening. Silver Cloud was in his usual place – in front of me – and he said:

"You must focus your energy onto me. Buffalo is a silent partner."

I kept looking towards Buffalo – who showed no expression on his face – and every time I looked towards him – I felt Silver Cloud drawing my vision back to himself.

Silver Cloud said:

"I too, had a protector, but I had to channel all my energies towards my guide!

Our protectors are our skin. They are always there – our skin is always there – and we take it for granted. The skin accepts that it is taken for granted. Without the skin, the physical body would not be in control. That is how important the role is.

In order to progress, we must channel our energies inwards and upwards. That is all I have to say. We shall practice this new direction."

Me:
"I don't like being cut off from Buffalo."

Silver Cloud:
"Buffalo knows this to be true and you will be letting Buffalo down – and all the work he has done with you – if you do not make the break. Buffalo will still be working with Wolf for a time – unspecified."

He will leave you a feather in your place.
When you see the three – you will know that Buffalo
has moved on. He will not forget you – and we will
permit him to visit.

Return."

Before I left "my place" I looked at floor and saw the
two feathers from Silver Cloud and Sitting Bull.
I "returned to my chair".

Several minutes later, I returned to "my place", asking
for protection from Wolf for the first time.

Silver Cloud:
"That didn't hurt – did it?" he asked.

I noticed that Wolf – who was younger and smaller in
stature than Buffalo - was standing by my entrance.

"And here is your feather" Silver Cloud said, as he held
a black feather out towards me. I was stunned – the
realisation that Buffalo had gone – flowed over me.
No "notice of intent" – prepared me for Buffalos'
departure. In fact I felt that the "notice" was cruel.
I was annoyed with Silver Cloud, who had kept on
about Buffalo's departure – only to delay that
departure, and I was neither eager, nor particularly
interested in getting to know a new doorkeeper.
However ungrateful that may seem to be – that was my
feeling at this moment.

It would be a short while later – as I got to know Wolf
– that I would acknowledge (to myself) – how easy it
was to work with him. I very quickly realised that our
vibrations were closely linked together.

This could only be as a result of the way he had been introduced to me – through Buffalo.

I took the feather that Silver Cloud was offering to me, as tears rolled down my face. The feather, which was about 8 or 9 inches long, had a blue spot on it – unlike any feather I had seen before. I stood holding it, by the quill, in my right hand – silently thanking Buffalo – and wishing that I could see him face to face – so that I could thank him for everything he had done for me.
Silver Cloud spoke:

"Say Hello to Wolf."

I was feeling sad and didn't want to speak – but managed to say "Hello" to Wolf.

Wolf:
"I am very pleased to be here and very happy to carry on the tradition of Buffalo."

Silver Cloud:
"Wolf is not as tall as Buffalo – I do not feel quite so overpowered – I had thought – if Buffalo should remain – that I would add more feathers to my bonnet."

Silver Cloud continued – despite my lack of reaction to his joke:

"The departure of Buffalo is a happy occasion.
You would be doing him an injustice if you attempted to pull him back." He was obviously reading my mind.

"You would be doing yourself an injustice.
We shall allow him to return and he can give us a progress report."

"Go and place your feather."

I walked towards the two feathers and bent down –
I placed Buffalo's feather in between the two already
there and stood up.

Silver Cloud, in reference to a trip that John and I were
making the next day, said:

"I am looking forward to our day out.
Wolf has led a sheltered life. He will enjoy visiting
these places with you.

So – we say Adieu to Buffalo and wish him Godspeed.

We shall meet tomorrow."

I reminded Silver Cloud, that because of the next days
visit to the farm of my relatives – I wouldn't be able to
visit him during the day, as was my practice.

Silver Cloud:
"We shall meet later on – at the turn of the day."

He then clapped his hands in a dismissive fashion,
saying – *"Be off."*

Me:
"Will you thank Buffalo?"

Silver Cloud:
"You already have.
My words could not express what your heart feels.
You were already prepared for the separation.
And now – Be Off – I have things to do."

I "returned to my chair."

As I mentioned earlier, John and I were going to visit some distant relatives of mine the next day, who live on a farm in Co Durham. As many of us know – family trees and distant relations – can be very confusing things – and this distant relationship, was no exception.

The précised version of this relationship – is that: the father of the "Aunt" that I was going to visit – was a cousin – somewhere down the line – of the grandfather of my mother. I hope you're following this!

My mum and dad had honeymooned with my "aunts", father and mother, back in ????.

After my parents had died, and as I was clearing their house, I came across my mothers' jewellery box. The wooden box has a print on the lid, which depicts the well-known beauty spot in Co Durham of, High Force waterfalls. Inside the box, I found the two train tickets – that had taken mum and dad to Darlington station – to begin their honeymoon.

My family had, had two holidays with the family, when I was about 9 or 10yrs old - which was the last time I had seen them.

As the years had rolled on, and following the deaths of the elder relatives - mum and dad had kept in touch with my "aunt" and "uncle", via letters and calendars, swapped throughout the year and especially at Christmas time. It was after the death of mum and dad, that I had found their address and telephone number. As Christmas quickly followed – I had sent a card and calendar – as was family tradition – and rang them on Christmas day – to wish them well. My "aunt" seemed to be particularly pleased that I had got in contact with them. John and I had visited my "aunt" and "uncle", who were now, both in their 70s, a couple of times and I had spent a weekend with them and their son - which had been a brilliant experience. They had all made us feel very welcome and their dry Northern wit provided plenty of laughs.

So, back to the story.

John and I had arrived earlier than had been arranged and so we stopped at a town a few miles away from their farm, and went to look around the shops. Whilst in a gift shop, I was amazed to see some Native American Indian statues on a shelf, and who should be one of them, but Sitting Bull, dressed in the finery of an Indian Chief. Needless to say – we bought the statue – and I beamed at the shop assistant, as she carefully wrapped it up, thinking to myself – "If only she knew!"

In a second hand shop, John was drawn to a black, wooden, lacquered box, with a dragon etched onto the lid - and another purchase was made.

With the statue and black box safely wedged on the back seat of the car, we set off to the farm where we spent a very enjoyable afternoon, and the homemade cakes that were offered to us.

We caught up on everything that had happened since our last visit and one of the things my "aunt" asked was, "Have you got a dog? Your mum and dad always had dogs." to which I answered "No, but we have talked about getting another one – but we're not sure whether we will or not."

John and I went with my "aunt," on a walk around the farm and the surrounding fields. I always love this part of the visit, whatever the weather.

As a child, tramping through the fields behind my home, with one of our dogs Shep, had been a favourite pastime, and up until the age of 11yrs – I had various school friends, who lived on farms.

My friends and I regularly spent the weekend at each other's homes - on an unofficial rota basis.

This had given me the opportunity to experience life on a farm – not to mention - the opportunity to ride their ponies! I remember thinking then – how strange it was – that when my friends stayed with me – they were content to visit the local town, go for a leisurely bike ride around my village, or play Tiddlywinks. Whilst - when I stayed with them - I wanted to "muck out" stables, feed animals, collect eggs, hose down shippons after the cows had been milked, and generally get "dirty". In my mind – the dirtier I became – the harder I had "worked". In fact, I enjoyed the farm life so much – that - at one stage in my early years, I had an ambition to marry a farmer when I grew up.

Until - that is – the reality sunk in – that - as a farmers wife - I would be expected to bring cows in from the field, milk them, clean up, AND make breakfast – all before 7.30am! EVERY DAY!!

But my love of the farm environment and walking round fields in my "wellies" stays with me.

As the afternoon wore on, it was time for John and I to say our "goodbyes" to my "aunt" and "uncle" and set off on our journey home.

At around midnight that same day, I "raised my vibrations" to find Silver Cloud, standing in "my place" wearing a pair of green Wellingtons.

"Had I been born at a later time, I would have liked to be a farmer – a custodian of land and animals." He announced.

I asked him if he liked the statue of Sitting Bull, to which he replied:

"It is not an exact likeness, but I appreciate the thought with which it was bought – a symbol.
I will tell Sitting Bull to come and look at it – if he is of mind, he will appreciate the thought."

I then asked Silver Cloud what he thought about John's black box, and he began a lengthy communication with John about the meaning of the box, and how John could use it. When Silver Cloud had finished his communication, John thanked him to which, Silver Cloud replied:

"One does what one can
Buffalo wishes us well for the future.
Wolf has done an excellent job.
The Badger needs some attention."

The badger that Silver Cloud was referring to, was a badger that had been on the side of the road, as we had driven home. John thought that he had clipped the badgers hind quarters with the car and although he had stopped the car and gone back down the road to look for it – the badger was nowhere in sight. But it obviously did require some distant healing, as Silver Cloud had indicated – so both John and I asked for some help for it.

Try as you may, these unfortunate incidents do happen – however careful a driver you may be – however it's comforting to know that Spirit, forever watchful – will always help if they can. We only have to ask.

14th November 1994.

When I arrived at "my place", Silver Cloud was seated at a table. I told him that it was taking me longer to transcribe the tapes, as the communication continued until the early hours of the morning. He asked me what I was going to do with the communications and I told him that, as we had discussed before – some of it would be passed on to the relevant people, and some would remain in my notebooks. As I finished the explanation, I found that myself and Silver Cloud were standing on a path which was in a forest. I asked Silver Cloud why we were there and the conversation went as follows:

"My mind projects the picture and you walk into the picture. Where would you like to go now?"

Back to "my place."

"You could have gone anywhere – why here?" he asked.

"Because this place is very important to me." I explained.

"We will go for a walk one day. You may ask me to take you somewhere."

"Can we go to see my wise men?"

As I finished the sentence we were transported to a big room, in which there was along table, behind which, sat White Cloud, Mr Shush, and another man, whom I didn't know – seated at the far end.

White Cloud:
"We are pleased to see you. What do you want to know?"

Me:
"What can I do with the communication I have written down?"

White Cloud;
"Keep the communication together – do not split it. Put it in a booklet."

Me*:*
"But people may split it."

White Cloud:
"They would read the whole and know the whole."

Mr Shush:
"You have come a long way since we met, there are many who have helped you."

Me:
"I can't think of any more questions. I didn't know I was coming."

White Cloud:
"We shall have another meeting."

Me:
"Who is the man down at the end of the table?"

At this point, Silver Cloud thanked them for the *"audience"* and I found myself back in "my place".

Silver Cloud:
"We must broaden your horizons. Now that you know you can ask – you may ask."

A question that a healer had asked me to ask, popped into my mind. They wanted to know the name of another healers guide – and so I asked Silver Cloud their question.

Silver Cloud answered:

"We shall not be assisting. The channel must speak to their guide. We will not be drawn – we have far more important work to do. Tittle tattle!"

It was obvious to me that Silver Cloud had been irritated by this request. I could feel and see, his irritation rising as he quickly communicated the following in response to my next question: "Why do you want to work so late in the day?"

Silver Cloud:
"It is convenient.
When other channels have fallen asleep – it is our opportunity to speak to their guides.
When other channels are not pulling – it is our opportunity to reach on high. We are Patient and Wait.
The channel that waits – is rewarded.
Those that pull without being invited are impatient.

Some do not use their guides – they are not led nor allow themselves to be led – they pull.
My channel will not pull.

There are those reaching very high, but then they begin to expect – on demand."

"This forces them into a dilemma when the communication cannot be received. They have no words to speak – so what option do they lay themselves open to?

This is painting a black picture of communication channels. I use it merely as an example of what a few are doing. By opening my channel later in the night – in your terms – when it is more convenient for us – my channel will be rewarded.

I do not hold with channels plucking out of the air – without guidance. There are those that disagree – but it is not my way.

And so we will continue to work late into the night, if needs be – but of course – it could be morning here!

Each step is a new day.
Each minute particle of information can be a new day.
We choose when the new day begins.
We can have many new days – in a short space of time.
You choose when the new day begins.
If we miss the opportunity for a new day – we can go back to yesterday – to find out, where, along the way – we missed the opportunity.
But, yesterday was yesterday – it's purpose – to move us to, today.
Yesterday – today was tomorrow.
Today – tomorrow is the future."

15th November 1994. Evening.

As I arrived in "my place" there were fireworks going off and Silver Cloud was slapping his shoulder. He looked like someone who had had a spark land on them, which had singed his clothes. He was obviously in a playful mood – but I was becoming wary of his "little games". Although they usually made me laugh – they also made me feel that I was being led "up the garden path". In simple words – Silver Cloud had a reason for everything he did or said – and behind every joke – there was a serious message – it was my responsibility to receive - and act on – that message.

Some, I was finding, were easier to understand and act on - than others.

Silver Cloud stood to face me and stretched his arms out to his sides. The fireworks instantly stopped.

The communication began:

Silver Cloud:
"I thought that would be a surprise. How can such dangerous things be so pretty.
They are a wolf in sheep's clothing!
But I did not light them for the morale.

I think we should have a list. I will create new things – it will be a challenge."

The next thing to appear, was an ornate fountain, complete with stone pedestal and spewing water.

Me:
"How do you do that?"

Silver Cloud:
"I think it."

The fountain disappeared and in his hand's, Silver Cloud held a large bunch of flowers.

The flowers looked like a cross between sunflowers and chrysanthemums

Silver Cloud asked:
"What do you want?"

Me:
"Do you mean now or the future?"

Silver Cloud.
"The future – what else is there?"

Me:
"I want to work with Spirit."

Silver Cloud:
"Where do you want to be?"

Me:
"At that cottage."   This was the first time I had really acknowledged that I would be happy to live in the cottage.

Silver Cloud:
"How do you get there?"

Me:
"By aiming for it."

Silver Cloud:
"Who will help you?"

Me:
"Me, John and Spirit."

Silver Cloud:
"Do you believe?"

Me:
"Yes."

Silver Cloud held out his hands towards me and said:
"What is this?"

I saw a brown butterfly fluttering in his hands.

Me:
"A Butterfly."

Silver Cloud:
"Has it always been a Butterfly?"

Me:
"No."

Silver Cloud:
"Which stage of it's life does it enjoy most."

Me:
"The one that its' at."

Silver Cloud:
"Why is that?"

Me:
"Because that is what it knows and is, at the time?"

Silver Cloud:
"Does it know the future?"

Me:
"Probably not."

Silver Cloud:
"If it does not know the future – if it does not know it is going to be the beautiful Butterfly – why does it carry on?"

Me:
"It has to."

The Butterfly flew away and Silver Cloud, who was now holding a staff, said:
"Wait" Silver Could banged his staff, twice on the floor. *"Stand in your place."*

I moved position, to stand in front of my feathers.

A lady entered "my place" from the door at the rear.
She was a lady of about 60yrs and she was dressed in a nurse's uniform.

She smiled at me and with a smile, both on her lips and in her eyes – she told me that her name was Mary and that she had come to give a message for John.
She told John that she had known him when he was a baby, explaining that she had worked in the hospital in which he had been born. She continued:

"I remember you
I saw the Light.
I am pleased to be able to come to speak.
I have come to say – I saw the Light attached to you.
I have come to say – the Light has grown.
That is all I have come to say.
Thankyou."

Me:
"She's gone."

Silver Cloud banged on the floor again.
I waited.

A frail elderly gentleman walked in with a message for John. I didn't get his name.

The gentleman:

"Tell him I am proud that he chose our family, because he really, is not one of us – he chose our family especially – I know that now – just tell him."

The gentleman left and once again, the staff was banged on the floor – this time to introduce Laura, a healing guide of John's.

And so, the evenings communication continued - giving John the opportunity to ask questions - regarding his patients.

CHAPTER FIVE

LOOKING TO THE FUTURE

16th November 1994.

I "raised my vibrations" and met Silver Cloud in my garden. This garden was a place that I went to during meditation, both with Silver Cloud, and with my previous guide, William. In this garden, there was a bench seat and it was here that Silver Cloud and I were sitting, when along came Armon, my uncle. It was, as always, great to see Armon and although our meetings – in real time – sometimes only lasted a few seconds – these meetings were always very precious to me.

Referring to the money struggles that John and I were having – Armon told me that we were "*nearing the end of the path*". Adding, that it had been necessary for John and I to walk the path – but that there was no need for us to be on it any more. Armon then asked me if I trusted him, to which I replied, "I do", telling him that he meant a great deal to me, as did Silver Cloud and everyone else in Spirit who was close to me.

Armon then reassured me, "*I will always be near to you*" - then he said that he would have to leave.

Silver Cloud and I remained seated on the bench and out of the corner of my right eye, I saw none other than Buffalo - approaching along the path.
Once again, I was thrilled and excited to see Buffalo and as I stood up to greet him, he grinned at me.

No more - the stern business like stance of my protector, no more - the teacher and pupil – but two friends meeting on a pleasant summers' day.

Buffalo said:
"You have grown a lot – since we first met."
I asked him how he was, and in reply, he told me that he was now working with his new channel – a female.

Sadly, this was the extent of the exchange between us, as Buffalo announced that he would have to leave – and leave he did, but I was very grateful that he had taken the time to visit me – I felt I was a very lucky person.

After Buffalo had left, Silver Cloud, who was now wearing a wry grin on his face - told me that Buffalo's new channel was *"a lot quieter"* than me, and with that statement – he turned his gaze towards the path.
I followed his example and saw the black dog ambling towards us.
As the dog reached us, Silver Cloud stood up and said:
"I will walk you to the garden door." The garden door was my entrance and exit to the garden.

I walked out through the door, and found myself in "my place", but I had entered it through the rear door – the door, through which Spirit entered when they came to communicate.
Wolf was waiting for me.

I looked onto the floor and saw my feathers lying there, and then I looked forward to the place from which I usually entered. It was strange to see "my place" from this other angle i.e. as Spirit saw it.
I could see a white wall of mist, in which, there was an archway - through which I usually entered.

I began to feel uncomfortable.

I felt as though I was on the wrong side. Wolf said: *"Return to your usual place."*

I moved towards the archway and then turned round to face the doorway through which I had exited the garden. Wolf then stretched his arms out in front of him, his fists were clenched.

I did the same.

Bringing his right clenched fist to the left side of his upper chest – Wolf dismissed me.

I copied his gesture and "retuned to my chair".

Wolf and I always used this greeting, both as a "hello" and "goodbye" - for as long as we were together.

That nightime I "raised my vibrations" as usual, but I didn't reach "my place". I could feel Silver Cloud around me, but I just couldn't reach him.

I kept trying to reach "my place" but my efforts were in vain. Then I heard Silver Cloud say, *"Trust me.*

At the same time I could see Silver Cloud, floating in the air in front of me. In his hand, he held what looked like a fairy wand – and with the wand - he wrote *"GOODNIGHT"*.

And then he disappeared.

Actually – this unexpected night off - from the communication, gave me time to ponder on those words of Armon that had been rattling around my brain since earlier that day – *"there was no need for John and I to be on this path any more."*

To me - these words could only mean that we would sell the house and use the equity in it to buy the cottage - OR – my £10.00 Premium Bond, that my mum gave me on my 21st birthday – was going to "come up."

This was great news! The end must be in sight!

During the day of the 17th November, I "raised my vibrations" and once again, I saw Silver Cloud floating around – surrounded by a huge white cloud.

He was obviously in a playful mood, I thought – anyway never mind, "I'll see him tonight and in the meantime – I'll practice my patience!"

Night -time.

I didn't succeed in reaching "my place", but I did see a pyramid with steps leading down from it. This reminded me of a dream I once had. A dream in which I stood with Armon, as we both watched a pyramid being built. Given that it took years to build a pyramid – I must have been watching a speeded up version of events and "Oh" how I wish I could remember how they had done it!

Anyway – back in my dream - I looked up at the steps and had the urge to walk up them. I began to climb them one by one and as I did so – Spirit were walking past me, down the steps. My notebook lists other things that passed by me, as I climbed those many steps – including:

A girl with ginger hair,

A girl with a bare arm,

A face sculptured in stone,

A totem pole,

A white panelled door (with something hanging on it) and lastly – as I reached as far as I could go –

The rear view of an Indian Chief, who was wearing a bonnet with feathers that hung right down to the floor.

From the 17th to the 20th November – I didn't manage to reach "my place". Neither did I see Wolf or Silver Cloud.

These long days were frustrating and upsetting. I had gone from the regular daily and nighttime's communication – to nothing, and – I was fed up with practising patience!

I was feeling the loss of both Wolf and Silver Cloud and my patience and temper were being severely tested.

I have never been – nor am I now – a naturally, patient person.

I CAN be very patient - with children and animals.

I CAN be "so laid back" - that I nearly fall over and you would think I had fallen asleep,

I CAN spend hours doing jigsaws – without the aid of a picture,

BUT –

Ill-mannered people,

Remote controls for televisions,

Computers that have a mind of their own,

Drivers who don't use their indicators when driving round a roundabout.

Sticky labels that "won't come off" – when it clearly states "easy peal",

AND –

YES – even Spirit – can - drive me to distraction!

However – on the night of the 20th November – after considerable effort, time, and a great deal of inner vibration – I saw Wolf and Silver Cloud.

Silver Cloud was sat with other Indian Chiefs, on desert land. They were sitting around a large fire, which provided an orange light, and in that flickering light, I saw that there were Tepees all around. I stood and waited – remembering the time when I had approached Buffalo when he had been with a group of Indians – only to be told – in abrupt terms to *"Go back."*

I watched as Silver Cloud removed himself from the circle and walked over to me.
Silver Cloud spoke:

"The chiefs are from different tribes. You have been allowed to come so that I could tell you that I am still here. To tell you where I am."

He then went on to say that he needed time with his Brothers – adding – *"The Brothers have all got channels – You are not the only one that is without.*

I will be back with you soon. Go with Wolf."

As I turned to find Wolf – the scene with the Indian Chiefs disappeared and I was in "my place".
I was having difficulty maintaining the vibrational rate and I began to slip away.
Wolf stepped nearer to me and said:

"Now that you have found us – you will remember."

As he spoke these words, I stepped backwards and nearly stood on my three feathers that were kept on the floor.

"Mind your feathers." warned Wolf.

I "returned to my chair" pleased that I had found Wolf and Silver Cloud but feeling guilty and embarrassed by my previous feelings of impatience, frustration and anger. The last few days had also made me question myself – "How much trust did I really show to them?" "How do I learn to be patient?"
On the afternoon of the 21st November, and as I "raised my vibrations" – I saw yet another flight of stairs.

These stairs were wide, shallow and curved round in an arc. I couldn't see the top of the stairs as they were clouded in mist – but I knew that if I reached the top - I would find "my place".

I began to walk up the stairs – raising my vibrations as I climbed. When I reached the mist - the arms' of Wolf and Silver Cloud reached out through it – and – asking that my vibrations be "lifted to the highest level" – I grasped their wrists and was pulled into "my place".

I thanked them both for their help and Wolf greeted me with his arm gesture. I returned the greeting.

I was continually and silently asking that my vibrations be lifted in order to stay in "my place" - and by way of response to this – Silver Cloud assured me that – with practice – I would find the new level of vibration, easier to maintain.

I made a note in my notebook, which reads:

"Although it is "my place" – it feels different."

That evening, as I was "raising my vibrations" for the evening communication – if there were to be any – I felt the presence of a Spirit that I did not recognise. At the same time – through my closed eyes – I saw a silver coloured "flying saucer".

Feeling apprehensive and with the presence of this unknown energy my natural instinct was to "return to my chair" – quickly! But, trusting and feeling, that Wolf and Silver Cloud were near and knew what was happening – I asked Wolf if I should carry on raising my vibrations and thus opening up to this energy.

Although I didn't hear any words from Wolf – I knew that he was telling me that it was safe for me to continue.

The following extract relates the conversation that I relayed to John – as this energy and I, conversed.

I had already explained to John that this energy felt new and strange to me. John – forever watchful when someone or something different was near - was sitting with his pendulum – ready to check for any danger.

The extract is an exact copy from my notebook:

Me:
"I don't know who this is – but they are from the dark side of the moon. The Spirit world is their bridge to this world. He comes in peace. He comes to make contact with this world – that is his plan."

"What world are you from?"

Ans:
"Planet. These things will be told at the appropriate time. I speak through Silver Cloud. Do not fear.
We have to have a spirit world, united with your Spirit world, on a higher level. We need your Spirits to communicate. A collaboration.
This is your life.
The story begins – the red planet.
We need one another to survive.
If your earth dies – our earth will also die."

Me:
"Can you tell me any more about the planet?"

Ans:
"All in good time."

Me:
"Can you give me a name?"

Ans:
"Peter the disciple.
I will return home.
Thankyou for your time.
I am pleased to meet with my channel.
Peter bids you farewell.
Reduce vibrations."

Me:
"I'm back in my place."

Silver Cloud:
"That was a special meeting place.
Peter will use you as a channel to pass his communication through you – to pass communication to academics.

He cannot come to our place – we create another place. It would not be fitting that he come down to our place – I will take you to their place – just a place higher up. It is surely an honour for Wolf – as his protection is vital – he has been well trained."

Me:
"I am losing Silver Cloud"

Silver Cloud:
"I have been channelling have I not.
You must learn to fly.
I will speak tomorrow.
Your friend – Silver Cloud."

The next day, (22nd November) I was hoping that I could ask Silver Cloud some questions about Peter but when I went to "my place" Wolf told me that Silver Cloud had *"Gone for afternoon tea"*.

Afternoon tea - lasted for 7 days.

During those 7 days, I continued to raise vibrations, still sitting every afternoon and evening.

Knowing that I had a sitting arranged for a healer friend on the 28th – I was beginning to panic about the continued absence of Silver Cloud. I pestered Wolf with continuous enquiries as to when Silver Cloud would return - to the point of exasperation – on both sides. My pestering culminating (on the morning of the 28th) in this reply from Wolf:

"You ask TOO many questions!
You will be able to carry on working in your place.
You have had your explanation.
You may go!"

As that sitting commenced, and although I only saw Wolf – I felt Silver Cloud return.

Trust and Patience Lynn – Trust and Patience!!

As to my questions regarding Peter – on the 29th of November – during the nighttime session – White Cloud came to communicate, through Silver Cloud.

I include part of that communication here.

White Cloud:
"On no account must any communication from Peter be released without permission.
I cannot say when the communication will begin – we are waiting for everyone to be ready at the same time. The timing has to be impeccable.

This is a vast undertaking and we cannot say, and we do not know when the alignment will be."

"I can say that Peter is delighted to have met his channel and is pleased and happy with his channel, and so we must all wait."

Silver Cloud continued that evening's session by saying that he had enjoyed his "holiday", adding:

"We have things to do here and there are times when we must go – but I am pleased to be back."

At that point – Silver Cloud told me to wait.

I didn't "return to my chair" to wait, but stayed in "my place" to raise my vibrations.
I recognised the energy of Peter moving towards me and raised my vibrations again.

Peter:
"It is I Peter.
I do not want you to be fearful of the communication nor fearful of the logistics of passing the communication to the correct receivers.
All communication will be given with explicit directions – to be followed exactly.
You are but a tool.
You will not be given our purpose in its entirety.
You are to follow orders.
If you do not know the purpose – then you cannot pre-empt the outcome. This has nothing to do with you.
You are but a tool.
I find my visit easier.
I take the opportunity of using the 3 channels as they are aligned. (White Cloud – Silver Cloud – Me)
You will not know my identity – only my communication."

"As time progresses, you may, if we deem it right – be given minor details of our purpose. Just know that you are part of a plan – you are all tools. If you do not obey instruction – you will be replaced.

I do not expect my channel to be replaced – but you know that you can be.

I am fading."

Wolf:
"Wait."

White Cloud returned and I asked him what I could tell people about Peter.

White Cloud:
"You can say that his name is Peter.
You can say that he comes from the dark side of the moon. You can say that he is One of Nine.
You can say that he has a message for the World, which will be delivered by The Nine."

Silver Cloud: in a very serious manner:
"You must not fall by the wayside – You will not fall by the wayside.

You must not discuss this matter unless instructed – or permission has been obtained – and this permission cannot be obtained from anyone – other than Peter."

Changing his sombre mood - which reflected my own – and speaking in a cheery, matter of fact sort of way – Silver Cloud continued:

"Well – I think that has cleared that up!"

"We will leave it for another day.
We have done much work today – valuable work.
You may go.
Goodnight."

I can't pretend that Peter's communication and presence didn't unnerve me – because it did.

Conversing with Spirit was wonderful – but – an "alien" from the dark side of the moon, telling me that he would use me as a channel – this, I found to be unsettling and scary.

My thought raced to those "what ifs".

What ifs – based on frightening stories I had heard about.

What ifs – based on truth or untruths.

What if he abducted me?

What if he wanted to do experiments with me?

What if I died when he had done what he wanted to do with me?

And yet – Silver Cloud, Wolf and White Cloud were part of this work, and I Trusted them.

So – taking my lead from Silver Cloud's calmness and lightness of attitude – I decided that I must Trust in the process - and their plan. I knew I had to treat Peter's presence and communication - with the same respect, gratitude and ease, as I did - all other communications.

After all – I reasoned – he was, "just another Spirit".

However – I couldn't escape the fact that Peters' energy – albeit channelled through Silver Cloud and White Cloud – was very powerful. He is an awesome Spirit. Putting the awe that I felt to one side - my inquisitive, basic nature turned my thoughts to –

"I wonder what he looks like?" "I wonder if he looks like any of those aliens that you see on the telly?"

I think of myself, as a person with a sense of humour and I attempted to draw on my humour, to remain calm and relaxed during those times when Silver Cloud disappeared – unannounced.

I tried to see the amusing side of my predicament – in the hope that my humour would prevent me from becoming angry and cross. Unfortunately – my humour is usually at the expense of others, but I can laugh at my own misfortunes – like the time when:

John and I were walking our Old English Sheepdog and Bearded Collie in the local park. The dogs were running loose and I shouted Trampas (the Old English) to come back to me. Trampas - who also had a sense of humour - turned and began to bound along the grass towards me. With his ears flapping up and down and his hair blowing in the wind – he lowered his head and quickened his pace. He was heading straight for me.

"No Trampas Nooooh!" I shouted in vain.

He ran straight between my legs and out the other side.

In a desperate bid to remain standing, I swung both arms, at speed, in an anticlockwise direction. I must have looked like a demented windmill.

All my efforts were in vain as I fell flat on my back with a thud. Now - whenever Trampas saw you sitting or lying on the floor, he saw it as a sign that you were in a playful mood.

Game on - Trampas ran at me again and plonked his ample weight onto my stomach - pinning me to the ground. With his tongue dripping and lolling out of his mouth – he gazed into my face and prodded me in my eye with his very wet, large nose!

John - a sensitive soul – laughed like a drain.

One theme that had been instilled in me, throughout my training with William, Buffalo and Silver Cloud – was – that the work of a medium was a serious business, which brought with it, certain responsibilities.

I felt that, with a few exceptions, I adhered to this rule.

It was, therefore, with some surprise and puzzlement – that I found, Silver Cloud was beginning to play games with me.

On the 30th November 1994, as I was "raising my vibrations" – I found that my feet were becoming very hot. So hot, that they were uncomfortable and I couldn't keep them still. Successfully raising my vibrations to a level that normally took me to "my place" – I found myself in another space. The space was empty – I felt as though I was standing in nothing.

My left foot in particular, was very hot and my attention drifted towards it.

"That is what you get when you sit too close to the fire. It is a big fire."

I asked who was saying these things and the reply was:
"It is I"

I said – "I don't know who you are."

Ans:
"Guess"

I was feeling irritated and uneasy, then Wolf appeared – he was laughing.

"A little puzzle" he said *"Play the game."*

Then he disappeared.

I continued to raise my vibrations and ask for Wolf to protect and help me. As my vibrations lifted, I arrived at "my place" where I saw a huge open fire, from behind which – Silver Cloud peered and said: "Peek a boo."

The noise from the crackling fire became so loud that I couldn't hear myself speak, let alone hear any reply. The noise from the spitting, blazing wood filled my head. Then, as if time had spun forward in one moment – the fire was out and all that remained on the floor – were the cold ash remains.
Silver Cloud was brushing the ashes together and generally clearing the place up.

"Where is your sense of humour?" he asked.
"Mind your feet!"
I jumped out of his way as his broom swept past me.

Perplexed – I asked him why this was happening, adding:
"I've come for the communication – is there anyone who wants to communicate?"
"You must learn to play" – he replied – "*Anyway, off you go.*"

Very puzzled by this encounter I just stood and stared at him.

"Go on – Go on!" he urged.

I returned to my chair – just in time to hear the audio machine clunk off, as the tape ran out.
On the next two evenings (1st & 2nd December) although I "raised my vibrations" repeatedly, I didn't get to "my place".

Eventually on the 2nd December, and after 2½ hours of "raising my vibrations" and "returning to my chair" – I saw Wolf.

"Silver Cloud has left a message for you"
he announced.
"Oh – what is it?" I asked.

"Goodnight." - was the reply.

Wolf then dismissed me with the words:
"You can go now – sweet dreams."

I was really confused by this change of attitude towards me and the thought crossed my mind that maybe Silver Cloud was fed up with working with me, that maybe I was letting him down in some way.
Whatever the reasons were for this change of attitude – I was sad. Sad - not to be receiving the communication and sad that I couldn't spend time with Silver Cloud.
My mediumship was a very important part of my day – it allowed me to block out the continuing and ongoing frustration I had with our money situation.
Regularly raising my vibrations resulted in my feeling energised and happy. My mediumship had been going – I felt – very smoothly - and I loved it.
I just couldn't understand the change in their behaviour.

3rd December 1994.

I "raised vibrations" and found myself on a patio area of what I knew to be the cottage. Silver Cloud was standing, looking out into the garden.
It was night, and as I followed Silver Cloud's gaze and looked into the darkness. I noticed that the garden was lit by many white "fairy" lights.

The garden looked quite magical.

I stood admiring it, absorbing the peace and tranquillity it exuded. I thanked Silver Cloud for arranging it, and for bringing me to see it.

As I looked at the lights that were furthest away from me, they seemed to grow brighter and twinkly, and as I focused on the glowing lights - I saw that there was a figure, standing, beckoning me to walk towards him.

The figure – a man – was dressed from head to foot, in a black hooded cloak. Feeling daunted by this presence and nervous of approaching him – I looked to Silver Cloud for a sign of reassurance.

Silver Cloud, understanding my nervousness – nodded his head – and we approached the man together.

It's a funny thing – but I noted then, as I had before – that when I was walking "in spirit" and on strange and sometimes dark land – I never bumped into anything – I never stumbled. My spirit always knew where the dangers were - "if only my life were like that" – I mused.

As Silver Cloud and I were about 7 or 8ft away from the man – Silver Cloud stood still – and I stopped walking. The man was over 6ft tall and was standing with his hooded head, bent forward looking towards the ground. The distance, combined with the darkness, meant that - frustratingly - I was not able to see his face. The man, neither spoke, nor looked at me – and it seemed to me that the three of us - silently - stood in that place for a long time.

So often - in silences I had previously experienced - a conversation would take place, or an exchange of energy and understanding. But during this silence I was not aware of any such exchange.

It was - quite simply – silence.

The prolonged silence began to un-nerve me and it was with relief that I heard Silver Cloud ask me
"what I wanted to do."
"Go to "my place" please". I replied.

My request was granted - and instantly – Silver Cloud and I were transported, safely back to "my place".
I asked Silver Cloud who the man was.
Silver Cloud told me that he was a man who had been watching me – and that the man was part of my future.
Happy with this simple explanation and unwilling to know any more details – I quickly asked if anyone would be coming to communicate.
But - I silently wondered - if the man had been Peter.

4th December 1994. My birthday.

John had bought me a CD that he knew I wanted – which was Julio Inglaise's "Crazy".
I love music of many genres and throughout my life – and especially since working with Spirit – I have increasingly used music as a tool to focus my energy. Spirit has also used specific pieces of music to communicate a message to me. They tell me directly what piece of music to listen to - or - they awaken a need in myself – to listen to a piece of music – until I have "received its' message". I use music to lift my vibrations, work through any problems, and occasionally – I prepare a compilation CD – for other people to use.

I had been playing "Crazy" all morning – loudly!
During the afternoon and with John present – I went to "my place" - Mr Bennet (a healing guide of John's) came to talk about music.

Mr Bennet said how he preferred Blues music. He explained how the tones of the music, open the chakras, thus allowing harmful, pent up, emotions, to leave the body.

"Blues" he said – *"Is Healing Music!"*

There was a party atmosphere in "my place" that afternoon, as John's guides, Mr Bennet, Kato, Laura – and my guide's - William and Silver Cloud – each spoke about their favourite type of music.

Kato said that his taste was *"mixed"*, whilst Laura – as John and I already knew – loved waltzes.

William said:

"Yes – but excuse me! – You can't beat a rousing tune. The orchestra playing – the choir singing."

I wholeheartedly agreed with William – as it had been Rossini's "William Tell" overture playing in the background – the day that William had come, and "grounded" me. The first meeting - that I had been aware of – between a "working" Spirit guide and myself. Silver Cloud announced that he liked nothing better than *"To shimmy"* and as if to prove his point – he spread his arms out, wriggled his hips and shoulders, and began to shuffle around "my place".

This encouraged everyone else to dance – and I watched and laughed as William, wearing his usual smart suit, and Kato, dressed in his judo attire – waltzed around together. Mr Bennet and Laura did the same.

Each of them, dancing to their individual - yet united - silent music.

It was a truly, wonderful sight to behold.

A sight that was interrupted - by the arrival at the front door of the house – by my sister, who had come to wish me "happy birthday".

Early that evening, my "aunt" from Co Durham, rang to say "happy birthday", and as our conversation came to a close – she said: "We've got something here for you – if you want it?" - "Oh – what's that?" I replied.
She laughed, and said, "We've got a puppy – if you want one." My brain took a few seconds to register what she had said and at the same time – I recalled my dream, the dream, where I had seen a black dog and her puppies - lying on straw.

My "aunt" went on to explain, that two of their working Border Collie dogs had been mated and produced a litter of puppies. The litter, which had been born on the 27th November, consisted of two dogs and two bitches. My "aunt" then said that my "uncle" had asked her to offer John and I one of them - as a present.

I was really excited and very grateful to both of them, for their kind offer. Especially so – because these puppies were potentially working dogs – and to a farmer – they were a source of income.
I said that I would speak to John – knowing – in my own mind – that the answer would be "yes please", and - trying to remain calm and rational - I told my "aunt" that I would ring her the next day.

I felt, this was one of those "meant to be" moments.
I felt that Spirit had organised and arranged the birth of the puppies to coincide with the desire that John and I had – to have another puppy.
And – not just ANY puppy.
But a puppy that had been bred by my relatives!

I felt very devoid of relatives – especially since my mum and dad had died. My family (apart from John) now consisted of one sister and two cousins - one of whom - had emigrated to Canada, and so – for me – the gift from a relative – was a very poignant gift.
And, I wondered - was my "uncle" psychic?
Did he communicate with Spirit?
Was he knowingly - "in" - on the plan?
I deduced that he must have been.

John and I sat, discussed how we would fence off a part of our large garden so that the puppy (as yet un-named) could explore the outdoors safely, and I began to plan what sort of bed we should buy for him.
We had decided that we would have one of the two dog puppies that were in the litter.

Thinking about dog beds' reminded me of our Old English Sheepdog – Trampas. When John and I got the puppy – Trampas - and anticipating the size he would become as an adult dog – we bought him a wonderful, very large, wicker bed. The bed stood on four wooden ball feet, the three sides and shaped front – were made of a sturdy, natural coloured wicker.

You could tell that Trampas was as proud of his sleeping quarters as we were – as he used to hide all his treasures in it. Treasures, such as chewed pieces of cardboard, remnants of bones and the remains of his plastic toys.

He was so proud of his bed and it's hidden treasures, that when I removed the bedding to put it in the wash – he would stand over me with a concerned look on his face. He knew that as I dragged the bedding out - his many treasures would be revealed as they fell onto the floor. Trampas would quickly scoop up, as many of the pieces as his mouth would hold, and return them to his now - empty bed.

Another sign that Trampas loved his bed – was that - over a period of time – he ate it! Eventually, Trampas slept on a hardboard base – suspended off the floor by four wooden balls – and surrounded - at each corner - by four, short, wicker stumps!

And so, here we were many years later – eagerly planning and anticipating - the arrival of a new member to our family.

Night-time 4th December 1994.

As I was "raising my vibrations" – I saw a teddy bear and I was told that it was, *"a very famous teddy bear"*.
The communication that followed, came from a person that I had watched on the television. His communication was for someone - equally well known - who he specified by name. I cannot relate his communication, as it is obviously private – but I can include the subsequent communication from Silver Cloud – which concluded that evening's session, and I will do so at the end of this chapter.

The question that arose for me – at the end of the session – was, "how do I pass this information on?"
After consulting with Silver Cloud – and being told who we must speak to about this dilemma – it turned out that: Unbeknown to us – John and I knew someone, who knew someone – who knew the "agent" of the person who was to receive the communication, and - to cut a long story short – the communication, which I had

typed and placed in a sealed envelope - was passed –
through three different people - on to the recipient.
A few weeks later – I was happy to receive a phone call
to say how much the communication had been
understood and appreciated.

I had had a brilliant birthday!
The gift of new music.
The visit of our guides - and subsequent party
atmosphere in "my place".
Interesting and surprising communication.
And a puppy!

I felt that the future was very bright.
I felt that I had a lot of good things to look forward to.

As promised – I will end this chapter by including the
communication from Silver Cloud – on the night of 4th
December 1994.

*"Just because somebody is rich and famous – it does
not bring inner happiness.*
*Being in the limelight and being an entertainer – one is
expected to perform at the push of a button.*
Eventually, the inner self is lost – lost within.
*There are many entertainers – people of notoriety –
people of recognition – who, when they arrive here –
have forgotten their true selves – forgotten their own
identity. They can only identify with the character they
have become. In some respects it is harder for these
people – because they have lost their true identity – and
have to find themselves again.*

*There is a price to pay for being in the lime light – for
being recognised – for being known for what you do."*

*"Those of you who find themselves in the limelight –
must hang on to their inner self. They must know "who
they are" and why they are and never loose sight of the
fact that they are who they are – and not – what they
have become.*

*This is a gentle reminder for all those who may find
themselves in the situation of being in the limelight.*

*You must, at all times, be in control of the spotlight,
yourself.*
*An entertainer such as ……… ……… cannot - through
pressure of work, a need to work, a willingness to work
– be in control of their own destiny.*

*When others press the buttons, when others pull the
strings – however willingly we allow the strings to be
pulled – we are in danger of losing the knowledge of
our inner self. Always, be true to the inner self.*

*As a leader of people, there were those who tried to
push my buttons – to make me function – to make me
decide – to make me lead.*
*But I NEVER lost the sight and the knowledge of my
inner self.*
I passed over – as the whole –
Knowing what I had done.
Knowing why.
Knowing the purpose.
Knowing the outcome.

*To be a leader – to be in the spotlight – to be on public
view – is a difficult and hard reality.*
*The reality of the situation that we find ourselves in,
superimposes itself over the reality of our true being –
hence the mask."*

"The leaders mask –
The politician's mask –
The mask of the comic –
The mask of the public face – hiding the private face.

We all need to return to our centre – albeit briefly.
In returning, we know our centre
If we do not return – we lose our way.

Retain and understand this information and draw on it – and use it – in the safe knowledge that you are drawing on experiences and wisdom of those, long since past, who wish to spread the wisdom to those who are willing to listen.

I hope you have had a nice day.
We have enjoyed it.
That is all today.
Tomorrow is just another day.

If you put the music on again – I will shimmy on out."

CHAPTER SIX

QUESTIONS AND ANSWERS.

On the morning of the 5th December, I telephoned my "aunt" to say that John and I would love to have one of the puppies that she and my "uncle" had offered to us.

She seemed to be very pleased at our decision and asked me if we wanted a dog, or a bitch – and without hesitation – I asked for one of the dog puppies.

My "aunt" invited John and I to go and visit them again – after Christmas – to select the pup that we wanted.

I couldn't wait!

6th December 1994.

John and I had been discussing how both our lives were changing, discussing the opportunities that were being shown to us by Spirit – the opportunity to work "full time" as a medium and healer – respectively.

At certain intervals – in the past 12 months – we had each expressed our willingness – to one another – and to Spirit – to change the path that we had previously chosen. The path that we had chosen and worked hard for - that of - commercial photographer and picture framers – owners of two commercial properties - with employees, and a large 5 bedroomed house, with 4 cars parked, side by side, on the drive - was becoming increasingly difficult to maintain. Our financial commitment to a further business – which was now struggling – added to the pressure that we both felt.

We acknowledged that Spirit had come to show us a different path and we were both willing and eager, to walk that path – with their help and guidance.

But – at this moment in time – life was a little "uncomfortable" and we both wondered "when?" and "how?" – the pressure would lift.

Nighttime.

Silver Cloud and Kato had obviously been listening to our conversation – and they both came to offer advice and comfort, that night.

Silver Cloud:
"Conditions are not perfect – only you know how imperfect the conditions are. When we are moved and settled – things will be on a smoother path, but we cannot control all outside influences and the pattern does not always follow."

Kato:
"We know that you can take on board – those things that are thrust at you.

A channel – in order to work efficiently – needs space and a certain amount of peace and tranquillity around them – and this is how myself and Silver Cloud, wish our channels to work. We are doing our utmost to help when and where we can but we are not all being – all seeing. We cannot control everything.

Silver Cloud and I, both wish our channels peace and tranquillity – although you have both proved that you do not necessarily need these benefits in order to do your work. But, if we are speaking of prolonged, day to day – a continual path – it is not beneficial for the channel to be working under extremes of pressure. Neither is it beneficial to the patient or recipient.
The choice has to be yours."

"Know that we are doing all that we can and know that we have plans afoot, but as Silver Cloud has already communicated – we are not all being.

The time will soon be here – when peace and tranquillity will be more available to you. We are talking a short time – but so much can happen in a short time – so many more pressures and a physical being must divide their energies into different directions – and be in a situation – where their energies are working at their most positive and effective.

The time is not far away from both of you but much work – still has to be done."

After Kato had finished his communication, Silver Cloud told me to *"Go back and wait"*, So I "returned to my chair" to wait until I was called back.

When I returned to "my place" I could see a very tall, thin man (6ft or more), dressed in a light grey suit. His hair was grey, with yellow tinges. He was standing at the rear on "my place" – not speaking. There was a strange look of expectation on his face as though he was waiting for me to recognise him. Silver Cloud, Wolf and this man – continued to stand in silence. I looked towards each of them hoping that someone would speak, but no one did.

These silences always made me feel uneasy – like a small child – I stood, nervously shuffling my feet, waiting for something to happen.

Silver Cloud and William had taught me that I must always wait in silence – until I was spoken to. But nothing was happening and now - as when I was a small child – I didn't find it easy to obey that particular rule. I found silences quite inviting and, as nobody else was speaking - I presumed - (although, very wary of incurring a telling off from Silver Cloud) – that I was being given permission to speak myself.

Taking one more look at Silver Clouds' motionless face and asking Wolf to protect us all - I asked the man what his name was and who his message was for.

The man took a step forward and instantly I recognised him. He was my great uncle – the father of my "aunt" in Co Durham. The great uncle, who owned the farm my family and I had stayed on for our summer holidays, when I was about 9 or 10yrs old.

The great uncle who let me help him to feed the calves and chickens and clean the dairy after the cows had been taken back to the field. The great uncle who had a large shed full of wonderful "things". Things like the cow horn that he gave to me and the deer's antlered head, which had been mounted onto a plaque. (Well – I was impressed at the time!)

The great uncle, who owned the big feather bed – in which my sister and I had slept. The bed was so big – and high up off the floor – that I struggled to get in and out of it! Causing much giggling between the two of us.

The great uncle, who used to sit with a few stems of barley, and wrap tiny pieces of coloured paper – around the ears of the barley – so that it looked like little lanterns. The great uncle, who, having noticed that my sister was irritated by a few warts on the back of her hand (which she had had for some months and had been treated with various potions) took her to one side to speak to her. Great uncle asked her if she wanted to keep the warts – to which she replied "No". He then said – "Well I will buy them off you" and reaching into his pocket – he handed her a penny.

A few weeks later - the warts had totally disappeared – and never returned! Magic.

I had many happy memories of this great uncle and was thrilled to see him again.

Great Uncle

"*You are bringing joy to my family and I wanted to come to say "thankyou".*

I have seen you with them, and it gladdens my heart,

You are very like your mother. Your mother did not have the benefit of knowledge and openings that you have had – but you are very like your mother.

When you were a little girl, your aura was bright and it may surprise you to know – that in my own way – I used healing on the beasts – all those years ago. But I did not have the benefit of knowing – but I found that if I laid my hands on – sometimes an animal would recover from sickness, and so I have known all along and yet not known – until I arrived here. I will continue to watch over you. You are very like your mother."

I asked him how his wife was and he replied, "*she is well and happy.*"

I then asked him if he knew about the puppy?

"*It was my idea – well it was your "uncle's" really.*

I shall watch you train him. Connect with his mind and he will do anything you ask. It is nice to see you – nice to speak to you – you took a while to recognise me.

You are very like your mother.

I will go now.

I shall be watching.
Goodbye."

After the visit from my great uncle had ended, Silver Cloud said in a criticising, irritated, sort of manner:

"You took a while to recognise him.
Instead of expecting them to come forward to speak –
you must tune your vibrations to them – rather than
expecting them to do all the work!"

This criticism really annoyed me – after all:-

Silver Cloud had told me VERY early on, and VERY clearly that: Spirit would enter "my place" from the rear and then come and stand in front of me – and only then - would they begin their communication.
I was feeling aggrieved as he continued.

"You know that, when they are here, we are all safe –
we are all protected, and so instead of wanting them to
come forward to speak – spend a little time tuning into
them – AND – if you had tuned into them – you would
have got him quicker. He wanted to see if you
recognised him – so you are not completely at fault.
You know that when you look at me and I do not look at
you and speak – there are two reasons."

1.   *"There is nothing to say."*
2.   *"You have work to do with that person – with that*
      Spirit."

"Just a little lesson."

Me:
"Was I right to ask Wolf to protect us all?"

Silver Cloud:

"As you know – when everyone is in here – we are all protected. But it is always acceptable to be mindful of just exactly what is occurring. That is: - That you are opening up to Spirit and that Spirit is coming closer to the earth plane. And so – it is not necessary, when we are in the "place" – but it is also correct to be mindful of just what is happening and – yes – ask Wolf for the protection for all – because you want everyone to be protected – don't you?"

Feeling that Silver Cloud was beginning to calm down, I said how great it had been to see my great uncle again. Silver Cloud replied:

"I feel that he has a soft spot for you.

Wolf and I have got work to do – we can not stand around and chat all day. If you are going to go down your path, as we discussed earlier – you are going to have to be quicker than this! I can't think why anyone thinks that you are so wonderful.

Goodbye".

Silver Cloud left.
I turned to Wolf and asked him what I had done wrong. Wolf replied:

"We both know that when he walks out of that door and has not dismissed you – it is our chance to speak.
Silver Cloud knows that you are keen to work and that has been something that he has worked for, for a long time – he knows you are on the verge – and he is quite emotional about it."

"He is not showing that emotion to you – but leaves me to explain."

I thanked Wolf for the explanation and asked him how he was?

"Well and bright. We do not ail here so I will say that I am bright. I have had my time with you. You must go."

I thanked him again and "returned to **my** chair".

Silver Cloud's sudden outburst and the unpredictable side to his nature that he was displaying - was really beginning to confuse me.
He seemed to be changing his own rules – and then - telling me off, when I didn't do things as he wanted them done, and – I reasoned to myself - maybe I didn't always do things exactly how he wanted – but – "There was no need to raise his voice and get "uppitty and stroppy." After all - I deduced - "You'd never catch me behaving like that!! Would you?"

Thank heaven - that Wolf had a more even temperament.

7th December 1994. Nightime.

I went to "my place" – Silver Cloud was standing still and in his right hand, he held a staff.
Silver Cloud banged the staff on the floor:

"I wish to speak.

It has been decided that – with your permission – that we shall – continuing from our conversation yesterday – continue down our path – post haste!"

"We feel that this is what you both want – we understand – that you understand – the problems that may befall – which can be off set, but – with your permission – we shall proceed.
Do I have your permission?"

John and I:
"Yes"

Silver Cloud:
"We have had a meeting – not just those that you know – but with others, and we have decided – with your willingness – that we shall not waste any more time – that we shall proceed on our paths. I have been chosen as the spokesperson because I am nearest to the communication channel.
But rest assured – there has been a meeting.
That this subject was the only agenda.
And it has been decided unanimously.
Well – does that please you?"

John and I: "Yes"

Silver Cloud:
"Right – we shall begin."
I was staggered at the abruptness of Silver Cloud's speech and – not being able to stop myself - I said:

"You are very abrupt."

Silver Cloud:
"I have been chosen as spokesperson and they are all around me now, to make sure that I deliver the message correctly – as was agreed. This is no joking matter!
This is your future we are speaking of – and – this is our futures we are speaking of."

"The Council have urged us – your guides and helpers – to put the situation to you – hence our conversations yesterday.

We appreciate your situation – we appreciate and know, that your situation is going to be altered. You must appreciate that your situation will not be altered overnight. You have already stated your willingness to continue with the work – to spread your horizons and to help others that are guided to you, and so we feel – your guides, helpers and Council – that with your understanding of the situation – there is no reason why we cannot push forward.

I would like to repeat that I am merely the spokesperson and that the team – as you call us – are all in total agreement – and are pleased that you have taken the decision that you have – we would not expect anything else from you. But – you always have the choice – the decision is always yours – never ours.
You have not surprised us.

This is the end of the message – we shall proceed from here.
With love.
Thankyou.
Go."

I "returned to my chair".

The content and speed with which the communication was delivered – left me reeling. I wondered whether there was some sort of double meaning in Silver Cloud's words - or - "Was he just speaking about our work?" The urgency to proceed – I found surprising.

I felt as though I was being pushed forward – with my obvious agreement – and yet – I also had the feeling that I had just signed a contract – without reading the small print!

A feeling that I knew only too well – having once signed (unknowingly) for a very expensive service contract. A contract that we didn't need and a contract - where - it took John's very "persuasive" verbal skills - to release us from.

I believed that – in the past – I had consciously, made very good choices and decisions for myself. Yet here I was, beginning to contemplate the possibility – that the consequences of my decisions – could "back fire on me" – that the control I felt I had over my life – was being taken over – both by circumstance and Spirit.

But - whatever happened – I trusted that Spirit would always be by our side – and on our side.

However – with the house as yet unsold – even with a price reduction – I began to feel insecure in my belief that we would sell the house "just in time" to appease the banks – thus ending our financial difficulties. The alternative was unthinkable.

When I returned to "my place", I found that it was a much more relaxed Silver Cloud - who greeted me.

Silver Cloud:
"Ah – Welcome – Come in.
They have gone now – now that they have heard the communication passed and received.
Well – this is the start – whatever IT is.
One word of advice.
Always manage to find some time for yourselves. Even if it is only minutes and don't forget to "return to the centre".

"Well – we shall have to wait and see what happens now. I must say – I am very pleased.

Ah – here is Mr Bennet."

John and I: "Good evening Mr Bennet."

Mr Bennet:
"Good evening.
*Well it is about time! (*Mr Bennet never liked to be kept waiting) *There is a lot more work we can be doing and we must find the time to fit it in.*
We don't want to worry about the other things – they will sort themselves out. We don't want to be worried about things like that – good grief! – if we worried about things like that all the time – we would never do anything."

Mr Bennet's communication was not helping the sense of foreboding that I was feeling and furthermore – Just what did Silver Cloud mean, when he mentioned "It?"

Mr Bennet continued:

"Anyway – I have to say that it was your decision and it was because of the decisions that you have made – that have allowed us all to progress. To really catch hold of the purpose of our lives – and the purpose of what we are doing – the purpose, as to why we are all together.

I must say – that I am very pleased and of course all those patients that are going to be receiving the benefits of healing – are going to be pleased – they don't know it yet – but they will be – and we know who they are – and they are going to be very pleased indeed."

Mr Bennet continued his communication by discussing one of John's patients. But at the end of that – he returned to the subject of our future:

"I feel that in the Spring we will begin to see a glimmer of hope – an improvement that will be sustainable.
Anyway – we are all very pleased.
Thankyou very much."
After Mr Bennet had left, Silver Cloud said:

"Mr Bennet – he breezes in – he treats this place as his own – he just walks in and walks out again."

Silver Cloud tilted his head, as though he had heard a noise – *"I think somebody else is knocking"* and turning to me, he said – *"Just wait there."*

Silver Cloud walked to the rear of "my place" - opened a door – and put his head through it. I heard his side of a conversation: – *"Well - No – We are very busy."*
It was really funny to witness this "everyday" type of conversation and I waited to see what would happen next. Silver Cloud popped his head back round the door and turning to me, he asked, *"Do you want to speak to William?"* That was like asking a child if it wanted an ice-cream with chocolate sauce on top.
"Yes Please!" I replied.

Silver Cloud poked his head back out through the door and uttering the words *"Oh – well you had better come in."*- he stood to one side of the doorway.

William walked in and greeted me with a hug and a large smile – which matched my own.
Releasing me from his hug – he said:

"They allowed me to listen to the communication – as I have been part of your progression.
Well – I taught you to communicate – nobody can deny that. So they allowed me to listen and to be present.
I am really pleased for both of you.

With Silver Cloud's permission – we will be doing more rescue work, as and when necessary. So I shall always be there and always be available.
I just wanted you to know that I was present.
Well I had better go."

With a bow towards Silver Cloud – he said: *"Silver Cloud has been most gracious – Cheerio."*
I just had time to shout "Goodbye" before he left.

The insecurity and questions that I had had, combined with my earlier confusion over Silver Clouds' - unpredictable behaviour, – dissolved as William had entered "my place". William's presence – as always – exudes confidence and re assurance – which is infectious. Whatever problem I may have – as soon as I see William – I know I will be able to sort it out. Even if the answer he gives is unexpected – or – something that I don't want to hear.

I knew then – that whatever the future held – William, Wolf and Silver Cloud had only my best interests at heart and - if William and I had the opportunity to work together again on a Spirit release – well that would be great.

As if he were echoing my thoughts – Silver Cloud said:

"Only we know, what we are asking you to do and it is only right that you have as much information as can be made available to you.
Your dedication is not in doubt, but we realise that you have a choice and that you have free will.
We would wish to help you with your choices and we are also very eager that you make the right choices.
But these choices that you must make – are exactly that – your choices to be made in your own time.

We cannot expect to take over your life as it is your life, but I repeat – that we are very eager for us all to be working together on a regular - as you would say – full time basis.

This, I have to say, is to enable us to carry out our plans and to help those people whom we know we are going to help – and those who may be a surprise to us.

There is obviously only so much – in the time allotted to us – that we may do. You can only be channels for as long as you are there – and are keen.
We have put a lot of effort into our channels – we will continue the momentum – with your permission.

There are many years ahead of us and you cannot imagine the amount and diversity of the work that has been laid out before you. We are as keen as you – to begin our path – and to fulfil the plan.

I shall go now.
Thankyou for your time.
Thankyou for your dedication.
You may go."

On the 8th and 9th of December I didn't see Silver Cloud and I was given no explanation for his disappearance - I resigned myself to the fact, that I would have to "patiently" await his return. During the afternoon of the 10th, and feeling that Silver Cloud was about – although I couldn't see him – I did see Wolf.

Wolf presented me with a feather – which I placed alongside the three others – on the floor of "my place".

As he handed the feather to me Wolf said:

"It is a tradition, that everyone gives you a feather.
You can go now – Go on!"

That evening I "raised my vibrations" and found myself, with Silver Cloud – in the cottage.

We were in the kitchen and Silver Cloud was looking around at the floor. He said:

"I am just wondering where we shall put the two dog baskets."

He had obviously been listening to my thoughts again! I had been wondering whether – in a few months time – John and I ought to get another puppy – as company for the pup my "aunt" and "uncle" were giving us, and the thought had crossed my mind - that maybe the dog that I had found in the hedge – was a sign that I should "rescue" a dog from a Rescue Centre.

Before I had time to ask Silver Cloud what he thought about that idea – I found Silver Cloud and myself were standing on the first floor of the cottage.

We were standing in a large room which had chairs laid out in it. The chairs had been placed in a semicircle. Silver Cloud sat – firstly in one chair – and then another. He looked as though he were trying to find the beat vantage point in which to listen to the imaginary speaker.

Jumping out of a chair, and heading towards the door, he said:
"Right – come and look at this."

I trotted after him, across a hallway, and into a smaller room.
"This could be a "healing room" he suggested.

Instantly – we were both back downstairs.

The whirlwind tour, took me into a *"dining room"* and a room - although *"small"* it would be suitable as an *"office"*. Back in the kitchen, and sitting at a kitchen table – Silver Cloud asked me if I liked the cottage?

I said that I did, adding that I wished that John could see it. Silver Cloud told me to tell John to *"think"* about the cottage, as he went to sleep – and if he did that – then he too would visit it.

I then asked if Kato had seen it?

"Of course – it has got to be right to work in – for both of you."

The cottage, was by now, very familiar to me. Familiar, in the sense that I felt "at home" in it.
Yet - unfamiliar - I didn't recognise it as a property that I had seen in my locality.

This unfamiliarity raised the question, "How are we going to find this cottage?" I decided to ask Silver

Cloud and, as if in response to my question, Silver Cloud pointed to a calendar that had appeared on the wall of "my place".

"What does that say?" he asked.

I looked at the pictureless calendar, and read out the month that it was showing – "March." There was no year displayed on the calendar, but I immediately assumed that John and I would move into the cottage, wherever it was, in March 1995. My immediate, excited, response to that assumption - was relief and happiness. The "knowledge" that - in 4 months time – all the uncertainty would be over, came as a very welcome surge of relief. I was so relieved – I forgot that my question had been "How?" and not "When?"
Still – at this wonderful moment in time – "When?" couldn't come soon enough for me!
I also deduced that it meant that very shortly – John and I would have an offer on the house! Brilliant!

As if echoing my happy feeling – Silver Cloud cheerily said:

"It is going to be a happy place."

Silver Cloud then spoke in a more sombre tone –
"What do you want?"

My reply, as always, was to work with Them, be free of debts and to live with John and the dog (or maybe, dog's) in this cottage.

Echoing the sombre mood of Silver Cloud, my thoughts reverted to the practicalities of such a move.
Would John and I be in a position to buy this cottage?

I plucked up the courage to ask Silver Cloud the question that I had been dreading to ask. "Is this cottage rented?" I knew that if his reply was "Yes" - that we would rent this cottage - it would mean that the house sale would not have happened. That would mean that the banks' would become increasingly difficult to manage and our finances – more difficult.

Regarding the house sale – my emotions had swung from – very belligerent – to desperate. I now welcomed any viewers with open arms - and with as much patience as I could muster.

I waited with bated breath for his reply:

"Does it matter? You will both make it "your own".
Go on – I will shut the door behind you."

I "returned to my chair" – pondering on Silver Clouds' non-committal reply. Nervously asking myself – "What will the future bring?"

The afternoon of the next day was spent channelling the guide of our dowser friend.

At the end of that communication, the guide was talking about "doorkeepers". My notes show that the guide had said that "doorkeepers" "*do not have names*."

For me – the names of my guides and doorkeepers were important. I took offence at his words – my mind racing with indignation, as he appeared to dismiss the important role a doorkeeper undertook. He seemed to be suggesting that doorkeepers were not important enough to be acknowledged.

After all – I thought: - Without the work that Wolf did – the visiting Spirit would not be protected.

That meant that he would not be able to safely channel, and – I reasoned – such an important person would have a name and – to use a person's name – showed respect! Jumping to the defence (as I saw it) of Wolf – I interrupted the guide by saying, "Well my doorkeeper has a name."

The guide instantly became angry and told me off for interrupting him. He too - became very indignant.
He continued with his communication and left, shortly after. I realised that by interrupting - I had shown disrespect to this guide.

My job was to pass the communication and only to speak when spoken to. Except that - only just recently - I had been told off, for not speaking – hadn't I? It was therefore - with some trepidation - that I "raised my vibrations" that evening. I expected to be told off again, by an irate Silver Cloud, and things didn't look too good – as I saw (for the first time) Silver Cloud standing in "my place" without his bonnet on.

I asked Silver Cloud if he was cross because I had spoken to the guide? His answer came as a surprise and somewhat of a relief – although there seemed to be a veiled "threat" at the end of it

"No No – but beware – do not pass comment – just deliver the message. If you are going to speak to him on a regular basis – as you are - it will help to develop a relationship with him – he will become a friend. You passed comment, rather than questioned. He is a friend of White Cloud – so he will tell White Cloud."

The thought that White Cloud, could at any time, come and tell me off – left me feeling a little nervous.

138

Silver Cloud has this uncanny knack of keeping me guessing! Which is why it is always important to me to heed every word he utters! I have learnt that EVERYTHING Silver Cloud says – is said for a reason. The hard part can be – working out the reason.

I remembered the phrase that Silver Cloud had spoken to me, early in our relationship. When advising me on how to pass communication correctly – he said:

"Say it – As is."

During a general conversation between myself and the dowser, that afternoon – he asked me;
"Have you ever asked Spirit what their world is like?"

I had never really thought to ask this question before – being content to wait for their communication which gave glimpses into their world – but I did, however, tell John what the dowser had asked.

The nightime communication began with Silver Cloud speaking:

Silver Cloud.
"I come from a world where all things are possible – over a period of time, and when I say time – I mean decades and centuries. But I also come from a World which would have no place in the Universe, if it were not for your world – and those like them.
Because without the contact between our World and your World – we would not achieve.

I come from a World where there is not sickness – where there are no wars.
Where there is love and understanding."

"But what would be our function if we could not pass to you – what we know?
We could only help one another in this vast space – and that would be a waste of our talents – if our aim was purely to help ourselves.

If our purpose was purely to help those who entered our World – all the work and preparation over thousands of years would be wasted. All the struggle and hardship – denial and ridicule - of those that have come before you – would have been for nothing.

We need the links – we need the channels.
I speak of all channels – to bridge the two worlds – to make our life meaningful and to give us a purpose.

We could be described as a race – a race of Spirits – as you are a race....."

At this point in the communication, the tape ran out on the machine – and John quickly replaced it.
Silver Cloud continued:

"... of the living and, as your purpose as channels is dual – in that your aim is to help those of your race – and to aid those of us in the Spirit race – so our purpose is dual channel.

We aim to aid and assist our own race and we aim to aid and assist your race. We are a mirror.
Your aims and purposes are our aims and purposes

The race of mankind is struggling into an ever increasing tunnel of darkness – through ignorance and greed – but mainly ignorance."

"We can see the potential disaster and we must all do what we can to halt the progression.

My World is not all knowing – my World also learns from other Worlds. I – like billions of Spirits, at whatever level, be they on the earth plane – in the Spirit World – or beyond. We all – must have the same aim – the aim to perpetuate the species. but not only that – but to create worlds in which the species can live.

That is my World.
End of message.
I will re-form."

That last sentence, *"I will re-form"* will give you some indication – that – as Silver Clouds' communication was being given – his, and my – vibrations - lifted higher. From my perspective – the vision that I normally saw – that of the man – disappeared, as he began to speak. Having experienced the dual channelling of Spirit before – when I "returned to my chair" – I turned to John and said:
"I'm not sure if those were the words of Silver Cloud – or someone higher up?"

I "raised vibrations" again and although I still couldn't see Silver Cloud – he said:

"When I speak and you know it is me – you can attribute the words to me.
When you are told it is White Cloud – you will attribute the words to White Cloud.
If it is apt, that you be told that the communication is coming from higher – then you will be told."

I reported to John, that I still couldn't see Silver Cloud, and Silver Cloud interrupted me, with the words.

"Well – I haven't told you to come back yet!
Give me 10."

I "returned to my chair" to wait for the 10 minutes, that Silver Cloud had requested, to pass.

When I returned to "my place", Silver Cloud was standing, waiting for me.

He greeted me with a, *"Good evening"*

I immediately asked him:

"Where are you – in conjunction with us?" A silly, unstructured question, I know, but experience showed – that Silver Cloud would know exactly what I was asking.

Silver Cloud laughed and said:

"If you imagine or visualise the World – and around the World, or encapsulating the World – a perpex shell – we are in the space between the edge of the World and the outer shell.
We are all around.
We exist within this space.
Which is why you can reach out – and we are there.

In essence – we are all around and we hover over our domain, but we have the freedom and the ability to pass round the entire globe, in this way – you can see through our eyes – you can see what we choose to show."

"There are those who may break free from the shell and travel outwards – and there are those who break free from the shell to travel down. But the downward spiral should be avoided – as a downward spiral, in any walk of life – should be avoided.

As we proceed along our paths' – we all travel further up and out – towards the rim.

Those that travel beyond – do so - to join with another World or Worlds. As, has been indicated to yourselves – other Worlds can be allowed into our World – the Spirit World – for the purpose of reconciliation and for the purpose of continuance."

Silver Cloud disappeared again – leaving me to reflect on his words of caution, regarding downward spirals. I was feeling, in regards to our finances – that I was on a downward spiral – a spiral that was rapidly, becoming out of control.

I also noted his reference to *"other Worlds"* – a reference to the prior visit of Peter.

When I returned to "my place", it was filled with a white, constantly moving, Spirit energy.

From the midst of the energy, came the words:

"It is the Spirit of knowing,
The Spirit of knowledge.
The One who answers the questions.
The reference library.

I am the One who answers questions
You must thumb through my pages.

I am the knowing spirit – of a One.

There is a Seeing Spirit".

143

"There is a Spirit of Pain
There is a Spirit of Healing

Each Individual Spirit, has the answers to the relevant
question. You ask the question – I show myself to you.
You ask a question on the philosophy of Healing – and
my counterpart will answer.
I am the reference library.

I am gone."

The energy disappeared - I saw Silver Cloud, who
continued with: -

"We here – are all Spirit energy – be we small marbles
of Spirit energy – or vast volumes of Spirit energy.

The Spirit energy that you have seen, is part of a vast
volume of Spirit energy. A place, where those above us
go for correct communication – if we do not know,
ourselves.

If I am unsure of the correct answer – I ask my Spirit
guide. My Spirit guide – in turn – will consult with the
Council. The Council will consult with one another and
may go to a higher authority. As your questions become
more personal to us – we shall reach higher, for the
correct communication.

We all have our own role – but we all have a
responsibility to transmit the correct communication.
So – we must strive to be pure in our transmissions – to
be true, and therefore – we must also be responsible to
the One above – and the One above – and those
above."

"With each question you ask – we rejoice in the opportunity to pass the correct communication as it is only through questions and answers – that we will all learn.

If you did not ask us – you would not take the opportunity to hear our reply. If you did not want to know – our communication would fall on deaf ears.

This is the work of Spirit.
This is the purpose of our being.
We have much work to do – and we digress.

I hope your questions have been answered fully.
We cannot add more at this moment in time – there is no more to say.

The channel may close."

CHAPTER SEVEN

"WE SHALL WEATHER THE STORM."

12th December 1994. Nightime.

When I arrived in "my place" – Silver Cloud was standing – cradling a baby. Surprised to see the child – I asked him why he had brought the baby to "my place".

Silver Cloud replied:
"I have brought the baby to show you – it is a Spirit baby – born in Spirit. It is a perpetuation of the species and is a result of "miscarriage" – cells that returned.
It is a little girl.

Although she is a Spirit child – she had to come to your physical world – but she was never meant to be a - physical child."

Me:
"What is the purpose of this? It seems to be a deliberate action."

Silver Cloud:
"She was born for a reason – and yet - not born.
Her path has been laid out before her – but because of her path – she must now grow in Spirit and not in the physical world.
She is special.

I will take the child away.
Come back."

I "returned to my chair" for a few minutes – until I felt that it was the right time to go back to "my place".
Having gone back – Wolf told me that Silver Cloud had gone *"To get something else."*

I waited.

When Silver Cloud returned – he was holding, in his right hand – a blue pyramid. The pyramid was shimmering and sparkling, and as I fixed my gaze on it – the pyramid looked as though it had life – it appeared to be moving around on the stationary palm of Silver Cloud's hand.

Silver Cloud:
"It is a key.
It is living – but not as you understand living."

At that point, I "saw" another pyramid, just the same as the one Silver Cloud held – being placed into another larger pyramid, that was in a hole in the ground.
Only the weathered hands and forearms of the person who was placing the pyramid – were within my vision.

Silver Cloud continued:

"It is life – it is alive.
It is a thought – it is thinking – it can think.
It is a life form.

It cannot die.
It must be – and is – protected.
It is not of the Spirit world and I have not got it – it is only being shown.
No one can possess it
There are many life forms."

"It will never be destroyed and if the earth were destroyed – it would still be there – living. If everything else in the universe was destroyed – those that belong – would return home and life would begin again."

As Silver Cloud, spoke the word "*those*" – I saw many small bundles of blue energy. In the centre of each of the blue energies – there were – what I can only describe – as – open mouths.

Once more, Silver Cloud sent me back to my chair – to await their call to return.

Several minutes passed – before I felt that Silver Cloud was ready to communicate again.

When I did return to "my place" – it was to find that John's Guides were standing in a line with two other men, who I did not know.

The Guides present, were – Kato, Laura, Mr Bennet, Mr White and the two unknown. Kato stepped forward and began his communication to John.

Kato.
"I have a message from home.

You are not to return, until your task is complete and you are a key – like the pyramid.
This message is being passed in front of witnesses and their work, is your task.

When you have completed your task – and you were given your task, before your left – only then will you return home.
You will pass through the Spirit world and greet your friends – but you will not stay."

"The knowledge that you have gained, of the physical world and the knowledge that you will gain of the Spirit world will be stored for the future – if necessary – for trillions of years, if necessary, and only if the universe destroys itself – will you be given another task.

That is a message from home."

13th December 1994.

On the evening of the 13th, and as I "raised my vibrations" – I was un-nerved to feel an energy bearing down onto me. Whatsmore – I could see that this energy was dressed from head to toe, in black.

The blackness, obscuring any features. My immediate response was to shout for Wolf and Silver Cloud – but because this energy was so strong and intimidating – I hastily "returned to my chair" and opened my eyes – folding my arms across my stomach in a bid to protect myself. Still anxious – I tried to raise my vibrations again. Still this presence was looming down onto me in a menacing way. It did not speak – it just leaned forward, into my face.

This action triggered a memory, back to the time when I had been on the receiving end of a physic attack.
The attack had come from a person in the physical world and had lasted the best part of three months.
It had entailed nightly visits from the person – whose aim was to dominate and menace me - in whichever way he could. That memory – that feeling of fright, intimidation and helplessness - mixed with feelings of anger and of wanting revenge - I knew - was partly responsible for my hesitation and panic.

Just the same feelings that had been present when I had seen Peter - dressed in black and standing silently - in front of me. The silly thing was, that the person who attacked me, never dressed in black at all and was always verbal. But the attack itself had been menacing, persistent and nasty. Somewhere in the midst of my mind – I had linked two things – black - and – silent, persistent spirit = danger. I felt that - at this moment in time – I was in the presence of all three.

Feeling that the energy had moved some distance away from me – and with Wolf's permission - I "raised my vibrations" once more.
The thought crossed my mind that this energy could be Silver Cloud, and just as that thought ran through my head – I heard the word - *"Boo!"*

My vibrations had delivered me to "my place" and as I looked around me, I saw Silver Cloud standing in his usual spot, and on his right hand side, I saw a wooden chair – over the back of which – was laid a black coat.

"I've just got in" said Silver Cloud.

With my heart still beating fast, as a result of being faced with an "unknown" energy, and, with the realisation, that it had indeed, been Silver Cloud dressed in black – I asked him:

"Did I pass your test then?"
Silver Cloud just answered with a shrug of his shoulders – then he said:

"You are still backing away."
Disgruntled – I replied: "Well it's not nice!"

"But Wolf told you that it was safe – you know you were protected."

I tried to explain that the black, when combined with an unknown energy, both scared and confused me, but Silver Cloud, seemingly, was uninterested in my excuses and said:

"If Wolf says that it is alright – you can relax."

"How can I relax – when this black is pushing down on me?" I stressed.

"But it was me inside it!
We are not criticising – because we know why – but you have got to get over your feelings! You have to get over your panic!
It is just a black coat."

The rest of that short evenings session was a question and answer session – John and myself, being the ones to ask the questions.

Expecting that Silver Cloud or somebody else would be waiting to communicate – I told Silver Cloud that John and I had no more questions to ask.
His reply was:

"Well – you had better go then."

I "returned to my chair."

During the next evening's session, in which Kato introduced John to an ancient Spirit called Mezulah – we were also introduced to Alexander.

I saw Alexander at the back of "my place". He was busy working at a carpenters' bench - planing a piece of wood by hand – the shavings from his plane were flying off in all directions and landing on the floor.

Alexander, then put his plane down and walked to the end of the bench – he was smiling. I saw that he was a man in his thirties, he was sun tanned and wearing a white shirt, with his sleeves rolled up to his elbows.

Alexander introduced himself by name, adding that he was a boat builder, from Greece. He told John and I that he had come to help both of us and that he would build us a boat to – *"sail on the beautiful blue sea."*

He went on to say that he built *"very good boats"* and explained that he would *"lead us through the tangle"* of our physical path. He then turned back to his workbench and said, *"I must get on with my work."*

At this point, Silver Cloud told John and I that Alexander had been brought in to *"steer us through the business side"* of our life, adding that he – Alexander – was *"only on temporary loan."* and had much *"charm and charisma."* John and I thanked Alexander and Silver Cloud for their help and guidance and Silver Cloud ended the session by saying: *"I think we have everything covered now – Yes – I think that is it."*

This was the second time that John and I had been assisted on our travel through life – with the aid of a wooden boat. The first was built by a man called Jose'. Over the years – the two wooden sailing boats have merged into one vessel. A vessel, which creaks and groans as it speeds along the top of the mightiest seas. A vessel which silently bobs on blue, tranquil waters, and a vessel which is always brought safely into harbour – by the expertise of the man at the helm.

As Alexander departed – Kylifah, the guide of our dowser friend entered "my place", and referring back to his channels earlier question regarding the proximity of Spirit, which myself and John had asked 3days ago – he quickly delivered the following communication:

"Is it not enough that you know that we are here?
Ask him where he sends the impertinent spirits – that he releases?
You know that the Spirit world exists.
We cannot be tied down geographically – we cannot be tied down – as to where we are.
We are all around.
We are Omnipresent!

You could not open an atlas and show where we are.
You could not fly a plane to reach where we are.

Surely – you are honoured enough – to know that we are there. There are too many questions asked, and not enough action!

Why do people ask continuous questions – merely to delay the action they must take?

It should be enough for you all – to know that we are there.

Where we are – is not the question.
What we are there for – is the question – and you know the answer.

There is too much time wasting – too much delay.
These questions need not be answered until you arrive here – and then you will know – you will not have the question."

"Silver Cloud, waxes lyrical – but I do not believe in such explanations. We are all here for a purpose and we must get on with the work in hand – and make haste – and not bother ourselves with the consequentials.

I thank you."

Kylifah swept out of "my place" and I could almost feel my hair blowing away from my head – as I stood in the wake of his departure.

Silver Cloud said:
"Well there you have it.
I do try to give explanations – if it is appropriate – understanding your natural curiosity. Guides such as he – do not see that explanation is necessary once contact has been made, and as he rightly says – explanations can be given at a latter date.
Please – by all means – give my explanation to the channel. If more questions arise, of the same nature – I would suggest that he ask Kylifah directly. And I shall await with interest – his answers.

Kylifah is somewhat unique and has very definite and determined plans, ideas, beliefs and understandings – and yes – I feel that we have all learnt a valuable lesson.

I thank the channel for the respect shown to him.
Well – I will go now to see how the boat is coming along.

Cheerio."

The following 10 days, where a very confusing time for me. Once again – Silver Cloud was "called away on business" and during his absence and despite occasional contact with Wolf and distant contact with Silver Cloud – I was – once again - visited by "unknown" energy. The contact with Wolf and Silver Cloud was spasmodic and on occasion – bizarre. I had many battles with myself – to keep focussed and open minded during this time. That dreaded word – patience – reared before me as I was once more put to the test.

Each night, I would "raise my vibrations" and record the outcome of my efforts in my notebook: -

16th December 1994.

I saw Wolf – but we are not in "my place".

Wolf has told me that Silver Cloud is at a "*business meeting*" and will be away for a few days.

I asked Wolf why I was not in "my place" and he told me that he and I will work at a lower vibrational level.

"Come back tomorrow night.
You may go."

17th December 1994. Afternoon.

I saw Silver Cloud and he said he hoped that I was "*behaving myself*" in his absence. He told me to work with Wolf. I saw, hanging in the air – the letter H – it was made out of green tinsel.

When I asked Silver Cloud what it meant – he replied – "*Maybe it stands for holly? Come back tonight and we will have something arranged.*"

I returned to "my place" that night – but it was empty. There is no more communication with either Wolf or Silver Cloud until the afternoon of December 19th.

19th December 1994. Afternoon.

I saw both Wolf and Silver Cloud. Silver Cloud was holding a Western style saddle and when I asked him about it – he just replied that someone had given it to him. Silver Cloud said that they had decided not to do any work over the last two days and when I asked him if he was back to stay – he replied:
"Yes – unless I get called away again."

19th December 1994. Nightime

Saw Wolf and Silver Cloud in "my place". They came and stood – one on either side of me. I felt as though an energy from above was being focused on us – then – Wolf and Silver Cloud stood away from me.
As they moved away, a tomahawk fell to the ground and landed with a crunching thud – into a thick piece of wood, which had appeared on the floor in front of me.
Silver Cloud stepped forward and removed the tomahawk from the wood – he handed the tomahawk to me, and I knew that I had to place in with my feathers, which were kept on the floor of "my place".

Silver Cloud then told me that they were *"modernising the system"* and that I was to be given a *"code word"* to be used by me – during my opening up procedure. This code word would be my password to allow me access to my place and to let waiting Spirit know that I was who I said I was. I found this new information quite bazarre and unnecessary, resulting - in my feeling uncomfortable and annoyed. These feelings were increased, when Silver Cloud then explained, that one idea for a code word for me, had been *"My little testy one"* – another - *"Thunder Dog"*. However, he added – I have decided to call you *"Fire Stick."*

Silver Cloud then said:

"Well – I think we have spent quite enough time.
You may go.
We will have more news tomorrow."

20th December 1994. Nightime

As I "raised my vibrations" I was aware of somebody standing to my right – they were dressed in a brown monk's habit. On my left – there was someone who emitted a very cold energy. This energy was blowing cold air into my face. I didn't recognise the vibration of either of them.

In my mind – I was immediately transported back to the night – some months ago – when John and I had been visited by a group of 6 monks. The monks – in Spirit – still resided at a disused Abbey, which was not far from our home. They had visited us because they were very unhappy about John's impending visit to the sight.
John had been asked by the new developers of the site – to dowse the land for them. The monks were very protective of the land and indeed rumour was that the monks had buried "treasure" on the land – many moons ago. Judging by their menacing reaction on the night of their visit – my feeling was - that the rumour had a lot of truth in it. Their warning – not to place any dowsing rods in the ground and not to disturb the ground in any way – was very clear – although they fell short of warning of the consequence of such an action.
However – they had been a formidable sight and a chilling energy - and the monk that was before me now – emitted the same power.

This power was doubled in intensity – as I realised that the cold energy that had been on my left - was also dressed in monk's habit. The two monks moved and stood a little way in front of me, then turned to face me. Their heads were bowed and hidden within the huge folds of their hoods. I was feeling very nervous as - to my horror – they looked up at me and silently - began to beckon me forward – asking me to follow them.

Panicking – I asked for Wolf or Silver Cloud to come but I heard or saw nothing from them. Out of the silence and from within the hood of one of the monks, came the words:
"They will not speak or help you."

The two monks and I stood in silence for a long while – during which – I relayed to John – what I was seeing and what was happening. John was, by now, busy asking - through his pendulum – if it was safe for me to remain within this energy. The answer was "yes".
Getting very fed up with the cold and this seemingly endless stand-off – I decided to take one step towards them. They – in turn – took one step towards me.

Having been around animals all my life, I knew that if you showed them that you were fearful – they could take advantage of that – and so I took a deep breath to calm my fears – gritted my teeth - and took two more small steps forward.
The monks disappeared.

Relieved – I asked for Wolf and Silver Cloud to come. There was no reply.
I "returned to my chair".

A few minutes later, I "raised my vibrations" once more. I arrived at "my place" and found that, placed on the floor - there was a giant plant pot – containing a leafy green plant. The atmosphere was very cold and I was aware of an energy present. I could feel it moving around me. I asked the energy, "Who are you?" and the reply came – *"The Ice King"*. I then asked – "What is the purpose of your visit?" to which came the reply – *"Nothing"*. Then the energy disappeared.

There was no sign of Wolf or Silver Cloud.

I hastily "returned to my chair".

I did not see or hear from Wolf or Silver Cloud for the next three days.

Not for the first time – I felt abandoned.

Not for the first time – I was confused.

Not for the first time – I felt as though I had let Wolf and Silver Cloud down. I continued to sit every day and evening but the result was always the same – nothing.

24th December. Afternoon.

I went to "my place" and was very happy to find both Wolf and Silver Cloud waiting for me. The extreme cold energy had disappeared – so had the plant – and things were back to normal. I told Silver Cloud that I felt that I had let him down because I had allowed myself to become confused and apprehensive adding that I knew that I had made mistakes and not followed his strict rules. I had known that I was being tested and believed that because Silver Cloud had been absent for several days - the longest time he had ever been away – I must have failed the test.

Silver Cloud answered my theories by saying:

"You have not made a mistake – you did what you had to do. Because you were put in a position – where you felt lost – and then were presented with 2 Spirits.
You did what you had to do.
No one can say that you made mistakes – you reacted.
An interesting exercise!

A training exercise for a communication channel.

There is no answer – to what is right or what is wrong in your action. It is an exercise and therein lies the difficulty – there is no right and wrong – merely a reaction.

You will meet them again – Or will you?
You must expect these visits – Or should you?
Take life as it comes."

Me:
"When I took a step forward, they moved away and disappeared."

Silver Cloud:
"They were always going to."

Me:
"Will you be there tonight?"

Silver Cloud:
"I might be – and I might not. My little testy one.
Off you go. I may see you later – or I may not.
Wolf has got a candle."

Silver Cloud then turned to Wolf, who was indeed, holding a lighted candle, and asked:

"What about the flower pot?"

Wolf:
"Whether it be a flower pot or whether you see me – it is still me. You could not see in the flowerpot.
The form does not matter.
It is the Spirit energy that matters."

Silver Cloud and Wolf then said *"goodbye."*

One lesson that I learnt from this communication, and a lesson that I have passed on to many other people - is – If you feel that Spirit is standing uncomfortably close to you – ask them to step back.
It is so simple to do, and IT WORKS!

At 11. o'clock that Christmas Eve, John and I prepared for the evenings' session. I was full of hope that both Wolf and Silver Cloud would be waiting for me. I went to "my place" and saw Wolf standing there, surrounded by swirling pastel shades of colour and light.

"Wait 'till 12 midnight." Said Wolf.

I "returned to my chair."

On the stroke of midnight I began to "raise my vibrations". As I soared upwards, I found myself on a sailing ship. The ship was not in the water – but flying through the air, and as I looked around me, I saw Jim, Kato, Mr Bennet and Laura – all healing guides of John, with Wolf and Silver Cloud. Whilst still holding my vibrational level – I quickly relayed to John – what I was seeing, and when I looked around the ship again – it was to see that John was also on board.
Silver Cloud spoke:

"We are all going to be together for a long time.
One unit with separate compartments – all with
different jobs to do – but we all fit together in the boat.
It is Alexander's' boat, it is very sturdy.

On this Christmas morning – a new year begins.
A new journey for all of us. The start of a new year.
New beginnings.

The team will stay together because each and every one
of us has got our own, and yet, collective path.
Alexander is up on the top of the mast – he is looking
for land.

So we have waited 'till this Christmas day to begin a
new year, and next Christmas day – allow yourself to
look back and see how you have travelled.
Here begins the story. Well – that is all from me.
Happy Christmas."

Kato:
"There is security among friends.
The team are gelled together and we all honour and
respect one another.
Sayonara."

Jim:
"Just to let you know – I have been chosen to steer the
boat from the front."

Mr Bennet and Laura in unison: *"Merry Christmas."*

Wolf:
"I have a very important roll.
I am at the rear.
I watch every body's back."

Alexander:
"I told you that I built sturdy boats.
It is rather a large one – there are many of you.
This boat will not sink, This boat will ride the heaviest
of weathers – the largest of waves. It will not become
waterlogged. My boats do not seep, and I am a-top – to
give the physical direction – North – South – East –
West – and those in-between. I plot the course.
I follow the stars and take the safest route.
I do not say that we shall not have storms – but we
shall weather them."

I continued to sit every day and night and received
communication from our "team".
At 11. o'clock on the 31st December 1994 – New years
Eve – Wolf - speaking in a formal and solemn way -
greeted myself and John, with the words:

"I would like to introduce your two Spirit guides –
Silver Cloud and Kato – they have come to speak."

I could see both Silver Cloud and Kato, standing apart,
but as they began to communicate, their energies
merged together. I could see that they were each
mouthing the words, yet, I was hearing one voice.
Their combined message was:

"We are here as your Spirit guides.
For the last few months, we have all been getting to
know one another, and getting together as a team.

We come tonight as one – yet two – to begin our
separate paths. Each channel will now begin their
journey on their separate path."

I was still having to put a lot of work into keeping my vibrations on a level with theirs and told Silver Cloud that "it was a bit difficult" to maintain the communication. Silver Cloud replied: *"You can do this"* and they both waited until I had regained the vibrational level.

Silver Cloud and Kato, continued:

"We are here to say, that as from now – we are officially your guides. We will each work with our own channel and each channel will now proceed down their separate paths. This is not a divorce of the team effort.
This is notice, that each channel must begin to work within their own sphere. This is where your new life begins.

Your two guides are together as one and as we separate – so your new paths begin. We shall continue as the Team – but – mark the beginning of your new life.

Happy New Year."

Kato, then said *"Sayonara"* and left.
Silver Cloud said, *"I will be back."* and he too, left.

Wolf continued the communication with the words:

"It has been decided that your guides will remain with you until their work with you is complete – this may take some time. The relationship that has been built – will now be built upon, further. Your guides welcome you on your path and on their path.

Thankyou.
You may return."

Just after Wolf spoke these words – the audio tape ran out – and I grinned in admiration once more - at their timing – as I replaced the used tape with a new one.

It was, by now, after midnight. I returned to "my place", to find that Wolf was waiting for me. He said:

"Your two guides have gone – they are happy to have delivered their message – and – I don't know about you but we are going to have a party."

It was then, that I saw Jim, John's doorkeeper. Jim was obviously eager to go to the party, as he urged Wolf to, *"Come on Wolf – come on!"* to which, Wolf replied – *"I will just see the channel off the premises."* Turning to me, he said*: "Silver Cloud, loves you very much, you know. Now – go on – because I will be late!"*

I prepared to lower my vibrations, believing that the evening's communication was over – but to my joy – Armon, my uncle, and John's mum, Elsie – came. I relayed this information to John and we both eagerly waited to speak with them. Elsie spoke first – to John.

"I am always watching – I have not been to visit for a while. I know the path that you are going down, and I am very happy, and I am happy for myself" *Laughing – she continued: - "I don't know whether you have missed me? I have been very busy."*

John affirmed that "yes" he did miss her, and then asked what she had been doing.

"I am having a wonderful time – so many things to see – so many people to meet – and although I have not visited for a while – I am still watching.

I am going to the party. Oh, we can have a laugh here. There is so much love – it is all around you and it is in everybody that you meet. I am very happy here.
I shan't be coming back (to the earth plane). *I am going to stay, but I know what goes on in the world. I can't do much about that – maybe you can?*

I'll see you son.
Bye Lynn."

Armon – to John:
"Your mum and I are great friends you know – we get on very well.
She has been helping me with some rescue work."

Armon – to me:
"I speak for your family in spirit. They all know how your path is growing. I came as their representative – to my "favourite niece." We will meet one day and be together and we will have so much to talk about – but not yet. The family wish you well. This is a happy day for both of you. I watch my little girl – I will always watch my little girl – she knows that. It is left to me to tell the channel to close. I tell the channel to close.
William sends his love to both of you.

I believe, you are known as "Fire Stick" – this is very apt for you – you are in safe hand's.
And now I tell the channel to close.
I will visit again.
Close.
Goodnight."

Silver Cloud - as promised - returned.

"What are you doing!?" he snapped - at myself and Armon. He spoke and acted, as though he had just caught two naughty children who had been found reading under the bedcovers after "lights out".

Armon and I grinned at each other – and said a speedy "Goodnight".
Silver Cloud turned to me and said – as only an American can say:

"Have a nice daaaay"

Adding sharply:

"The channel WILL close!
GOODNIGHT!!!"

As I scurried back to "my chair", I swear I heard Silver Cloud snap a light switch off in "my place", as he left.
Like any indignant parent might – in a bid to stamp it's authority over two disobedient children who should have been asleep, hours ago.

CHAPTER EIGHT

1ˢᵗ – 7ᵗʰ JANUARY. 1995.

1ˢᵗ January. 1995.

On the evening of New Years day, and as I raised my vibrations – I began to feel a cool, vibrating energy. As I continued to lift my own vibrations, the coolness changed to heat. This hot energy began to swirl with increasing speed and was concentrating its attention, around my heart chakra. Feeling the need to ground – I asked that Wolf or Silver Cloud would help me. In answer to my request, Silver Clouds placed his hands on my feet and as he did so – I felt my feet, sinking into the floor. This assisted grounding, gave me the opportunity to focus on my heart chakra, and as I looked at it – I saw a thread of energy, emanating from the ether, which was entering my heart. The heat reverted to cold, and I could feel a very precise cold spot, within my chest. My vibrations continued to lift – and the energy continued to swirl around me. I recognised that the energy – was Peter – the Spirit from the Alien world.
The communication began.

Peter.
"I know you find it hard to comprehend, that I am not of the Spirit world, that you know. This is not a matter for concern. I am not concerned.

My molecular construction, is of no importance, at this moment in time. The link that we have made, is the important factor."

Me;
"Am I speaking directly to you?"

Peter:
"Do not think that you are so great that you are speaking directly to me. I am speaking through White Cloud and Silver Cloud. I am not concerned that you cannot comprehend. I am happy if you would think of me as one of your Spirits' – for the time being.
The thread means that you are mine – and any other work that you may do, when not in my use – is of no concern of mine – suffice to say, that when I demand that you work for me – everything else will be forgotten – set aside.

When asked – you replied that you would dedicate the rest of your life to the work of Spirit and the Spirit world. I am part of that world.
Ultimately – your dedication is to me – know it."

That is all I have to say.
The channel may be released to the work of its guide.
Farewell."

White Cloud:
"I will take the opportunity to speak – as we are stacked, still. We wish, that you feel safe within the task that has been set before you. There are many, within my community who are supporting Silver Cloud, Wolf and yourself – in your endeavours – both, as a day to day communication channel and in you other work.
Neither Silver Cloud nor myself, carry the burden of the production of the channel, and the progress of the channel, alone. We have much support, above and around us, in this matter."

"You are correct in saying that you are a tool – but you are not a tool to be misused – abused and discarded.
When your physical life is over – you will continue the work in Spirit, and therefore you are a treasured commodity.

You have the added insurance of living with another channel, who understands that you will have to do, as you are bid – thus creating a harmony in your physical life – to assist in Peter's task.

The channel that you live with, is stable. Should you show signs of becoming unstable – you have a built in stabiliser. You are being looked after on all spheres. His reward from Spirit, for his role – is to live with a communication channel.

We in Spirit – thankyou.
Now I must leave.
Goodbye."

Peter always leaves me with a chill down my spine.
I know what he expects me to do – and roughly – when and where - he expects me to do it. I know that I am not the only channel on whom these expectations fall.

I continue to wonder what the outcome of his expectations – relating to myself - might be, and still –
I do not have his permission to relate all that I have been told. I do know – because he has told me – that if I break any rules – I will be replaced.

So – for the purposes of telling this story – I have - with their permission – included Peter's communications – to the extent that I have. I know that there is at least one other communication of his, that is to be included - and

171

then – just as in the years that have followed – Peter will fade into the background.

To re-emerge – at a time of his choosing.

As I have looked through my notebooks – in order to write this chapter – I see that on some evenings – I didn't see Silver Cloud of Wolf. On these evenings – I would sit for an unspecified time – and continue to raise vibrations. Other evenings were taken up with channelling for John and his patients and for two other channels and their patients. I also did sittings for a few people. Most of this communication is private to the individuals and will therefore – remain so. However – I will rely on my Team – to highlight those communications (or parts of) that they want to be heard. So - as I continue to narrate the story – you will notice that - unlike the previous pattern of the "day to day" format – there will be gaps in the dates. These gaps were filled with the communications as described above and time spent just "raising my vibrations".
I continued to "sit", every day and night.

2nd January 1995. Evening.

When I arrived at "my place" I heard Silver Cloud say to someone:

"This is my channel – Fire Stick."

Into my vision, came a tall native American Indian – he was carrying a stick.
Holding the stick towards me, he said:

"I have brought you a gift – I am Geronimo.

You are one of many channels working for the Indian, and Silver Cloud has invited me to come to "say hello".

On behalf of the Indian – I would like to thank you for the work that you are embarking on.
Your admiration for the Indian race has been noted and I like to visit the white channel. I am grateful to the white channels who work with the Indian.

I still suffer – in my heart for all those who suffer from racism – it is very near, and dear, to my heart.
Because my people suffered so much I still feel the arrow in my heart. One of my duties in Spirit – is to work against racism – not just because of colour – but because of the way of religion and way of life. This is one of the things that I want to stamp out – and so you will understand that when I come to you – as a white person – I give my gratitude – you show no racism. So I leave my stick, as a reminder of my visit. I see that you have a collection of gifts – I hope you will add my gift to your collection."

Looking towards Silver Cloud, and silently asking and receiving permission to approach Geronimo – I stepped forward. Geronimo held the stick out towards me, and taking it, I placed in on the floor with the feathers and tomahawk.

Silver Cloud, clapped his hands together twice, and said; *"You may go."*

I "returned to my chair", for a few minutes – before returning to "my place".
Silver Cloud was waiting for me and began to speak:

"Geronimo is a great friend. We do still - even in Spirit – collect as a people – we live as a people. We have the need to be together as a people, and we always will.

We feel that to be the Indian, is to continue the responsibility of our forebears – to remain as a people – even in Spirit. Our existence, when in the physical world was guided by Spirit – as was that of our fathers and their fathers before them – and so it must continue in our life in Spirit. It is through this amalgamation, that we can reach our own people in the physical – as our fathers did and their fathers did and their ancestors did – and so we must continue – it is our way.

When the Indian passes into the Spirit life – they join our community – with the freedom to experience other civilisations – but they belong to our community and it is only right that we all live together, and as I have said – we carry the responsibility of our forefathers – in guiding our people, still on Earth.

You are lucky, that I have chosen you as a channel.
Some of us, choose different nationalities as our channels – instead of our own people – as this is only right – so that you may experience the close proximity of us – and we of you. I could have had a very obedient squaw! But – it is part of my evolvement – my rough path – that I chose to work with a white channel.
But – I am capable - and able of overcoming the many misdemeanours of my channel.

I am strong in my ability – and to be fair – no one has ever told me that my life in Spirit would be an easy one, and now the channel is functioning at the correct vibration – the channel may go."

"I sometimes feel – if it was not for Wolf – I would walk off the job. Do not believe all that Wolf tells you – he gets carried away.

I will tell you more of my people and the work we have to do, at another time. Thankyou for calling.
Say Gooodnight to Wolf
I will be waiting.
Now – Go on!"

4ᵗʰ January 1995. Nightime.

As I "raised my vibrations" I felt a great deal of cold swirling energy around me, and after some minutes of waiting for clarification of who it was – I heard the words: "*Stop me.*"
Realising that the words were those of Silver Cloud – I said; "Stop."

Silver Cloud:
"I wondered how long you would keep me floating round there?"

Relieved that he was in a good humour – I relaxed and smiled, as he continued:

"You are becoming a more patient channel – but – you must still ask for what you want – rather than sitting and letting "it" go on around you. There was a time, when you would have been shouting "Wolf!" and "Silver Cloud!" and demanding that you be given an explanation. Now, you have become more patient – but you must still ask some questions – but as "Fire Stick" and not "Thunder Dog."

175

I was thrilled to bits to hear these encouraging words.
At last – it seemed as though the words Lynn and
Patience – did belong in the same sentence!
No more – that dreaded "P" word. I could only hope
that I could maintain my newly found status – that of
being a "patient person!"

Later that evening, Silver Cloud gave the following
answer – in response to the question from John –
"Would practising opening the brow chakra, help to
develop clairvoyance?"

Silver Cloud:
*"In raising your vibrations – after opening the chakras
– Spirit will guide you. Your function is to make
yourself ready to receive communication at whatever
level – in whatever manner would be of benefit to you.
Your part in this, is to make yourself as available as
you can – to prepare as much as you can – to receive
the information. Be that pictorial – verbal, or feeling.*

*The work is never finished, because the channel can
always reach higher and the possibilities can be
endless, but you must start with the energy centres and
attuning yourself with your guides and helpers, and
when you are in a state in which you can receive – you
will receive – because they are ready to send."*

John:
"So – if opening up as a healing channel – I am also
opening as an "anything" channel?"

Silver Cloud:
"Anything else you are capable of receiving."

John:
"I have seen things in the past – parts of the body – I assume that that is to help with healing – Is that something I need to ask for?"

Silver Cloud:
"*No.*
If it is their will, that you receive this and you are prepared and ready to receive it – you will receive it.
If it is not applicable – one assumes they will not send it. Maybe they have not decided whether you receive in pictures, or whether you receive verbally. Maybe one helper would send in one manner and another would send differently, but, all they can ask, is that you make yourself ready to receive whatever.

You are a natural healer and so when healing – naturally, all this occurs.
It is a natural gift – but – the visualisation and the hearing and understanding – is a further aid to your healing – and this must be worked on, if you want to receive the pictures, or hear the words.

My channel has the natural gift of communication BUT – the channel has had to add to that natural gift in order to access higher. You have been a healing channel for many years – without you knowing – so the healing channel is not in question – the other abilities can be quite easily learnt."

At this point in the communication – Kato, Laura, Mr Bennet and Mr Mcdonald – all healing guides and helpers of John – entered "my place". Kato stepped forward to speak:

177

Kato:

"Good Evening.
Your ability as a healing channel is not in question.
Myself, and the helpers behind me – all have our
individual task to perform. As your healing guide, I
have arranged for the helpers to be gathered. I have
brought them all together to assist me in my task. They
are doing my work for me at this moment in time and I
step back as I put each one in place. I ask that under
my guidance, you work with each and everyone.
I want you to know that I am always there – although at
this moment in time – I stand back to allow them to
perform their tasks with you. They are helping me on
my path, as well as fulfilling their own roles and your
roll. I ask that you work with them and allow them to
communicate with you in their individual ways."

Laura:

"You are already able to communicate with me – me,
as I have grown up – you as the channel. You know
when I am there – and you hear me – and this has been
a natural growth."

Mr Bennet:

"I prefer the direct communication through the
channel. But you can feel my presence.
My strong presence – when not healing – will indicate
that I wish to communicate and I will communicate
through the channel." (Lynn)

Mr McDonald.

"You will continue to feel my presence – but I will
communicate through the channel." (Lynn)

Kato:

"I have brought together a very able and somewhat jolly team of helpers. I wish you to enjoy the communication and nearness of us. I will be there, and we will work together. In the meantime – work with the three – not forgetting Jim (doorkeeper.) I shall be away for a few days, planning our journey together.
I thank the channel.
I thank Silver Cloud.
I thank Wolf.
If you need me – then ask. I will not be far.
Good day."

As Kato and John's team left – I remembered the forthcoming London trip that John and I had planned. In a few days time – we were going to visit the psychic artist Coral Polge.
I asked Kato if he would be with us on that trip?

Kato:
"I am hoping that I can come – I am the team leader!"

I had already asked Wolf and Silver Cloud – in the hope that Coral Polge would be able to draw their images. I was very excited about the outcome.

I also took the opportunity to ask Silver Cloud what he thought about our (John and I) decision, to have two puppies from my "aunt" and "uncle".

Yes – we had decided to have two!
On returning from visiting the litter of puppies and choosing one of the males', we thought - on reflection - that it would better for him to have some company.
I rang my "aunt" and "uncle" to ask if we could buy a second pup. Their reply was "Yes" - we could choose

179

another one – but – "No" – they would not take any money. When asked which pup we wanted, we said that we would like a little female – "the one with the crinkly ears" – "the one who had puddled on the carpet!" And so, John and I were eagerly awaiting the phone call – the call that told us we could go and pick up "Jack" and "Jill", and bring them to their new home. The call, which would herald a new era.

Both John and I were very touched by the generosity of my "aunt" and "uncle" as we continue to be – to this day. Silver Cloud's thoughts on our decision to have two puppies instead of just one – were as follows:

"There are plenty of us to watch them.
None of us would wish to grow up alone – be that a human being – animal – bird. Nothing in nature grows alone – nothing in nature can grow alone – it would fade and die. A living being that is capable of pain and emotion, should not grow alone – it should be with it's own species. As a general rule – a human being, could not be totally happy in the continuous, close proximity of another species – without one of it's own, and, likewise – an animal – although much loved – is happier and grows more readily and openly, with one of it's own species. If a tree is planted on it's own – it sends out seeds and they grow into saplings – and so the tree creates it's own species around it.
A tree could not live without others – it would not grow to its full height – it's full dimension.

The puppies will be happy and thrive.
Does that answer your question?"

I took that as a "Yes – Good Idea!"

6th January 1995. Afternoon.

When I arrived in "my place" – Silver Cloud was sitting on the floor. He gestured an invitation for me to sit and join him.
"I believe you wish to speak to me?" he asked.

I wasn't surprised that he knew that I had a question to ask. After all, he was always with me, always knew what I was thinking, always knew what I was feeling – knew me better than I knew myself, but every time he pre-empted a question – I would always smile to myself. It was my reminder that "Yes" – Silver Cloud was always with me, even on those occasions when he was "away on business", and Silver Cloud always allowed me to ask my questions in my own time.

Me:
"I wondered if we could move the afternoon sessions to the morning?"

Silver Cloud:
"What do we use these sessions for?"

Me:
"To join our energies and be together.
If we could move it to the morning – at the start of the day – maybe you could give me some advice on what was going to happen that day. We could join our energies ready for the day."

Silver Cloud:
"But I am with you during the night – when you are asleep."

Me:
"Maybe we could use the morning so that you could explain what had happened during the night – while I can still remember some of it."

Silver Cloud:
"*Mmmmm*
I would have to change my schedule."

Me:
"Yes – but if you are already with me during the night – and if we used the morning – you would be free during the day."

As you can no doubt tell – I really wanted to move the session – for my own convenience. I had been "sitting" at 4.00 o'clock, every day for months, and sometimes I found that it was inconvenient – as it would be when John and I went to London, and, when we went to pick the puppies up. Silver Cloud – although he knew this – and also - what the outcome would be – was not going to make it easy for me.

If I had been open and honest about my reasons –
the conversation would have been a lot shorter!
The conversation continued:

Silver Cloud:
"*Wolf would have to change his schedule.*"

He called Wolf to come and join us.

Wolf:
"*You must ask for protection at night.*"

I agreed to do that.

Wolf:
"Maybe it would be a good idea to change to a morning session – we are already together at night."

Silver Cloud:
"I will give you my answer tonight.
Well – we have discussed that – you may go."

I stood up to leave – saying that I would see them later that night.

Nightime. 6ᵗʰ January.

Silver Cloud:
"Wolf *has persuaded me, to allow you to commune with us, in the morning. This is for practical reasons and I have been swayed by Wolf."*

Me:
"Thankyou."

Silver Cloud:
*"Don't thank me – thank Wolf.
It would fit with Wolf's agenda – so – we will change our 4.00 o'clock meeting to a 9.00 o'clock meeting.
I shall give you some latitude."*

Me: Not being an early riser, and with a feeling of panic – I asked:
"How much latitude?"

Silver Cloud:
"We are considering your nightime movements."
He paused to consider them for what felt like and eternity and then said:

"Within half an hour of your waking.

Wolf can be very persuasive.
Come back."

So – I had been given the decision. Now all I had to do was to rush round every morning and be "in my chair" prepared to receive communication - within half an hour of opening my bleary eyes. Great!
You know that phrase – Beware of what you want – because you just might get it – I think that it applied to the situation I now found myself in!

When I returned to "my place", Laura, one of John's helpers was there. With her, was the little blonde haired girl I knew to be Angela. On the 22nd September 1994, Angela had come to ask me to pass a message to her mother. I thought Angela was about 4yrs old.

Laura:
"This is Angela and she is a friend of mine. She will be with us sometimes, on "work experience".
I have taken her under my wing. She is a lovely child, and like me, is growing up in the Spirit world, so, I have been spending some time with her. She likes to see the animals and so she is going to come – when we see the animals."

Me:
"How are you Angela?"

Angela:
"I like being with Laura – we play games – but not with the animals."

"Laura says – when I grow up, I can look after the animals and you're having puppies. Can I come and see your puppies?"

John:
"Of course you can."

Angela:
"Laura says I must behave myself but we play sometimes."

Laura:
"I hope you like our little helper – she will come with me sometimes. The love and friendship that I received when growing – I now give to a little girl."

John:
"She is a lucky little girl."

Laura:
"We are lucky to have her in our midst.
She is 4yrs old.

*Anyway do not worry about the dog (*ref. to a dog that John had been helping*) as long as they feed suitable portions and quantities – for such a young dog – she shouldn't have a problem."*

John:
"That's good news."

Laura:
"Come along Angela."

Angela:
"Bye bye."

John
"Bye."

Laura:
"She is a thumb sucker.
Bye."

Laura took Angela (who was sucking her right thumb) by the hand and they walked away.

Silver Cloud:
"When that child came to deliver her message – she entered everybody's hearts, and Laura knew of her, because of her circumstances of growing up in Spirit.
Laura asked Kato to permit Angela to visit occasionally, when healing with the animals.
Kato has given his permission, as long as the child is not a disruptive influence.

That is enough – turning my place into a nursery.
Any questions?"

One question, we did ask Silver Cloud, that evening, was – "Can we help everyone – whom we come in contact with?"

Silver Cloud:
"We are always guiding people to channels – else – why would we put all the time and effort into the channels? But – we cannot make people want to listen – we cannot make people want the healing. But – everybody, who crosses your path, is crossing your path for a reason, and it is for you – to find the reason – to know the reason – and – if necessary – to offer the services of both channels."

"There is so much need amongst those around you – be they people that are known to you – or strangers, and you both have the facility to assist – if required. You have the responsibility to offer assistance.

We cannot insist that you do this – we give you the tools to do this – and trust that you will use the tools – and not put them to waste.

Every person who crosses your path, is an opportunity and it is up to you to vocalise – on our behalf.
If we could speak directly to those people – without using the channel – we would. If we could heal those people without a channel – we would."

John:
"We know someone who is in distress – could Lynn give him some guidance from you?"

Silver Cloud:
"Everybody who is alive on the Earth – has someone in Spirit – without exception. If that person cannot be found, at the allotted time – or it is deemed – that until such time – the person can accept what is being given from Spirit – then nothing would be forthcoming.
It is not for the communication channel to judge whether communication would be forthcoming. It is merely the choice of the communication channel – to make themselves available for anyone and everyone – if it is to permitted by the doorkeeper and the guide.

If my channel asked for some help – do you not think that I would give it if I could? – or – I know a man who can. I have spoken in the past, when it has been necessary and when I wanted to."

"I am in complete charge of my channel – as Kato is, with yourself. The mind of a communication channel is taken over for brief periods of communication. The mind of a healer and counsellor – of a true healer and counsellor – is continually asking for guidance – and the guidance will come.

We do guide people towards your path, but – on the larger scale – literally everyone that crosses your path, as you walk forward - you have all been guided to the same spot, at the same time – be this, in the street, on the road, in a restaurant - you have all been guided to be there at the same time. Not everyone is meant for you. Maybe, they are on their way to somewhere else – another destination? Maybe, you are on your way to another destination? But – you criss cross – on a busy street – and eventually – you will stop. You will turn to them and say – "There is a reason, as to why I bumped into you", and they may say – "That's strange – I felt the same way" and then, you will know that you have arrived at your destination."

John:
"This is very deep."

Silver Cloud:
"I am a highly evolved guide – so I do not speak for the sake of speaking. I am also a friendly chap – with the common touch. I understand that you have many questions – work with those that you know and listen to those that you know. They know, what is best for you and your future path. The questions that you ask, are interesting – some – you know yourself – are not necessary – I do not mind."

"It is only in repeating answers – that you may learn. The team that has been placed around you, is sufficient and plentiful – for you to proceed down your correct path. They have all the experience and knowledge and more – they welcome questions, and although the questions, at this moment in time – are not directed at them – I speak on their behalf – I want you to know this. Nothing that I pass to you – is against their wishes – or against their thoughts – particularly, Kato.
If I cannot answer – it is because I cannot answer.
If I will not answer – it is because it is not my place.
But, we can only learn through question and answer – and so we welcome your questions."

Qu:
"You have mentioned in the past – Communication between the Spirit world and other Worlds – can you tell us more?"

Silver Cloud:
"No. Suffice to say – there are other Worlds – as you know – and we all need to co-operate with one another – yet each – within our own Worlds. We each have much to do. That is all I can say."

Qu:
"Can you tell me the difference between the Spirit of an animal and the Spirit of a human being?"

Silver Cloud:
"A Spirit is a Spirit – be it human or animal or a tree."

Qu:
"Does the Spirit of a tree, remain as a Spirit of a tree?"

Silver Cloud:
"What else would it be?"

Qu:
"When you show yourself to your channel – it is as a man – but – when you are not showing yourself to your channel – are you in a different form?"

Silver Cloud:
"Light."

Qu:
"So a tree is not a tree – in Spirit – but light?"

Silver Cloud:
"Yes – we would not be able to move for trees!
Spirit is an energy."

Qu:
"Would the Spirit of a tree – reform into the physical as something else – or as another tree?"

Silver Cloud:
"It would reform – as sustenance again – in the plant life. I am not a tree – Nor - have I ever been a tree.
Each Spirit energy has it's own structure. The Spirit learns many things – but – the Spirit of a man would not wish to become a tree – to stand motionless. What would he do with the knowledge he had learned in a previous life? A human being would not wish to return as a rabbit – because he would not be able to use the knowledge gained and the experience gained – they are not a rabbit's experience, The human beings experience – must be continued. Rats, show resistance to a poison – the knowledge of their metabolism is passed on to the next generation."

7th January 1995.

John still had unanswered questions about the spirit of a tree – and he asked Silver Cloud:

"Does the Spirit of a tree, come back as another tree – or as something else?"

Silver Cloud:
"The Spirit of a tree – returns as a tree – in order to meet it's full potential. The potential – the things it has learnt. A tree would not want to be a blade of grass BUT – the Spirit of nature – as a whole, when brought together – understands the structure of it's counterparts."

Qu:
"Are we healing the planet?"

Silver Cloud:
"There are many aspects to healing the planet. Healing man – healing nature – healing ones environment – the prevention of toxins escaping into the atmosphere.
They are many fold, but all is not lost – if – individuals are aware of the need for healing. The power of the individuals – is in the uniting of the individuals.
One thought – one hope – one plea.
But the destruction of the planet is being affected by many different… …
Return."

At this point in the communication, Silver Cloud stopped speaking and asked me to wait. Realising that someone else wished to speak – I remained, concentrated, and continued to raise my vibrations.
The next words that I spoke – were the words of Peter.

Peter:

"The healing of the planet, is one of the reasons why I am forced to communicate.
We shall discuss this subject many times.

Your planet must survive – it is imperative for the survival of others – as each World – not known to you – must survive – in order for the Universe to continue.
The answer to your question is No – not enough is being done and it is an urgent task – and this is the path and my reason for being.

As Silver Cloud has already stated – the destruction of the Earth and it's causes in particular – are many fold.
The destruction – being brought about by many misdemeanours. There is only a certain amount of revitalisation that can be achieved from your Spirit World – and this is a slow progression.

The urgency is now upon us. We must end the physical destruction – but this too, is many fold –
I speak of wars
I speak of pollution
I speak of desecration in the literal sense.
The very destruction of the earth on which you walk and the destruction of the air – of which you breath.
The task in hand is tremendous – but the basic flaw – is man himself.
The greed.
The ignorance and the lack of care – both for nature – the air – the seas – and ultimately – for each other.

As you can see – your question is not easily answered and this is the unfortunate predicament that you find yourselves in."

192

"I will endeavour to answer the question – but – the answers are so many – that the question, as a whole – "Are we healing the planet?" cannot be answered with a single answer – until we understand the break down – the many problems that face us all.

To begin in answering, and by way of a recommendation – I would say that we must begin with the people. They must firstly understand the destruction that is creating havoc in your world – has repercussions on others.
But in our beginning – we then raise many questions.
Do we begin with an end to war? Do we begin with a reduction in pollution – both of the earth itself and the air surrounding? Do we begin? – Can we begin, to create an environment in which man has not the need to destroy another countries environment?
Where do we begin?
As you can see – there is not one answer, because there are too many questions. Too many problems.
Where do we begin? But the problem is man.

If we can reach as many souls – and we must reach many souls – all over the World. But then – there is the question – having reached – where do we begin?
It is up to as many of you – that it is possible to reach – to begin with you're own environment. To make more people aware of the destruction. Be that, the care of litter – the landfill sites, which produce methane and other harmful gasses – the destruction of the earth itself – that you walk on.

Do we begin with the picking up of a piece of paper?
It is up to each individual to do what they can – within their own environment.
To pick up the piece of paper."

193

"To lobby the packaging companies, not to produce the paper to be dropped. To stamp out racism – to make the passage of the life span, as fair for the white as the black – for the rich and the needy.

Do we begin with the seas?
The answer is – we must begin at all points.
We need a vast army of people – enlightened within their own capabilities.

In time – given the opportunity – your planet can be healed.

In time – given the opportunity – your planet can revive.

In time – given the opportunity – your planet must revive.

Each person – each life – must do what is within their realm – their experience, and they must reach out to the extent of their perimeter, to do what they can – within their perimeter. If they live by the sea – then surely their priority would be the sea. If they live within the sight and sound of industry – then surely their priority would be that industry.

I shall return to give a more detailed plan and detailed instruction. But not one person can answer the question. Not one World can answer the question.
This must be a giant task of many Worlds – each with their own problem – but united in their willingness to survive.

Thankyou."

CHAPTER NINE

THE QUESTIONS CONTINUE.

9TH January 1995.

On the morning of the 9th – I woke from sleep – feeling
a sense of doom. I remembered dreaming of standing in
a grey, dead landscape and my mood - on waking –
reflected the greyness and I felt as though I was still
walking in that landscape. At 9am, I sat and "raised my
vibrations". My low mood was overwhelming my
ability to reach "my place" and although I continued to
try – I failed to reach my goal.

My low mood also allowed me to be-moan the fact that
– still – we had not had an offer on the house, and over
the Christmas period – there had been no viewings.

March, was very close now and my lack of patience
and my anxiety were beginning to dominate my
thoughts. Knowing that Silver Cloud would be near – I
asked – "Are we still moving house in March?"

There was no reply.

My mood sank lower and I "returned to my chair".

That evening I reached "my place" and found Wolf,
waiting for me. Wolf told me that Silver Cloud was
"Not back, yet" – but added: *"An old friend has come to
see you."*

To my joy – Buffalo walked in.

Buffalo:
"Hello. I was just passing.
Are you behaving yourself?"

Me:
"I think so.
Can you be there when we go to see Coral Polge?"

Buffalo:
*"I will have to ask permission.
I have moved on now and I am enjoying working with
my channel.* I will go now – Silver Cloud will be back.
And you behave yourself."

Wolf:
"Go back and wait."

I was grateful that Buffalo had taken the time and effort
to visit me - seeing him again had lifted my spirit.
When I returned to "my place" – Silver Cloud was
there, resuming our conversation of two days ago, ref.
our questions about "people crossing our path" - he
continued:

Silver Cloud:
*"In my opinion – people cross your path – and it is up
to you to see a reason and to seize the opportunity – if
there is an opportunity. But I speak as a communication
guide and cannot speak for the healing guide of the
other channel.*

*There will be times when an offer of help will be
rejected and this is built into the system – as it
strengthens the character of the channel.
It also assists the guides, in hearing the reaction to the
offer of help, they can take this information and use it
to their advantage and the advantage of the channel."*

Me:
"Can you explain that?"

Kato:
"Good evening.
I was coming to speak, but I will explain the reasoning behind what Silver Cloud has said.

In studying the reaction of those in the physical – to the offers of help – it enables Spirit to have pre-knowledge of the various reactions. In this way – we can guide those who will accept the help, more readily.
This is not to say, that we should, or would, discount every opportunity, but – if we in Spirit, can work more closely together – we can cut the rejection rate.

Having – ourselves – been in the Spirit world for great lengths of time – and only working with channels who have a thirst for knowledge – and a willingness to help – one tends to forget the negative reaction.

As guides – we are working with positive reaction – with our channels.

The negative reaction, surprises us – as it is a long forgotten memory – and maybe it is through the rejection of the channels help ....."

Me:
"I have lost him."

Kato:
"I am being called away. I should be in another place.

Suffice to say – that the rejections are necessary, so that we in Spirit can learn, and through that rejection, and our learning, we can assist the channel to offer help and the help of Spirit – in a more direct way."

"If the channel understands that we in Spirit, can assist one another – the channel could ask their own healing guide for assistance – as to the right passage, to reach the patient, but – you do live in a negative world, and not everyone – indeed many – will accept the healing energy – or the communication. And therefore – rejection is inevitable – but this is not part of the path that you are on.

I am sorry – I have to go."

10th January 1995.

9am. John was present.

Silver Cloud:
"I have brought Alexander." (The boat builder)

Alexander began his communication in response to my question that I had asked Silver Cloud: - "Are we still moving house in March?"

Alexander:
"I did not realise that it would be so difficult.
I understand your frustration. I was given the time-table of March and I thought that we were on schedule.

I have to say – that there is a delay – but that is not to say – that when we do find a buyer – we cannot speed things up."

Me:
"What is keeping people away?
Is it the price or the time of year?"

Alexander:
"You people are very unsure and uncertain. You live in an uncertain world – which does not create stability."

Me:
"Do we drop the price?"

Alexander:
*"It does not create stability.
I am still working for you."*

Me and John:
"Thank you very much."

Silver Cloud:
*"Well – you have things to do.
Go and do those things."*

11th January 1995.

John and I went to London today, to see Coral Polge.
She drew the images of Wolf and Mr Bennet.
John and I were thrilled to have the images – although I personally, was a little disappointed not to have an image of Silver Cloud. I was very tired due to the 5am start that morning and by 11.00 o'clock that night – I could hardly keep my eyes open. Try as I might – I couldn't retain my vibrations for long – but I did maintain them long enough to receive a posy of dried flowers from Wolf. The next day, when I spoke to Silver Cloud – I said how pleased – yet disappointed I was with the drawings.

He replied, jokingly – *"Wolf and Mr Bennet are the most forward of Spirit's."*

Our trip to London, and our journey on the Underground System had made John and I – firstly - thankful that we did not have to use this system of transport every day, and secondly – we wondered if there were any harmful effects brought about by the energy/ley lines and railway lines in general?

On the 13th January – John had the opportunity to voice some of our questions, with Silver Cloud.

Silver Cloud:
"Any questions from either of you? – John?"

John:
"Can people have problems – when they are catapulted down these straight lines?"

Silver Cloud:
"Yes."

John:
"When the lines stop what happens to the energy?"

Silver Cloud:
"It is trapped."

John:
"Does the energy go beyond the physical lines?
The people who live on a direct line with it – are they affected?"

Silver Cloud:
"Yes. As you know – negative energy travels through the earth."

John:

"I suppose – you have got the lines that are set into the earth – you have got the overhead electric cables – and you have the people that are in-between them."

Silver Cloud:

"The network is necessary, and there are those that spend their time down there – and the homeless, who sit and absorb the energy. Mankind did not apply itself to this problem – it is a great problem – not just in your country, but in Japan and America – where you will find great crime problems.
Carry on."

John:

"I saw a programme on the television, which said that in an attempt to find out some of the problems that mankind is causing - they have put a new satellite into orbit. The satellite beams radar off the earth in order to get a three dimensional plan.

Is this attempt to stop pollution – actually causing pollution itself – because of the radio waves? And mobile phones are used all over the place now."

Silver Cloud:

"It is seen from Spirit. The communication systems of the world are a hazard, and yet, even in our work – the communication systems of the world are necessary.
As a channel would be given a message to be sent some distance – we cannot expect the channel to walk the distance. These are great problems.

We have a guest. – White Cloud."

White Cloud:
"I am pleased to see you."

"There are those in your world, who know of the things that you speak and their plan, is to find the physical evidence that people may understand – hence those that have placed the satellite. Their intentions are honourable. They are driven through their own discomfort in what they see, and feel, and know of the pollution – throughout the world and the Universe beyond. They must use whatever technology is available to them and although there is not yet a satisfactory way of recovering satellites – or indeed – in some cases, there is no endeavour to retrieve the satellites – they are polluting the very Universe that they are attempting to save.

But – as was discussed the other evening – each person must do what they may – within their own environment and within their own capabilities, and as was discussed the other evening – there are many places to begin."

At this point – my vibrations were lifted further.
The following communication is not attributed to any named person. All I was told when I asked who was speaking, was.

"The words that are being spoken, are coming from on high."

Anon:
"It is up to each individual to do what they can – within their own capabilities and within their own environment, and so we must excuse further pollution, as we know that this pollution is being created through the best endeavours of the creators.
Each major city, throughout the world, is a hub hub of mixed energies, and these energies have no escape. They are like a tornado – going round and round."

"The negative energy spreads outwards and upwards and you will find that within the centres of cities – people are driven to crime – depression – ill will towards each other, and this – in the main – is caused by the negative energy, that has no escape.

The city of London, with its' vast array of underground tunnels – cannot escape this vast array of underground tunnels. They are necessary for the inhabitants to move to work – to live their lives.

Where do we begin with this problem. The planners, un-beknown to themselves – have attempted to address the problem by removing the people to the outskirts – but now there is a move to bring the people back – this is not good. In the outskirts you have an escape.
If you live and work within the centre of the major cities of the world – you have no escape. This is why, in the future – motor vehicles will have to be removed from these cities – as the negative energy and the pollution has no escape – we cannot allow the further pollution by means of motor vehicles, and therefore – this is one beginning – which of course – necessitates the people being transported underground.

But – as long as they can escape to the outskirts – they have an escape. We have to accept that in many cases – the pollution of the Universe is necessary – in that it will give the information. It will teach others and – hopefully – show others, in the physical sense – as – seeing is believing – the damage that is being done to the Earth and to the atmosphere, above and beyond it.

Thankyou."

14th January 1995. Nightime. John is present.

As I was "raising me vibrations" an energy that was "roundish and grey" charged at me. Then I saw a green man walking towards me, with his hand, outstretched. The man walked right past me – turned – and came back towards me – then he disappeared.

An array of images continued to appear and disappear around me, causing me to duck and dive, as they swept past me. The other images, included, a pair of hands resting on a silver topped cane – an elderly man and woman sitting on a park bench - a bear's head – a white lighthouse – and a "beige cone shaped thing".

Silver Cloud:
"The picture show is over – did you enjoy it?"

Me:
"Well – not really – what do they all mean?"

Silver Cloud:
"There are those that will be coming to pass their messages and they will find the words difficult. Not the speaking of the words – but coming to speak to communicate with their loved one.
They will really be pleased to come – but yet – if they haven't' communicated before – it can be awesome.
So – they will create a picture – to introduce themselves to their loved one. They will use their memory to create a picture – which you can describe – as a gentle introduction. We know that you – as a channel – prefer to speak directly – but that is no concern. Our only concern – is to present the message – so your feelings in the matter, are of no concern, and therefore – we shall be working in this manner."

"You must understand that loved ones have been parted from the sitter – in some cases, maybe for many years. You must understand that the sitter may be apprehensive and may be un-believing. Therefore – if a mother or uncle came and said "Hello – I am your mother – I am your uncle" – this would be too harsh an introduction.

You have been trained to pass the communication directly – as you are given the communication – but – you must also understand and not lose sight of the fact – that the sitter may well be a sitter for the first time and the communicator, may well be communicating for the first time – after what could be decades in the Spirit world.

It is all very well, to pass the communication of a highly evolved guide or helper – that is the easy part of a channels work. The difficulties arise when dealing with the loved ones – as the communication will take many forms. You may also find that you are asked to stop the communication – by the sitter. In which case – we shall have to pause and wait until we are able to continue.
The showing of the picture and the describing of the pictures – is a gentle introduction to the message.
The difficult work is about to begin.

Wait."

When I raised my vibrations – a few minutes later - I saw John's grandmother.
As a loved one of John – she had come to assist with my training – for which I am very grateful – and the following extract is once more – directly from the transcribed tape recording:

205

Me:
"I am not in my place but I can see your grandmother and a little brown dog.
It seems to be an experiment."

Silver Cloud:
"You would say the words – grandmother – little brown dog."

Me:
"Sorry John."

John:
"I understand."

Silver Cloud;
"If you had said the words – John would have known."

Me;
"She's got a bag of sweets with pear drops in."

John:
"Yes – I had forgotten."

Me:
"She's holding them out in a little white bag."
"I also feel that I am sitting squew wift – I feel as though I am facing the fire. I don't know whether that is connected to your grandmother?

John:
"She used to keep pear drops in a cupboard by the fire and she had to move a chair to reach the cupboard."

Me:
"I am on the right hand side of the fire place."

John:
"That would have meant something to me."

Me:
"Ok – I'm turning back again now. She's got an apron on – cross over bodice – she's put the sweets in the pocket."

Me:
"There's something funny about a clock on the wall."

John:
"I don't remember anything."

Me:
"Do you connect clocks with your granddad?"

John:
"No."

I saw the clock clearly now – it was a clock that had a moving picture of the sun and moon behind a glass window. A clock that – as a child – used to fascinate me – when we went to visit my aunts house.

Me:
"That's not for you – that's for me. It's my Aunt Elsie – the sun and moon clock used to hang on her wall."

Silver Cloud:
"Your grandparent and aunt have been pleased to assist, they have been pleased to be able to help and we give them our thanks. This has been a demonstration of the type of communication we can expect from loved ones and it is important that you do describe as much, in fact - everything of what your see – accurately."

Me:
"Ive seen a black money box with a hand. I know you had one."

John:
"It doesn't matter that you know I had one."

Me:
"What do I do now."

Silver Cloud:
"Ask who is showing the money box."

I asked who had brought the money box – and I saw and heard Elsie – John's mother.

Elsie:
"Hi son."

John:
"Hi mum – nice of you to pop in and lend a hand."

Elsie:
"They asked for volunteers."

After a short visit with John – Elsie left.

Silver Cloud:
"Well – our volunteers have gone now – it has been a useful exercise."
To John – *"Thankyou for your co-operation.*

The channel may go and we can have an early night.
I am quite happy this evening,
Off you go.
Goodnight."

As I said before – I am very grateful to John's grandmother and also my aunt and mum in law, Elsie.

Spirit give their time and energy – unconditionally and I continue to be touched by their care and generosity.
I also remain grateful to John – for his ongoing help, encouragement and patience.

Given that "loved ones" have this happy knack of showing an obscure, hovering object to a channel – by means of introduction – I have to publicly say how much I admire a good stage medium – who can stand for 2hrs and deliver meaningful messages to their audiences!

January was an odd month.
The nightly sittings continued – sometimes there were long nights of communication and then, for a period of two or three days – I would see images.
On the 16th of January – my notebook reminds me that I caught the flu virus – leaving me unable to "raise my vibrations" – although I tried every day.

The good news was – that the end of January brought the call from my "aunt" and "uncle". We could go and pick up Jack and Jill.

They were two months old and settled in very quickly.
Two beautiful puppies with their own distinct characters, and once I had got them housetrained – I would be in seventh heaven!

9th February 1995. Nightime.

Instead of arriving in "my place" – I found myself sitting in a canoe with Silver Cloud. We travelled down a wide, blue river, which was edged with rocks, and I could hear the water flowing over the rocks as we travelled. The banks of the river were not steep and Silver Cloud steered the canoe over to one of the banks. As we both got out of the canoe – we stepped into "my place" – and sat down on the sandy floor.

Silver Cloud:
"Sand has many uses.
You can draw in it (he made a circular drawing as he spoke) Women can clean pots with it.
It is one of Natures carpets.
Each tiny grain – though separate – working together.
Each tiny grain – different from the next – with it's own pattern – it's own evolvement. Each tiny grain of sand, evolves over billions of years, at different rates, at different times – in different patterns, and yet – when you look at the whole – it is like one – the same.

As each grain of sand evolves – so a star evolves in as many numbers – hidden from view.
Each grain of sand has a star.
The star reflects it's light to the grain of sand.
The sand reflects it's light to the star.
As the Earth evolves in this manner – the firmament is likewise evolving.
The grain of sand has a mirror in the sky.

Now we look at sand differently.
You cannot see the mirror in the sky – but you can see it's reflection."

10th February 1995. Nightime.

Silver Cloud:
"Any questions?"

John:
"What could you tell us about "Miracle" healing?"

Silver Cloud:
"Contrary to what happens on the Earth – the Earth is a beautiful place – linked within the Universe.
If you could scrape all the bad – all the things that are going wrong – the aura of the Earth would be a very beautiful thing. The Earth itself is a beautiful creation – a gem amongst gems – and very colourful."

John:
"I've seen pictures of the Earth taken 20yrs ago and more recent pictures show it is duller."

Silver Cloud:
"The Earth's aura is clouded."

John:
"I'd not thought of Earth aura."

Silver Cloud:
"The aura is the energy.
You cannot see it – but one day you will."

John:
"What can you tell us about "miracle" healing – compared to prolonged healing?"

Silver Cloud:
"I will have to get someone to answer this."

"This question is hanging in the air.
I will go and see if I can find someone.

It is not what you know – it is who you know – and in
my case – I know both.

I have brought Harry Edwards to speak with you."

Harry Edwards is the World famous Spiritual healer –
who – in the 1950s/60s – regularly filled halls to
capacity – to give healing to his audiences.

Harry Edwards:
"Hello.
Your question regarding the so called miracle healing
is an interesting question.
In my case – I can say that those patients that were
brought to me – came very much as a last resort –
because in the time we are talking of – when I was
working – healing and hands on healing, was very
much frowned upon, in certain quarters.

I had the gift of healing, to show to the world that
healing, indeed could take place. I had the pleasure on
many, many occasions – to heal instantly and give
miraculous results. I worked with powerful healing
guides. I was a natural open channel and many of my
case histories were of an arthritic nature. The healing
in these cases can be most successful – as is a simple
matter of breaking the deposits around the joints.
This can be effectively done, through Spiritual healing.

The question of illnesses, stemming from emotional
disasters – emotional crisis – is something that has
come more to the fore – now that the healing process is
more generally accepted."

"This is giving the healer the time to work with the patient, on a one to one basis – and it could be said that the healing that is taking place today – is a truer form of healing. It heals the mind. Hopefully the symptoms of the illness, will not return.

If – when I began on my long and sometimes arduous path – I had to begin to convince the patient and those witnessing the healing – that the illness stems from emotion – from past life – as I now understand it – I could not have produced the remarkable achievements that I did in my many public displays of healing.

I had many patients who I saw repeatedly – they would return with either the same complaint, or a differing complaint. These patients have sadly, not been written into my books and into the many articles written about me. The world was not ready for long drawn out explanations of the origins of illness, and the World was not ready to wait – or willing to wait – to see the end and final result.

There are healers who continue to work as I did – to continue the process of awareness.
There are many more healers and counsellors, who are working in reverse – beginning with the origin.
These healers – and there are many – and growing in numbers – will never be at the forefront – as they work quietly and alone with their patient.

The World needs the two differing ways of healing. The World still needs to see the miraculous recovery with their own eyes, but – underlying that issue – the greater need, is for the healers and counsellors."

*"My patients benefited enormously from my contact
with them. I helped many, many more people – and this
work continues. Sadly – it will always be the miracles
that are written of, but you know the art of true healing.
With the right Spirit guides and with the willingness to
heal – a healing channel can be used in the public gaze.
But – I repeat – the patients would return with the
symptoms recurring – or with differing illness.*

*The gift of healing – given to both groups of healers –
is a gift indeed to be cherished, and one group, must
not look at the other group, and covert their gift.*
*The gift of speaking, is a gift from God – it is a gift that
thankfully – the majority of people in the World are
given. The healer, who also has the gift of speech and
the gift of hearing their guide – is doubly gifted.*

This is my view.
This is my opinion.
This is my understanding.

*I am pleased to be able to communicate my
understanding.*
I return to my Spirit home."

John:
"Thank you very much for your honest answer. It has
been a great help to me."

Harry Edwards:
"I return to my Spirit home."

11th February 1995. Nightime.

As I "raised my vibrations" – I was taken back in time.
To the time when I was about 4yrs or 5yrs old:

I was sitting on the swing in the garden, and dad was pushing me. As I was swinging – as that 4yr/5yr old - on that summer's day – I found myself sitting on the cross bar of dads' bike:

I had been allowed to walk to the end of the road – to meet daddy who was riding his bike – on his way home for lunch. He stopped and lifted me onto that very cold and uncomfortable cross bar and we cycled home.

The tyres of the bike, throwing up the little stones on the road. His knees, sticking out to the sides - to avoid knocking me off.

The next image – was of my Big "Noddy" toy.

Red and blue and cuddly – his blue eyes staring out at me, from his rubber face – the bell on his hat, jingling.

I was crying – because I wasn't allowed to take Noddy shopping. I knew I wasn't going to win this argument and I was cross, as I sat him on the chair in the living room - whinging - as mum and I walked out of the front door leaving him all alone in the house.

Now – I am 3yrs old – and I'm using a spoon, to dig a hole in the garden. I'm chattering to Armon (my uncle in Spirit) and we have heard Mummy coming, so he has gone to hide from her – leaving me giggling as I see him peeking out from his hiding place.

I toddle after him – the hole forgotten - we are now playing hide and seek.

Transported back in time once more:

I am about nine months old.

I am lying in my pram, in the front room.

With one hand on my fleece rug – I am pinging the rattling lambs that mummy had fastened to the pram.

I can see little blue sparkling lights on the ceiling.

Armon is by the side of the pram, and I struggle to sit up to talk to him. Then - I heave one leg and then the other leg over the side of the pram to escape my restraints and so that we can play on the floor. But it's not easy because my straps refuse to free me.

As I dangle over the edge – with Armon holding my feet - mummy walks in. She snatches me up and puts me back in the pram softly slapping my leg and saying "No", but Armon and I are laughing as mummy leaves the room, closing the door behind her.

I am back in "my place" and Silver Cloud is smiling at me.

Silver Cloud:
"Memories from the archive – being run as a film.
The channel may go."

Mum and dad must have been run ragged by my antics and they must have felt as though I was laughing at them as I toddled away giggling - but - it was uncle Armon's fault! Honest!

15th February 1995. Nightime.

John had had some communication with Jim – his doorkeeper and following that – we had another visit from Angela – the 4yr old who had grown up in Spirit.

Me:
"Little Angela is here."

John:
"Hello Angela. How are you?"

Angela:
"Very well."

John:
"Do you like the puppies?" (John and I felt that Angela had been playing with the puppies. We had both felt her energy around and - we suspected – it was Angela who was putting a tennis ball under the writing bureau out of site!)

Angela:
"Yes. They went to bite me – but I stopped them."

John:
"Are you enjoying being with Laura?"

Angela:
"Yes.
The children today (ref.: - to children in a school that John had visited today.) – *The children wouldn't be naughty if people weren't naughty to them.*
I'm not naughty.
The children – the children don't want to be naughty and at home – we don't learn to be naughty – we learn to be good and to be kind and I'm a good girl.
The puppies are naughty but Laura says puppies have to be naughty.
Laura's my friend."

John:
"She's our friend as well."

Angela:
"Laura says you're going to see some more children. You're going to heal the children, and if you can't – they're coming here and we will make them better."

John:
"Will you be there as well?"

Angela:
"Laura says I can come.
Laura says I can help."

John:
"I'm glad – I'm sure you will be a big help."

Angela:
"I'm going to listen.
Mr Bennets my friend.
Mr Bennett gave me a flower."

John:
"That's nice – what colour?"

Angela:
"Yellow."

John:
"Nice colour."

Angela:
"Sunshine.
Bye."

John:
"Bye Angela – thanks for coming."

Angela:
"See you again."

Laura:

"As you know – I am keen to work with children – and they will be there for us to work with – and for.
As Angela, so eloquently said – the children do not have the intention of being maladjusted. The children are forced to be maladjusted – it is a gradual process of indoctrination – neglect – ill treatment and mis-understanding – inappropriate care and the strains and stresses on the parent – being shown in the behaviour of these children.
A modern day malady.

In order to reach the child – the child must be removed from the negative influences – so that the true child can be reached and the child can gain understanding – as to its behaviour – and a re-conciliation with the parent or guardian, or influence – that has caused the negative attitudes in the child can begin.

If something has happened to a child – and then as the child grows into an adult – it carries the same fear, phobia or misunderstanding, in order to dissolve that fear, misunderstanding or phobia – you have to take the adult back, to the child.
The benefit of regression is two fold:
They have the understanding of what happened – and this may be a memory that has been blocked, and – they also have the benefit of being the adult – and seeing the consequences of their action.
So – very quickly, they can reconcile."

John:
"Is regression into past lives, sufficient to correct the Karmic imbalance – or is there more to it than that?"

Laura:

"The regression will find the problem in the previous life – but that will have manifested itself in the present life – and therefore we have another problem."

John:

"Do you have to recognise both problems – or will getting to the root of the first problem automatically sort out the second problem?"

Laura:

"Nothing is automatic. The second problem may be a differing problem – which needs to be reconciled in a different way – needs to be dealt with separately. Unless the person has an instant remembering or realisation that – "yes" the problem in a previous life is the cause of their problem – they are still stuck with their present problem. Some – do not carry previous life's problems forward into their present life."

21st February 1995.Nightime.

Those present where John and two friends Moira and John, who had attended a course with him that day. They had come for an evening meal and were keen to participate in that evenings' session – hoping for communication from loved ones.

Silver Cloud:
"Good evening.
Question and answer – You have a question John."

John:

"I was discussing with some friends – the importance of water to people and the environment – what can you tell us about water?"

Silver Cloud:
"Water is life.
Water is life giving and water is cleansing.
Water is a mirror – if you look into water – you will find your soul.
Water is the eye of the soul.
Water is being contaminated."

Me:
"Peter has come to speak."

Peter:
"Peter the guide.
Water is a very precious element – as it gives life and nourishment to the smallest of creature and plant.

The water on your planet is being wasted and contaminated and therefore, it could be said that you are destroying the very soul of your planet. As a pool of water – when gazed into – is the mirror of the soul – then the water surrounding your planet and the water which infiltrates the surface of your planet – is the soul of your planet – because of it's life giving qualities.
We have spoken before, of the wanton destruction of the Earth – and you raise a very good question.

If the entire water system on the Earth and surrounding the Earth – is eventually polluted – to it's own destruction – What is left for your Earth?

I am not the healing guide and I will not speak of the healing properties of the water. I come to say – that the water is life itself – to you, yourselves – and to the planet.

I leave you now."

I then received the loved ones for our two friends –
after which – Angela visited:

Angela:
"Hello.
I wanted to come and say hello because everyone else
has been coming to say hello and I wanted to come to
say hello."

John:
"We're glad you did."

Angela:
"*Thankyou.*
They wouldn't let me go today (on the course with
John) *I couldn't go with you today. Laura said I*
couldn't go."

John:
"Never mind."

Angela:
*"Hello" (*to Moira – and she waited for a reply)
"Hello" (to John – again – she waited for a reply)
"I'm a good girl I am. I have to be good – Laura says.
Anyway – I wanted to come and say Hello."

Me: to John, Moira or John.
"Have you got a question for her?"

John:
"What have you been doing today?"

Angela:
"I've been to school."

John:
"What have you been learning?"

Angela:
"I've been drawing a picture. A Giraffe with a long neck and spots."

John:
"What have you done with it?"

Angela:
"Don't know – just drew it"

John:
"Have you shown it to Laura?"

Angela:
"No – I forgot."

John:
"I bet it's a nice picture?"

Angela:
"I'm a good drawer. I went in the garden and saw some flowers."

John:
"What colours?"

Angela:
"Allsorts."

John:
"Was it sunny in the garden?"

Angela:
"Oh yes – there was this big green thing."

John:
"What was it?"

Angela:
"A big green thing – leafy thing."

John:
"A bush or a tree?"

Angela:
"No silly. A big leaf thingy – thingy.
You're silly – it's a leaf with holes.
I'm going now."

John:
"Thankyou for coming – see you again soon."

Angela:
"I'm going to find Laura now,
Bye Silver Cloud."

Silver Cloud:
"Well – I hope you all enjoyed that – I can't get rid of
her. (Angela).
Well – you each have had communication this evening.
I hope it has been meaningful – as this was the
intention. There will not be time for more questions this
evening.

The channel may go."

24th February 1995.

A friend, who is a healer, had joined John and I for this evening's session and whilst we were waiting for our friends guide to come – we were visited by a Japanese gentleman: -

"Good evening.
I am a healing guide – I do not have a channel – but I am – I was, and still am, a herbalist – using the ancient crafts – dating back centuries.
I speak to both healing channels.
I come with the agreement of the channels guides.
You will ask for me by name – Dmoro.

I was on the Earth in the 15th century and therefore you can surmise – that I have much knowledge.

I take my leave.
Good day."

Silver Cloud:
"Dmoro was a peasant – but very skilled in herbalism – he helped a lot of people and that is how he earned his meagre living – by selling medicine, but – he also gave it to those that were poorer than himself.

He is a very small chap – a very kindly man, and he will be allowed to pass information – using one word – a certain sort of tea – it will become very clear to you."

John and our friend – were then invited to ask questions, and one of the questions that John had, was about a small child - whose spirit – John had been aware of - as he had been healing a patient.

Silver Cloud:

"The child is in a coma, but the child is playing, the child is completely unaware of the trauma. The coma patient travels, and although – in some cases – is aware of the anxiety of it's loved ones – it is incapable of comforting it's loved ones.

This child has been in a road traffic accident – this child has been hit by a car, and whilst it's physical symptoms are being brought under control, and whilst the physical ailments are being treated – the Spirit of the child is removed.

Until the physical symptoms can be borne and accepted by the Spirit of the child - the child will remain separated, but when the physical body has had time to recover – the Spirit will return to the physical body, then the loved ones will begin to see an improvement.
This can take a short time – this can take many weeks – and in some cases – months. The Spirit of the physical being, has to accept what has happened to the physical – and when the physical has accepted the trauma – and when the Spirit is able to cope with returning to the physical body – the Spirit will return.

The Spirit of the child, is a happy Spirit – but – obviously, the Spirit needs to return to the physical body - as the physical body cannot be maintained indefinitely, and therefore – those who are maintaining – need to see an improvement – and the Spirit must return, in order for this to take place.

The child will awake to tell stories of things that he has been doing and places that he has been – and he will be told – "That while you were sick – you were dreaming."

Silver Cloud then added these words:

"A channel can be likened to a tree – whose major root, goes very deep into the earth – it's other roots – spreading out, to stabilise the tree.

As the tree grows – with each passing year – a circle within the trunk of the tree is produced. The progress of a channel - who reaches up and who has the initiative to discover and ask – can be likened to the tree – that also reaches up to the Universe causing - it's branches to spread far and wide.

In this way – a channel can be likened to a growing healthy tree. It's root, embedded deep into the earth.
Its growth – although estimated – cannot be totally pre ordained. It is only the willingness of the branches to continue to spread – that each circle of the trunk can be developed.

The continued enthusiasm of the branches to reach out – ensures another year in the growth of the tree."

CHAPTER TEN

COLOURS - CHILDREN
AND A "CHOSEN" RACE.

1st March 1995. Nightime.

White Cloud and Mr Shush were waiting to speak.

Mr Shush:
"We are your future.
You must step forward towards us.
You have no need to cling to the past.
The past is not your life.
The past has been a stepping-stone to where you are
now – the point of your arrival.
The past is immaterial, as you are not now – the
conditioned person that you were in the past.
Walk towards us.
Your past life has been lived for others.
Your past life has been conditioned by others.
You will now throw the conditioning and control away.
Peace be with you."

White Cloud:
"You must be your own self and as you move to a new
location – you will be the new self. You will throw off
the overcoat and discard it as rubbish and leave the
overcoat behind, and as you step forward and move to
your new location and your new life – you will not even
remember the overcoat. You have lived your life for
others and now is your time.

The move to your new location is symbolic, as well as
practical. The symbolism will be lost in the mists of
time. We wait for you to move to your new location."

"In the meantime – you can begin to cast off the past –
by way of preparation. Enjoy your work.
The channel may go."

If you remember – March was the month that I thought
we would sell the house – leaving us debt free, then
Alexander said there was a delay.

Hearing these two communications, today, made me
think that the move was imminent again, yet both Mr
Shush and White Cloud were speaking of more than
just moving location – they were asking me to discard
"rubbish". I didn't understand what the "overcoat"
signified – and why did I have to put my past behind
me? I could only hope that my newly discovered
patience would assist me in whatever the future held.

6ᵗʰ March 1995. Nightime.

During this session a gentleman – who said his name
was Imarla, visited us. My first sighting of Imarla – an
Asian Indian – was of this gentleman, sitting in a cross
legged, Yoga position – and floating in the air.
In his hand – he held a small bell – which he rang once.

"Tell him to listen for the bell." He said – directing his
words to John.

Me:
"Are you a healing guide?"

Imarla:
"I am a healing guide – but healing of the mind.
Healing through guided meditation – similar to
hypnotherapy – but – not the suggestive meditation."

"Meditation, resulting in a hypnotic state – but self-hypnosis. He (John) will be given the ability to guide his patients through a meditation – thus walking them through their past experiences and their past trauma – but it is they that will do the walking, with a free Spirit – not an induced state of hypnosis. Thus – the patient will become - self healing – through the guidance."

Me:
"He is not to be a guide for hands on healing – as his life experience – on a personal level – was to remove his Spirit from his physical – and this is what he wants to teach."

N.B.
John later studied hypnotherapy and became a Hypno-psychotherapist – both practising and tutoring.

8th March 1995. Nightime.

As I "raised my vibrations" that evening, I saw, firstly – a highly polished, round wooden table with 3 feet attached to brass wheels. Secondly – I saw a lady dressed in a fur coat. She looked as though she was very affluent - both in dress and manner, and told me that she was a "titled" lady – adding:

"I am very pleased to make you acquaintance and pleased to visit your humble home."
She added:
"I like the table – be it of simple construction.
It really is too warm to wear the coat – but it was expensive. No one seems to appreciate the amount of money that it cost. I will move on."

As the lady left – I found myself standing on the landing, of what I understood to be a block of flats.

I heard a noise and looked in its' direction. I saw a man walking down some steps, which led onto the end of the landing. The man began to walk towards me and as he came nearer – he held out his hand, inviting me to shake hands with him – which I did.

There were three noticeable things about this man.

Firstly – his appearance. He was stooped and unkempt and a little smelly. Secondly – he seemed to be drunk.

And thirdly – as he mumbled a *"hello"* – I detected a Scottish accent.

The Scottish gentleman and I then had a lengthy conversation. He began by telling me that he had lived in the flats and described himself as, *"a drunk"* – going on to say that he was not often *"in work."*

He stated that it *"was the drink that killed me"* but that when he arrived in Spirit – *"They treated me the same as her"* I knew that the "her" he mentioned – was the titled lady in the fur coat, that I had just met.

With added speed and fluency – the Scottish gentleman went on to describe his arrival is Spirit by saying:

"It didn't matter to "Them" that it was the drink that killed me. I didn't do much with my life and now – I can see the error of my ways.

It wasn't all my fault but I have to take responsibility for it. I have let go of the things – the people – who made me like I was.

It was funny – because I thought it was me - but I know now that it wasn't just me.

The wife wouldn't recognise me now."

As he said those words he metamorphasised into an upright clean and well dressed man.
He continued:

"I want to come back – to prove to them that I can do it right.

I'll be off now – cheerio."

With those words – I was once more standing "in my place" and Silver Cloud was waiting to speak:

Silver Cloud:

"We see the results quicker – of the healing and counselling – when we are addressing Spirit that is without it's physical envelope – as is the case of the gentleman that you have just spoken to.
He has understood the reasons as to why he was as he was – and has come, very quickly – to accept the reasons for his behaviour, and also – to pass forgiveness to those who created him."

Silver Cloud directed these next words to John:

"When you are counselling a patient in the physical – they do not have the benefit of being able to communicate directly with those who have passed over – who have played a part in their misdemeanours.
If you find that a patients' behaviour stems from that of a parent, and the parents before that – you cannot think "I will go and speak to them". There will not be a mediator between the two.
So, you see the problems before you. Time will have to be set aside, when dealing with these deep rooted, emotional problems – as you already know."

"You have spoken to the young man – who has   - through his own evolvement – been able to see a chink of light – at the end of his own particular tunnel.

Hopefully, you can go back – to give the patient the benefit of remembering the experience, and using their adult knowledge and using the counsellor – they can – as we have spoken before – come to terms within their own lifetime – of the reasons for their behaviour.

There are those in Spirit, who know what work has to be done - and they will strive with their best efforts."

Addressing both John and I – Silver Cloud continued:

"I have used the two different people – to show that – when you pass into Spirit – you are as your were when you left the physical world.
There are those that are willing and eager to change and to make amends. To be given another chance if they feel they may need another chance. That is their request and entirely a matter for themselves.
There are those that are still attached to the Earth and their own possessions. They feel that because they had possessions – including servants who catered for their every need – that they were happy.
They feel that because they told people – who were always willing to serve them – that they were in a true state of happiness. Eventually – they will learn that they too – will become the servant."

Laura entered "my place" and asked John if he had any questions.

John:
"Have you seen that boy who is in a coma?"

Laura:
"Yes. He is returning from coma but he has a long way to go. Perhaps you could ask for more Distant Healing. I would be quite willing to go back and see him."

John:
"What can you tell me about sending colours whilst Distant Healing, for example – gold light. Do I visualise it or just ask for it to be sent?"

Laura:
"The gold light is a healing, protective, all enveloping light. It gives a sense of peacefulness to the aura.
The sending of gold light has a disarming quality, so the answer to your question is "yes" ask for the gold light."

John:
"What about other colours. I assume healing energy is blue?"

Laura:
"Yes – bluey white.
One can send any colour of the rainbow.
The blue is healing energy. Pink is renown in the physical world – as being the colour of love.
I don't think it is appropriate to send love without a purpose. Green is the colour of regrowth – again – this needs to be sent with some explanation as to why you are sending it. Sending the colour of regrowth means – you could wish someone well – you could wish a change for the better, in their situation.
Yellow is rather a harsh colour. Yellow could, maybe used to brighten an aura – to revitalise an aura.
But – would it not be better to ask for "Healing energy"?"

John:
"You are saying – it is not for me to decide – it is for me to ask?"

Laura:
"To ask for the appropriate colour."

John:
"It is interesting to know they are used."

Laura:
"They are used – but in multiples – in a cacophony of colour."

John:
"If healing energy is blue and white – is the white a combination of colour?"

Laura:
"The white represents the Spirit energy – the pure white. Within that – as you say – there may be colour so finely graded that the colour could not be seen.

I do not feel the need for you to break down the colour – to send distantly – although I have given you one or two of the colours and told you what they represent to us. Trust in your Spirit guides who know the appropriate healing energy to send."

The next day – 9th March – during the nightime session, John asked his guide, Kato, for some advice.
John was thinking of going on an Earth Energy course, and he wondered if Kato thought it would be a useful course for him to attend.
Kato's answer was very typically – non-committal.

But, as I believe it applies to all of us – at some stage in our lives – I wanted to share it with you.

Kato:
"It is not my place to tell you what not to do.
I can – however – tell you what to do.
I would suggest, that if you feel that you are being diverted against your will – then cease.

I would not forbid anyone.
It is not my place.
I would not advise anyone to cease the gathering of information.

I would advise – that their instinct tell them if the information was relevant to them at this moment in time, and do not forget – that because you may find that this information is not relevant at this moment in time – the information will come again – if it is relevant."

24ᵗʰ March 1995. Nightime.

Wolf was alone, when I arrived at "my place".
He asked that the, now mounted and framed, image that Coral Polge had drawn – which we had hung on the living room wall – be hung in the hall of our new house, when we moved.

Sensing that he wished to speak further – I acknowledged his request and waited for him to speak again.

Wolf:
"When I lived in the physical world – I was not a very Spiritual person.
I hunted."

"I did not speak to the Spirits, and it is only since I passed over – that I have been on a Spiritual path.

I always knew the Spirits were there – but I was young, which is why I am pleased, now, to be a doorkeeper – at the entrance to the Spirit world, and it gladdens my heart – that there are many people of your race, who know and acknowledge the Spirit world.

I was not a Spiritual person when in the physical world, I left that to others – although I had great respect for those that knew of the Spirit world, and to some degree – I feared what they knew.

The chiefs and medicine men were held in great esteem and, with some fear, because of what they knew – and because they could speak to the "Great Ones".
And so – in a sense – you may say that I envy you – as you too, have access to the Spirit world, and I feel that my life in the physical world was empty – in the sense that I went out and hunted – I looked after the animals – I got drunk – and, I'm ashamed to say – I did not behave in a Spiritual way at all.

So I have had a lot to learn and I have had a lot to come to terms with, since I myself, have been in the Spirit world, and this is why I am pleased to be a doorkeeper, because now – every day – I can see those in the physical world, communicating with those in the Spirit world – of which, I am now a part.

And so it would be an honour for me – if you could hang my likeness by your doorway, and when people ask – "Who is that?" – you can tell them, and you can tell them what a changed man he is – for:"

"When he lived in the physical world – he was drunk a lot of the time – when not hunting or fighting or looking after the cattle – his only excuse for his behaviour was youth."

"I had not much thought of the future – as in those times – the future could end the next day.

My one regret was that I dishonoured those in Spirit, who were attempting to help us and lead us out of the torment. I felt that I had been dishonourable, but I hope now – that I make amends for my dishonour.

The channel may go."

What I will tell you about my doorkeeper Wolf is: -

He is a loving, caring, honest, reliable and humorous man. He has unconditionally protected Spirit visitors, clients, and me, thus enabling the communication to take place. His unfailing protection and nearness – has given me the confidence to walk safely on my personal path with Spirit.

That is who Wolf is to me.

26th March. Nightime.

I "raised my vibrations" as usual and as I arrived in "my place" – I found myself in the presence of an Asian Indian gentleman. He was waiting to speak.

And so - upon finding this stranger in "my place" and with Wolf and Silver Cloud not visibly present – I asked him who he was and if he wished to pass communication? He answered:

"My name is Induru."

My routine was to wait and see if there was going to be any communication before I switched the audiotape on – and this cue came from Wolf and Silver Cloud, but seeing this man standing there waiting for me, and sensing his impatience - I hurriedly bent down and turned the audiotape on, then I sat back in my chair to receive his communication, which I knew was for John.

He began, what was a long continuous evening's session and I include it in its entirety.

Induru:

"My name is Induru and I do not enjoy being kept waiting.

I have been told that I must use this channel – I am not used to your ways and I will know – at a future date – to wait and be recognised.

I have come to say that I disjoint my limbs – and through the disjointing – one feels the disablement of a useless limb. It is through the disjointing that one can understand the feeling – of a missing limb. It is an art form – that not everyone possesses. I would dismember all my limbs during meditation – and through this action – I felt an affinity with those who had a missing limb or a useless limb."

"I have spoken to Katamoro and he has told me of your decision – and so when the patient presents itself and it is applicable to me – I am happy to work through you."

John:
"Thankyou."

Induru:
"I apologise for my lack of patience. I am not used to communicating through a channel. I do not understand the niceties involved – but I appreciate the channels recognition."

John:
"Can I ask a question?"

Induru:
"I was leaving."

John:
"I will ask you again then."

Induru:
"No – you may ask now."

John:
"Your energies are for people who have had an accident or surgery – wheelchair bound or bedridden?"

Induru:
"You listen well."

John:
"Do I ask for you by name or do I need to go through Kato?"

Induru:

"No – you ask for me - as I believe I am a member of your team and as such, am available when you ask.
You will ask for me by name. I realise that there are others around that are helping you – I have said that I will not work with the others. I may have to reconsider, but – for the time being – when faced with the accident or limbless patient – you will ask for me by name."

John:
"I shall do that. Thankyou."

Induru:
"Good day."

Mr Bennet:
"Good evening.
I thought that I would come and clarify that last point.

This may be discussed again in the future – but in the meantime – I would say that all your so called "Normal" healing patients that come to you – and this does include arthritic and those that are minimally injured – I will be there.

What we have agreed – at this point – is that those patients who are in wheelchairs or bedridden through accident or injury and where the mind is somewhat superficial – if I may use that word – that is not to minimise their feelings and the depth of the hurt and pain that the patient is feeling – but to say that the problem in the mind is purely because of the physical ailment – So, I am saying – in these cases - and you will know these cases – you will ask for Induru."

John:
"You are saying that the pain in the mind is brought about by the physical injury – not the other way around?"

Mr Bennet:
"Exactly. And so I speak for the team, when I say that Induru will be asked for by name – for those patients – and those patients alone."

John:
"I appreciate the clarification."

Mr Bennet:
"He is a welcome member of the team but is not yet used to our ways and no doubt – he will become used to our ways.
Thankyou."

John:
"Thankyou Mr Bennet."

Mr Bennet:
"I thank Silver Cloud for allowing me to come."

Angela:
"Hello. I've come to say hello."

John:
"It's really nice when you do that."

Me:
"She's come on her own."

Angela:
"I don't like that man – he doesn't say hello to me."

243

John:
"He will once he gets to know you – like Mr Bennet."

Angela:
"Mr Bennet's my friend – He (Induru) *doesn't say hello to me – I don't think he likes children."*

John:
"He'll get to like them."

Angela:
"I've come on my own.
*Jim (*John's doorkeeper) *likes me and I like Jim – he's funny."*

John:
"Does he tell you jokes?"

Angela:
"No.
He does things - he hides things for me.
He says –"Which hand is it in?" and "It's not there."
I don't know how he does that."

John:
"Maybe one day he will show you."

Angela:
"I don't know how he does that."

John:
"I don't know – he's never shown me. I think you're very lucky that he's shown you."

Angela:
"Well – it's not there – it's in his hand – and it's not there – and it's gone!
You're going to see some children."

John:
"Are you going to be there?"

Angela:
"Yes. Laura says when. Those children are poorly.
I was poorly. I'm not poorly now – it's not nice."

John:
"Being poorly?"

Angela:
"No. I was poorly and my mummy cried.
I'm not poorly now, and there was flowers at the funeral – cos I saw them."

John:
"All different colours?"

Angela:
"Yes. Lots and lots and there was a teddy bear – a yellow teddy bear."

John:
"Have you got the teddy bear?"

Angela:
"No. I've got a doll – dolly."

John:
"Is that the dolls name – dolly?"

Angela:
"Dolly.
I don't like that man. Laura says he doesn't see me –
that's why he doesn't say hello."

John:
"Well – there you go – you can understand why he
doesn't say hello if he can't see you."

Angela:
"*I can see him – he can't see me."*

John:
"I bet if he could see you he would say hello."

Angela:
"*Mmmmm."*

John:
"One day maybe he will see you and he will say hello."

Angela:
"I might be big then.
Silver Cloud says I've got to go now."

John:
"It's been nice to talk to you.
Thankyou for coming."

Angela:
"*I came on my own."*

John:
"You did.
Say hello to Laura for us when you go back."

Angela:
"I don't want to go back on my own."

John:
"Is there somebody who can take you then?"

Angela:
"I don't know."

John:
"I bet if you ask Silver Cloud he will find somebody."

Me:
"She's asking him."

Angela:
"Silver Cloud says if I go to the door – my granddad's there."

John:
"Oh – that will be nice won't it – you won't have to go back on your own."

Angela:
"I'll go and see.
Bye."

John:
"Bye."

Silver Cloud:
"Angela was one of those children who couldn't be helped any more, in the physical – by the knowledge of the doctors and physicians who fought so hard to help her."

"She is living proof, is she not, that recovery is there for all, and when recovery is not to be – in the physical – you must know that recovery in the Spirit world is complete, and know that the Spirit and soul of that child goes on and grows – and they develop.

I am speaking of the children who – develop as they would in the physical – their knowledge and understanding grows – all be it at a faster speed than the physical, but as you can see – their knowledge grows – very much on a parallel with their life on the physical – had they been permitted to stay in the physical.

So Angela, is an example of how their growth continues and also – of how the children in the Spirit world, readily accept, that they are growing in the Spirit world and not in the physical world, to them – it is still the growth that they had wanted. To a child – it does not make any difference to them – that their growth is to be in the Spirit world and not in the physical.

The Spirit of a child is very accepting of its conditions and surroundings, and as long as that Spirit is allowed to grow – then the Spirit is happy.

It matters not – to the child – that they have been denied the life in the physical – I am speaking of young children – as long as they are not denied the growth – then they will remain happy. It is the denial – that would diminish the light of the Spirit.

But those of us in Spirit, and those of us in Spirit who have been here for many thousands of years – have grown to understand that the Spirit of a child must be allowed to grow."

"Therefore – when a child is in Spirit – it learns and experiences things, that it would probably experience and learn in the physical. We try to nurture the child to develop and grow in the Spirit world, as it would in the physical. In some respects – you could say that the Spirit child is held back.

Obviously, the potential for the Spirit child is to learn at a speedy rate and to learn of things that only the adult mind – in the physical – can learn.
The potential is there – for that young Spirit to learn very speedily – but this would not be right – as each Spirit must not be denied the right to be child like, and so great care is taken over the young Spirits and those that pass from the physical into the Spirit world. Great care is taken so that the might grow at a similar rate – as if in the physical world – until – it is deemed that the child can accept more knowledge – greater knowledge – more readily – more quickly. There is not a time limit or a certain age put on the……"

White Cloud:
"Good evening.
The children in the Spirit world are not subject to the rigours of having to gain so much knowledge, by a certain age, or within a certain time, and when it is deemed fit – that the Spirit is able to grow more rapidly, and grow into adulthood – then the information that is given to the Spirit of that child will be given at a higher level and with greater speed.
That is not to say that we do not have adolescents…"

At this point – the audiotape had to be replaced.

"…but as you have already witnessed with Laura – a child can remain a child for as long as that child…"

"...wishes – or for as long as it is deemed fit that they remain as a child. A child can appear as a child – when if fact – he is an adult. These are complicated ways – of which we cannot go into. Suffice to say – as Silver Cloud has already spoken – the child Spirit that passes into Spirit – is allowed to grow naturally, and then – at some stage – that child can move to a higher level of understanding – and hence – you produce the man.

As you know – we do not have fixed years, fixed decades, fixed time limits – as is necessary in the physical world – so the children that you may see, in your capacity as a healer – who pass into the Spirit world - will continue to grow as they passed – at whatever age they passed – and so their life continues.

Thankyou."

Silver Cloud:
"It seems I am not able to finish my sentences.
I thought I was explaining rather well."

John:
"So did I."

Silver Cloud
"But there are always those that know more, and there are always those who can pass the information more precisely, and there are always those who feel they have spoken and have not been heard and wish to be heard. And there are always those of us who will stand aside for the words of the Great Spirit.

I hope this information has been useful?"

John:
"Very."

Silver Cloud
"We have no more communication to pass.
The channel may go."

During his work as a press photographer, John had - in his professional capacity - visited the opening of a couple of children's hospices, and spent time with terminally ill children and their families. I know that there had been one child in particular, who will always stay in his memory.

John had spoken to his team about his willingness and commitment to work with such children – as his team seemed to be indicating that he would, and on the 28th March 1995 Kato and John had a discussion through me, about this work. I would like to share (with John's permission) a small part of that conversation:

Firstly - Mr White - a guide who receives those who have suddenly passed over, through trauma.

Mr White:
"Although I am a receiver of those passing through trauma – I have experience in these matters. So rest assured that there are those that I know, who will be waiting to receive the children. This is all part of your "extended team" – the team in Spirit who you do not know – and the team in Spirit who you will not know as each are individual and individual to the child."

"But they will know you and so they pass their gratitude now – for the work that you will be doing in the future."

Secondly – Kato

Kato:
"We are all thankful for the children – for in their short lives – there is much that we may learn from them – much that they can teach. Your experiences with these children and the inspiration that you will gain from the children themselves – their families – their siblings – would perhaps be useful in book form – to give inspiration and to raise much needed funds for the hospice, in that way – the children's short life would give so much to others.

You will find that you will gather drawings and poems and the written word – and in your physical life – you have the capability to get these works published.

On behalf of the Spirit world – we say Thankyou."

John and I have yet to fulfil this request personally, but we suspect that hospices are perhaps using this type of publication to put in the public domain – in order that the words of the children are heard and to raise funds.
I use this space to make a personal plea:

"Please, if you can – support the wonderful work of hospices all around the world."

As Kato said goodbye that evening – Angela came to say hello:

Angela:
"Can my picture go in your book?"

John:
"It will take pride if place."

Angela: Then began to describe her picture.

*"A cow. It's head's like that (*she tilted her head to one side*) and this big horn (*she indicated with her hand, how the horn came out of the middle of it's head and then, as if repeating an earlier conversation with someone – she indignantly said):*
It's not a rino..sa..rar..s – It's a cow."

John:
"With one horn?"

Angela:
"My picture could go on every book and you could put my name on."

John:
"Smashing idea."

Angela:
"I'll send you the picture – from Angela.
Bye."

Angela went skipping off.

30th March 1995.Nightime.
Earlier this evening, I had spent two and a half hours with a young man who wanted to have communication from his mother.

The fact that his grandmother and others came instead didn't seem to interest him. He had put a lot of heavy, negative energy, out into the room and I had really struggled to pass the communication.

Even though I knew that the communication was relevant to him – he kept repeating the words, "No I don't understand any of it."

I was tired and fed up with his attitude and at 11pm that night – as I "raised my vibrations" I was desperately asking for Silver Cloud. I heard the words "*Will I do?*" – and recognised the vibration of White Cloud.

White Cloud:
"You coped with a difficult situation adequately.
There will be more similar situations.
People are coming for communication – but they are also coming to experience and test the channel.
It has been of a valuable nature.

They have been of help to the Spirit Mary and she wishes you to know that she is grateful for her communication. The sitter will probably not cross your path again, so – know that you have done your work – you have passed communication and you have given some "food for thought."

Those that come to test the channels and Spirit – are a valuable addition to our life's' experience and as you know – we learn from our life experiences."

I was grateful to White Cloud and his words – especially the ones that said – "*The sitter will probably not cross you path again.*" Thank goodness for that!

1st April 1995. Nightime.

As I "raised my vibrations" I felt a very strong vibration around me. It was not an energy that I recognised. I could also hear chanting and drumming – but knew it was not the chanting of Native American Indians. As the chanting continued, the words "Ancient People" and "half man/half Spirit" came into my head. Whoever it was, and I knew it was male – it kept repeating the words "half man/half Spirit" and the more I listened and raised my vibrations – the nearer I was to him. Then he began to laugh in a mocking way and, echoing the words of Angela – I thought – "I don't like that man!"

I can't describe the man as I did not see him clearly – but his energy was very strong and I felt uncomfortable in his presence – yet – I had a job to do – so I continued to tune into his vibration.

He began to speak in a loud derogatory manner – and here are his words:

"You are not Spirit – you are physical man with Spirit. You have forgotten Spirit.

You do not know what it is – to be half man – half Spirit. You cling to your Spirit to save your souls – so that you may be immortal. Your last chance at survival. You must continue to cling and grasp and use your Spirit – else you will die forever.

The Incas know. The Incas will always live.

The Incas are the last race of the true Spirit people.

The Incas are the last chosen race.

Those that follow are made by the Spirit world.

The Incas were deceived.

The Inca will not be annihilated."

"We are the chosen race to populate the planet Earth – so therefore we must return in our thousands – as our right to the planet Earth. No one – no Spirit – will deny us the right to the planet Earth.

We come to help now – not to destroy.
You must cling to your Spirit to save your soul – to be immortal – else the planet would die.
If you were not to return to the new Spirit home – you could not return to the planet Earth – to nurture it.
The planet would die. This will not be allowed – it is our planet and you will not destroy it."

At this point, the energy appeared to fade away – and then it returned:

"I am Banjou – immortal, the Spirit of the host.
Cast out from it's physical being – deceived.
Deceived by the Gods who said we would never perish – and the host bodies perished.
We will not be deceived again – Never.
The Gods promised immortal life.
We expected immortal life on the planet Earth.
We were deceived.
We come to help – so that you may not be deceived.

We, were the chosen race."

CHAPTER ELEVEN

PROTECTION - VISUALISATION
AND CUTTING CORDS.

2nd April 1995. Nightime.

After the communication between John and Kato had ended that night – a flowing river appeared in front of me, and Silver Cloud sailed into my vision. He was sitting in a wooden framed canoe, which was covered in animal skins.
Silver Cloud stopped the vessel and said:

"As you paddle down life's rivers – it is always better to take your guide with you. It is also lonely in a canoe for one. In a canoe for one – who would you blame if you took the wrong course? – I speak hypothetically.

Of course – the Indian is very skilled at building canoes. The English people have rowing boats."
(He turned to John, and continued)

"So your team have acquired a rowing boat – as they know how to build one. Kato does not sit on water – Kato would probably – walk on water. So – your team have acquired this rather, over large, rowing boat - to seat you all – and so – there is your vessel."

John:
"Right."

Silver Cloud:
"The three English, guides and helpers will take a turn in providing the momentum."

"So – I will paddle off – and leave the English team in my wake. The canoe is also quieter than the squeak of the oars, the canoe has stealth – the oars announce the arrival. This is why the Indian has the canoe.

I will slide off. The others have already given themselves away.
The channel may go."

I have often sat in the canoe with Silver Cloud – my fear of water and lack of swimming ability gone, and the peace that I find, combined with his wise words – enable me to truly experience tranquillity.

After receiving some communication several days ago, I had been asked to give a copy of the transcription to a friend of ours – so that he could pass it on to someone else. On receiving the communication, a request had followed – "Would you please sit for me?"
This lady had been experiencing happenings, and receiving small pieces of information – usually during her sleep - she was anxious for explanations.
The most striking happening - was that she would often wake up with a "sun tan." Her feeling, and mine, was that the person who had given the communication would have the answers to her questions.
That person was Banjou – the Inca.

I reluctantly, and with some trepidation – agreed to do a sitting. I can't say that I was looking forward to the experience. I didn't feel at all comfortable in his descending, menacing, energy - and his delivery and his words, left me cold, however – I had passed the information on, as requested, and I had a duty to agree to the sitting. That was - after all - the reason my team and I had worked together for hours.

On the night of the 3rd April – Silver Cloud was waiting for me:

Silver Cloud:
"I wish to speak to you.

You are entering a difficult time.
You will be passing words that you will not want to pass – and passing words that she does not want to hear. You will feel as though you want to stop the communication – but you cannot – it is your job.
You will be watched - and watched over.
Mr Bennet will assist if necessary.
It (the experience*) will not drain your energy but you may need to cleanse your aura."*

Silver Cloud added:
"I may need to replace some of my feathers myself."

John was then given the opportunity to ask Jim – his doorkeeper, a question.

John:
"Is the tingling that I feel – you trying to get my attention?"

Jim:
"It is an indication that there is someone there.
Mr McDonald has to be introduced – rather than introduce himself – so if you would acknowledge his presence by asking for protection for him.

I am affording protection to the Spirit world as Wolf protects those individual Spirits who come for communication."

"Because the channel does not recognise – does not know – the number of Spirit involved – it is put upon the doorkeeper – to recognise the Spirit individually – and to afford protection.

As you know – doorkeepers are able to afford protection without the recognition of a channel – but – the recognition of the channel, forges the link and so aids the protection. Wolf is becoming an expert at affording protection to those Spirits who move around and mingle – unlike the protection given to Spirit guides – who come to the channel and are static – as they come for a particular purpose.

But the Spirit who are gathering and may not know that protection is needed – as they come in haste – they are not used to descending, and maybe do not realise that they must have protection, and so – the doorkeeper has to be – on behalf of the channel – expert in his work – refined and precise – as a mother hen gathering her chicks."

John:
"Yesterday – before I went into that house – you advised me about asking for a particular energy – to repel negative energy. It wasn't until I got there, that I realised the negativity of the people as well.
Which was the stronger – the people or the place?"

Jim:
"The negativity – as you say – surrounding the house, has attached itself to the occupants, and it has become threefold in its' strength. As the occupants have retained the negativity – it is concentrated in its' strength."

"There is negativity surrounding the dwelling and the occupants are drawing the negativity The negativity sticks. My job, is to be aware of the problem and to make you aware – and to give protection and advise on the protection that is necessary for you. If you had absorbed the negativity – you too, would have been negative – although you are not negative – it sticks."

John:
"Should I use the same protection that you told me to ask for – when I dowse over the plans of the house?"

Jim:
"Correct – it sticks."

John:
"Sticky stuff this negativity."

Jim:
"It is all part of the learning process. I could have been remiss, in not informing you of the system."

John:
"I was aware that you were doing something – and for some reason – I didn't ask."

Jim:
"We are all learning.
Angela knows that she needs protection and she turns to me to ask for it.
She is very wise for her age and is learning fast.
I will go.
Cheerio."

The evening session was coming to an end, which heralded the return of Silver Cloud.

Referring to a meditation that John had done earlier in the evening – where he had been on his rowing boat – Silver Cloud directed his words to John:

Silver Cloud:
"I hear you stepped into the boat?"

John:
"Yes – I was very chuffed. It was quite a step for me."

Silver Cloud:
"Well – these boats can be very unstable when one first steps into them."

John:
"Kato stayed on the bank."

Silver Cloud:
"He would not be seen dead in a rowing boat!
It is unbecoming to a Samurai and furthermore – I would say – that if he got in it – there would be no room for anyone else. He functions better on the land."

John:
"It was great."

Silver Cloud:
"No doubt you will hear them coming again.
The channel may go."

4th April 1995. Daytime.

Today I went on an adventure with Silver Cloud.

We travelled in the canoe across a lake and headed for the opposite shore – where we disembarked. After sitting for a while, we walked through a wood, which had many young trees growing in it. Yellow primrose and tiny purple flowers were growing all around us.

We came to a clearing and I was thrilled to see several tepees, which had been erected in a circle.

I followed Silver Cloud into one of the tepees and was surprised to see White Cloud and Mr Shush. Silver Cloud and I sat with them on the earth floor and - just as Silver Cloud and I had "joined our energies" before – we all sat in silence – just "being".

White Cloud then stood up and walked out of the tepee – we all followed him and - as it was time to leave – we said our "Goodbyes". Silver Cloud and I retraced our steps and as we reached the wood – I turned back to look at the clearing – all the tepees had gone.

We travelled back across the lake and to the landing stage, from which he had picked me up. Silver Cloud said that I must "*go back now*" – so I got out of the canoe. He didn't follow me, and as I walked up the landing stage I wondered which way I should go.

Leaning up against a tree, was Armon (my uncle).
Armon said:

*"Focus on the future and know that you are not alone.
We all walk with you.*

Wolf will take you back."

Looking to my left – I saw Wolf standing – waiting.

As I looked at him – I was un-ceremoniously plonked back into my chair!

That is one of many trips that I took with Silver Cloud. I never knew when they would happen – where we would go or what we would see. Very often, we went to one particular place, a place where the ground was sandy, the river icy cold and the trees were tall. A place where the sun beats down onto the sand and you can feel the heat as you walk, a place where the sky is cloudless and a vibrant blue, and a place where we would walk and talk - or sit in silence - listening to the river, as its' clear water bubbled over the rocks.

4ᵗʰ April 1995 Nightime.

As I prepared to go to "my place" – I saw a man who was cutting through a piece of metal with a power saw. The noise was deafening, and the orange sparks flew all around him This vision was replaced with a man who was blowing molten glass out from the end of a metal rod. The globe that he produced, glowed orange. My attention was drawn to the sound of metal being struck with a metal hammer. I turned to the direction of the sound – and saw a blacksmith - hard at work over his anvil. Next – I heard the sound of wood being sawn, I looked to see a carpenter – sawing through a plank of wood, with a hand saw.

The visions disappeared – and Silver Cloud was standing in front of me.
He began his communication:

Silver Cloud:
"Each one provides a service - each individual puts themselves into the service which they provide, although the previous trades people that you have seen - all have a product at the end of their line - so the medium and healer, also have a product they produce."

"One being, communication, the latter – a restoration of health – be that physical or mental.

So – you are providing a service and producing a product – although the product that you provide is not entirely your own – it is a product of Spirit energy.
Nevertheless – you will be seen – as providing a service – as the carpenter who produces a table or the blacksmith who produces a poker. It is a job of work – for which you have undergone training – and for which – you will undergo further training – and will gain experience as you travel along."

To John, he said:

"The taking of photographs is a hobby – I feel you raise your hands in horror. The taking of photographs will be a release – an opportunity to work on the physical level – although – as we have noted – you work on the physical and the spiritual at one and the same time.

You have both committed to being "full time" members of the Spirit association – and as such – any activity on the periphery, will be a hobby – will it not?

We understand that you still have many difficulties before you – I speak the Truth – I also speak with a suggestion of jest, but – whatever befalls, within the next two months – your horizon, is that of beginning again – a new career, and so – whatever befalls – is seen as a stepping-stone towards that new career.
And your previous job of work, will become a hobby.

Kato and I are awaiting on your first day of work."

"And although we are not impatient – we too - feel that we are now dragging our heels, and there is no reason to stop us beginning our new day."

Me:
"If we are dragging our heels – what can we do?"

Silver Cloud:
"Propel yourself forward."

Me:
"How?"

Silver Cloud:
"Take bigger strides."

John:
"This is what we were talking about the other day."

Me:
"Bankruptcy?"

John:
"Not particularly – just physically getting on and doing."

Silver Cloud:
"Your new day awaits."

Me:
"He is stood with his arms folded."

Silver Cloud:
"You must speak amongst yourselves."

John and I had discussed the possibility that we may be declared bankrupt in the future. We could not find a buyer for the house, and we had overstretched our finances with business loans. Interest rates were climbing – and the banks were now bouncing the occasional cheque and charging us £30.00 for the privilege of doing so. Their action escalated over the coming, months which only exacerbated our situation and eventually – our situation became dire.

To cut an arduous story short – after a long battle with the banks' - and during the summer of 1996 – John and I took a *"longer stride"* and declared ourselves bankrupt. We lost the house and business in the process. Happily – we did manage – by means of selling many possessions – to pay all our small creditors – leaving two banks to fight over the proceeds of the eventual sale of the house. Good for them!

I apologise for telling you the outcome of our finances at this point in the story – but – not liking "guessing games" myself – I thought it best to resolve the mystery now. However – any communication about the house and new location – will be included in the following chapters – so you won't miss out on anything!

Back to the evening session of the 4th April:

Angela:
"I haven't sent you my drawing for the book."

John:
"No"

Angela:
"For the children."

"Jim's going to help me – not Mr Bennet – Mr Bennet will send the wrong picture. I want the cow."

John:
"I'm looking forward to getting it."

Angela:
"When you move house – when you move house – can I come?"

John:
"I hope you will."

Angela:
"There's a little corner – I'm going to sit in."

John:
"Where is it?"

Angela:
"I'm not going to tell you. I'm going to sit in it and I'm going to watch the people coming – but I'll be a good girl. I'll watch them come and I'll watch them go. I'm going to peep through the letterbox. I'll see them coming and they won't know I'm there – but I'm going to be good – but I'm not going to tell you where I'm going to sit. When you move house, you're going to do some important work and I shall be very quiet then – else Laura – Laura won't let me come – but I'm going to hide, I'm going to peep through the letterbox – where the letters come – and I shall see them coming. Anyway, I'll send you my drawing."

John:
"Have you done any more drawings?"

Angela:

"I've been with people – no time to draw. Can't draw every day otherwise you'd have – you'd have too many drawings and you wouldn't know what to do with them. You give them to your friends – and I've got a lot of friends – and you give them to your friends – but then – then you've still got some left over – drawings – so I've not done any - and you're my friends and so I'm going to send you one – of the cow."

John:

"That's brilliant."

Angela:

*"And Jim says we must keep it flat – so I've been taking special care of it and keeping it flat – a bit got – a bit got bent – but it doesn't matter.
So anyway – I'm going now."*

John:

"It's been smashing to talk to you."

Angela:

*"I came on my own
I'm going on my own."*

John:

"Thankyou for coming"

Angela:

*"Bye.
Bye Silver Cloud.
Bye."*

Silver Cloud:
"We know where this dwelling is and it is for you two to find it. We shall give you a map. So the channel may go and you must watch and wait for the map.
The channel may go.
Goodnight."

As I told you earlier – I had agreed to sit for a friend of a friend, in order that she may have some questions of her's answered by - Banjou the Inca.

I did sit for her and passed his communication – and as was usual – the communication was taped. I gave the tape to the lady to keep – therefore, I have no transcript of it – and as the communication was personal to her – it wouldn't have been included in these pages. However, prior to the sitting - on the 5th April, Banjou came once more – at the beginning of that evening's session. His energy was very heavy and descending – causing me to have difficulty in breathing. I felt as though he was trying to take over my body. And remembering him talking in an earlier communication about "hosts" – I became increasingly anxious.

Wolf, Silver Cloud and Mr Bennet were all in attendance. As I struggled to breath, and with my duty to pass Banjous' communication also bearing down on me – it was 15 minutes before we all reached a "happy distance" which enabled me to speak his words.

His words were as follows.

"The Incas are honourable.
We come to protect our planet – as is our right.
Without us, the planet would not survive and I know this to be true. These Spirits that are around you now, are but a shadow of former man. They say that they are true Spirit – as things were meant to be."

"They say that they have transformed into Spirit, as this is the meaning of life – they are misguided.
They are a pretence. They stand round you now, as your guardians – they do not know the truth.
Only the Inca knows the truth, and that is why we must return to the host – to save our planet. I shall not return again to tell you more before you are lost.
I am gone."

Silver Cloud:
"Pass the energy through you."

I welcomed the short break that Silver Cloud gave me and used the time to regulate my erratic breathing and also to cleanse my aura of Banjous' energy. I did this by breathing out through my aura and dispersing his energy – with the help of Wolf and Mr Bennet – harmlessly into the atmosphere. John and I spoke about the communication and expressed our thoughts', that Banjou was an "earth bound" - "stuck" unhappy spirit, and I was very relieved that he would not be using me again as a channel, after the sitting that had already been arranged in a few days time.

I went back to see Silver Cloud – who – on my return to "my place" - handed a feather to me – another one for my collection.

Silver Cloud:
"You are correct in saying that he is "earthbound".
We do not recognise his words.
There is truth in what he communicates – regarding the planet – in that – we in Spirit, wish to help you living "on the planet - to help you to recognise the destruction through the pollution."

"And yes – we in Spirit come in order that we might help you save and restore the planet to its former glory. The difference occurs in that we do this for future generations – this is our Universal belief.
We have had an interesting communication……"

Peter:
"I have come to endorse the words of Silver Cloud, and to say that those of us outside your Universe – work with the Spirit world with which you are in contact.
The Spirit world which, you know to be true.

Those of us outside your Universe, wish you to know that we are there to help and assist, and that the visual aids that we have – show us that the planet Earth is indeed, in need of help and assistance. This is why we come – to aid the planet Earth, so that it can continue its' path within it's own solar system, which, in turn, aids the path of other planets in similar solar systems.

The planet Earth is not a possession.
The planet Earth is part of a Universe.
The planet Earth belongs - by right - to the Universe which has a far greater control than any race – any inhabitants. You merely borrow a millimetre of space on the planet Earth – while you choose to live.
When you leave – you leave your space to the next generation. This has been for many generations – and this will continue.
Each speck of life – whatever race or creed – merely borrows its' tiny space – and then must leave – to vacate that space for another generation.

This is the truth – as it has been for billions of years – and this cannot be denied – this cannot be altered."

"We see, from where we are – how the planet Earth fits within its' own solar system.
It retains its' rightful place.

Know that we are there – and that we watch – and that we see the whole, and because we see the whole – and because we are part of the whole – we know it to be true. You must believe. There are those who cannot – but they will not change the whole.
Never.
Peter."

Silver Cloud:
"The channel may go."

Having met Banjou and heard his hostile words and felt his mocking arrogant energy – I wondered why I had ever been scared of Peter's presence at all!
Peter is a friend.

The next day – the 6th April – Silver Cloud shared with us, his advice on "listening skills".
As I prepared to go to "my place", I felt a very sudden and sharp pain in my lower back. I felt as if – when I tried to move to relieve the pain – I would find that I was unable to. I thought to myself – "This is what John must have felt like when he had his slipped discs in his back and neck"

Silver Cloud:
"Is it (the pain) *your imagination or is it a reality?"*

Me:
"It's a reality.
No it's not – I haven't got a slipped disc."

Silver Cloud:
"Is it your experience – to have suffered the consequence of a slipped disc?"

As he spoke – Silver Cloud was pacing back and forth – slightly stooped – with his hands clasped behind his back. He reminded me of a lecturing professor.

Silver Cloud:
"What would you say to someone – sat before you – who said they had a slipped disc?
Could you – in all honesty – say "I know how that feels"?"

Me:
"No"

Silver Cloud:
"Therefore the art of listening – is not to say "I know how you feel" – because, quite clearly – you do not.
It would be more honest to say – "I do not understand how you feel – as it is not within my experience – but I know if you were to share that experience with me – I would begin to get some understanding of what you have experienced."

Beware of platitudes.

Beware of likening the experience of a person – to a similar event in your own life – as the two experiences are not the same. You cannot say –"I had a similar experience – I know how you feel" – because a similar experience – is not the same experience – and you are two different people."

"And so – all you can ask, is that they share the experience with you – in order to make you understand how they felt and how they reacted, and the counsellor will try to make them understand – the reasons as to why they reacted in the way that they did.

If I were to say I had a pain in my neck – you would not understand – John would understand – but his understanding would be different from mine – as the experience would not be the same.

The art of listening, is a difficult task to attempt.
One should listen with an empty mind."

The sitting where I would communicate the words of Banjou was imminent and to my consternation – on Sunday the 9th April – Banjou returned.

He was in a really disagreeable, angry mood. I was very reluctant to pass his communication and asked Silver Cloud if it was really necessary for John and I to hear his words.

Silver Cloud – looked at me in silence.

That look - his eyebrows raised and head slightly tilted to one side - reminding me so much of my dad and his attempts to silently chastise me. That look – that told me that I must channel Banjou.

I struggled to "raise my vibrations" to his level and by now – his energy was swirling around me – oozing his impatience. It was with relief – that Wolf, Silver Cloud, Mr Bennet and Kato - positioned themselves between myself and Banjou.

I felt their protecting, calming energy wafting all around me, and their intervening energy meant that Banjou had to move further back. I was very grateful for their combined presence and, from behind their protective shield – I received the following communication from Banjou.

"You are not worthy of my words."

Silver Cloud intervened and stopped him speaking.
Then – after some words exchanged between them both – Banjou continued:

"I will not speak to you again to give my personal message. I will speak to my host (the sitter*) – my words are lost on you.*

You surround yourself – you are closed to my words – you are closed to my knowledge – and you spurn my intelligence. I shall speak to my host via your voice – reluctantly. I am prepared to address my host. Only I know when that will be.

I have come to save your soul – as was my intention – but you are lost to me. You are misguided and I waste no more time – as my time is precious.

It is in my hands when I address my host – no one dictates to the Inca.
The Inca is above.
The Inca must find its' own communication channel.
The Inca must be permitted to speak.
We will find our own communication channel – where we are not hindered – but where we are in control.
You are lost."

Banjou left.

Silver Cloud:
"I thank Kato and Mr Bennet.
There is strength in the unity of the team - a strength
which connot be penetrated. Unity can be a fearful
thing – when seen from the other side."

Kato:
"We are pleased to show our unified front.
The content of the communication is very deep seated,
it has not been dispelled, dispersed, broken down or
rearranged. Neither – has any explanation been able to
alter the thought process of this particular Inca.

We must provide a unified circle in which the
communication can be passed – for the well being of
the host. I can only echo Silver Clouds' good advice –
the communication channel must pass it through –
through the healing process. A healing channel passes
negative energy out through its' aura to dispel it –
likewise – the communication channel – at times – will
have to pass communication which it does not wish to
remember – and the way to "forget" – is to pass
negative energies and thoughts – out through the aura.

I wish the communication channel to know that when
we are needed – or – if we are needed again – we shall
be pleased to assist Silver Cloud.

The Inca believed that they were the chosen race.
The Inca believed that anything they wanted – they
could have. They believed that they were promised this.
They believe that the promise was broken.
The promise was not made.

They were given reassurance that to live their life in a
certain manner – would bring them the Kingdom of

Heaven – but a promise was not made, and therefore you can understand their way of thinking – thinking that they have been deceived and cheated.
The Inca will not communicate within the Spirit world.
The Spirit world – as they found it – was not the world that they wanted, so – they return in some numbers to attempt to achieve their aims on the planet.

They are eternally in turmoil, they must eternally, return to the Spirit world and hopefully – those above us – can convince the Inca not to return to the planet Earth. They have had their time – their time is past – they have left their mark on the planet Earth – and for any race – that should be reward enough.
To leave your mark on the planet is indeed an honour – that is their reward – but they do not see it.

I take my leave."

Silver Cloud:
"I cannot add to the words of Katamoro.
I am indeed grateful for his assistance.
The channel may go."

20th April 1995. Nightime.

A healer friend had joined John and I for this evening's session – during which – there had been some discussion surrounding the death of another healer.
Kato, our friends guide – who I will simply refer to as "T" and Angela gave us their insight into the Spirit world.

Kato:
"As channels – unless you can see it – you can only believe that our world is a beautiful world."

"And to the healing channels, I say that you must believe – that you must know – that those spirits that you assist in releasing from the physical plan – arrive into this beautiful world – where there is a greater capacity for knowledge and understanding – where there is time to sit – to absorb – to meditate – free from the physical shackles that you carry, and that we have all carried with us on the physical plane.

Know that the spirit of those patients that are lost to you – pass into an everlasting world – where their spirit is totally free. Free to learn the things they wish to learn – to experience only those things that are good for them. To travel in the blink of an eye.
Know this to be the Truth, and in knowing this – you will not grieve – other than for a short space of time.
You grieve for the physical loss – but know that they pass into this beautiful world.
This will assist you in difficult times.

Know that some day you will be in the position where you may ask to meet again – and this is the knowledge that you have. The knowledge helps you to do your work. Hold onto this knowledge. Never let it go – then the hurt will not penetrate too deeply.

As your patient leaves you – you must rejoice – as indeed they will rejoice when they arrive and meet those waiting for them."

T:
"Hold the knowledge of the continuation of life and the beauty of the Spirit World.
Hold it within your aura – and those that are sensitive – and those that move within your aura – will feel part of what you feel."

Angela:
"I'm a good girl."

John:
"Have you been painting?"

Angela:
"No. Mr Bennet has been telling me a story."

John:
"Was it a funny story?"

Angela:
"Mr Bennet laughed.
Sometimes I don't understand Mr Bennet.
Have you got my picture?"

John:
"No not yet."

Angela:
"Well I gave it to Jim and Jim said he would send it to
you – my cow.
It will be crumpled now."

John:
"I'm sure it will flatten out."

Angela:
"Laura said, if I'm good – when you see children – I'm
going to come.
Laura said – when I grow up I can be a healing guide."

John:
"Would you like that Angela?"

Angela:
"Yes – because I was sick and my mummy cried – but I'm all right now.
Why did my mummy cry – 'cos I'm here now?"

John:
"She didn't know that at the time, did she?"

Angela:
"Yes – but I'm better now – didn't my mummy want me to be better?"

John:
"Of course she did."

Angela:
"I like it here – I'm going to be a healing guide.
I think I would heal old people like Mr Bennet – 'cos the old people, they get sick and Mr Bennet is an old man. He's not as old as my granddad – he is very old.
Laura's' like my mummy – she holds my hand.
And Jim is like my daddy 'cos he plays with me and he does tricks."

John:
"What sort of tricks does he do?"

Angela:
"Well – I've told you – it's in his hand and it's not – I don't know where it's gone – I've told you
So – when I'm grown up and I'm a healing guide – will you be there?"

John:
"I don't know – I might be."

Angela:
"Well - then you can help me
Well – you can stand there and watch me – when I'm
grown up."

John:
"I shall do that."

Our healer friend:
"Can I watch as well?"

Angela:
"I don't know. You'll have to ask Laura.
Silver Cloud says I've got to go.
I'm going on my own."

I saw Silver Cloud move forward to steer Angela towards the door at the rear of "my place". A truculent Angela, snatched her right arm away from his impending grasp, and shouted:
"I DON'T NEED ANY HELP SILVER CLOUD!
I can go on my own.
Bye."

As Angela left – Silver Cloud said – in a exasperated yet humorous tone:

"When that child is grown – we shall all be very old!"

21st April. Nightime.
The Eve of John's birthday and Silver Cloud gave him this advice:

"On your birthday, wake up as if you have just been reborn. Experience as if you were experiencing for the first time. The birthday is a rebirth - Happy Birthday."

22nd April 1995. Nightime.

As I "raised my vibrations" that evening, I felt a different vibrational energy about me.

The energy was cold – firstly around my legs – and then it crept up my body – concentrating around my solar plexus. At the same time – I "saw" an image of a womb with two ovaries on either side. I heard a man speak with a German accent, and as I concentrated my vibrations towards him – I saw a middle aged distinguished gentleman who wore a white, neatly trimmed beard.

He introduced himself as Klaus, and told me that he *"understood the psychology of the growing foetus."* At first – I passed the communication on to John by repeating his words and as it is written in my notebook in the third person – I shall just copy it here, as is:

"He is able to communicate with a foetus and through the communication he can begin the healing process.

A beautiful concept – to be able to begin the healing process on a psychological level – before the child emerges into the world. This is done by communication with the spirit of the foetus.

The spirit of the foetus is willing to listen and capable of understanding – as the spirit of the foetus was once an adult and it is only when the next life commences – with the birth – that the spirit is a child, but, while the spirit is within the foetus, it remembers past adult life – but being born with no speech – no understandable communication and total dependence on another adult – the knowledge of the previous adult is trapped.

And the only way that the adult can emerge is by the child growing."

"But, the spirit of the foetus has full understanding – which becomes less, as the embryo develops into a helpless creature. The knowledge of previous life evaporates, as the spirit of the new child takes over and begins to grow itself. holding within it – the knowledge of the previous life."

Because I had been channelling Klaus's words for some minutes – we had become closer in vibration. This meant that Klaus could now speak directly through me. He continued:

"Therefore – one can communicate with the spirit while the cells are in embryo form – one can begin the healing process."

John:

"If there is a correction to be made – then that correction can be made then?"

Klaus:

"On a psychological level – not physical.
What must be – must be.

The spirit of the embryo knows what goes on around – outside in the physical world. One can communicate with the spirit – to be told what has happened to the mother – while the mother was carrying the embryo.

The child, when born, relates to the mother – as the child has experienced what the mother has experienced. So – the mother will accept the new-born child – and the child – within the aura of the mother, (its way of recognition of its parent) – will have an understanding. Not necessarily a firm bond – but a recognition of understanding."

"The child – when born – has to be given to the father – to be within the father's aura – so that a recognition can be developed. The child does not recognise by sight – the child feels the vibrations of the aura – then recognises by hearing and distinguishing sounds.

A child – when crying – can be passed around a group of people – and when it returns to it's mother – it ceases to cry. Occasionally – it finds a similar match – a match of vibrations within the aura – where it will find comfort and ceases to cry.

You will learn more of these things, because in the work that you will be doing – you will need to understand how the child is linked to the mother – in order to assist the child and mother to part.
The letting go.

I shall visit again – Klaus."

The evening session continued with more communication for John, from Kato.
Some of that communication related to the effects of negative energy within the aura. In particular, John wondered whether the "cold like" symptoms that he had been suffering in the last few days – were a sign that negative energy that was trapped within his aura.

Kato:
"The negative energy which you are withdrawing from your patients – invariably escapes through your aura. But – you can expect – as healers – to have a build up of "negative" ions from time to time."

John:
"Would it help if I did a visualisation to cleanse the aura?"

Kato:
"Admirable – and the immersing in water. We will do some work on cleansing the aura through visualisation and immersion in water at the end of the day."

Silver Cloud:
"I go and sit on a hill and let the wind blow through my feathers."

John:
"Would that work?"

Silver Cloud:
"Yes."

John:
"It would work if you think that, that is the intention of being there?"

Silver Cloud:
"Exactly.
Even we in Spirit have to cleanse ourselves as negative energy can be trapped within our vibrations, and so – even we in Spirit have to attend to our preening – but not as often as a channel should!"

The next day – and still relating to the cleansing of the aura – Silver Cloud, in his professor mode, began his communication on the subject of:

"Water."

"The colours in water reflect the colours of life.
The colours in water – as the light shines through it – is
as a mirror of the colours within the aura, and so, for
cleansing the aura – immersion in water is truly
beneficial. Even though the water available to you is
not pure – it still retains the properties of life within it.
I am very keen on the purification by water.
I thought you would like to know that.

The cleansing of the aura – using the visualisation that
you use, is a refined idea of the cleansing properties of
water. The beads of light that you use – are like the
droplets of water. You must use what you are happy
with – but water would suffice."

John:
"What happens to the negative energy once it has been
removed from the aura?"

Silver Cloud:
"It disperses into the atmosphere, but – because it has
been withdrawn and because you are asking your Spirit
guides and helpers to remove the negative energy –
with their help and through its dispersal – its effects are
diminished. The negative energy is weak."

25th April 1995.

Today – the house and myself both felt as though we
were surrounded with negative energy.
John had dowsed in all the rooms, and discovered some
negative energy in the upstairs bedroom that I used as
an office. To dispel the energy, John had done some
visualisation work in it and the room now felt better,
and as I had a sore throat – I asked for healing from
Spirit and Mr Bennet had come to give that healing.

Nightime.

Khylifah, the guide of our dowser friend was waiting to speak:

Khylifah:
"One of the dangers of unnecessarily – living in a large abode – is that the rooms are not used. Unless you enter them every day and walk through them with your positive energy – then there is inevitability – a build up of negative energy.
Why do you live in such a large abode?
It is too large for your capabilities – you cannot begin to utilise all the rooms that you have."

John:
"We are going to change that situation."

Khylifah:
"Well – it seems rather strange that two people should want to dwell in such a large abode. It is not good for a dwelling to have rooms that are not used and never entered. These empty rooms harbour negative energy.
People who live in large houses are creating for themselves – coves of negative energy – useless space.

You must make amends and utilise the whole premises for as long as you remain here. One thinks of the large families of yesteryear – living in cramped accommodation, but as a general rule – those families were happy – cared for one another – grew to be caring people, and this is because all the space within their dwelling was utilised.
Granted – there was a mixture of emotion – but a large family can live in a small dwelling and remain happy."

"Too much space is not necessarily good for an individual – unless the space is utilised.

I have come to give you my judgement, and this is a lesson that you could pass to those in similar circumstances. One only has to think – and apply ones mind to the situation.
Good day."

Silver Cloud;
"As you empty your dwelling of possessions and goods no longer required – the house will indeed feel lighter, so, you must press on. Only take with you – what you will need in your next abode – because in your next abode – you will be using the rooms on a daily basis.
Continue to cleanse the room – not in visualisation – but in a more practical manner.
The channel may go."

26th April 1995.

I had spent some of the day, walking in and out of the rooms in the house in an attempt to put my positive energy into them. I was finding it difficult to remain positive in our present circumstances – no house sale – lack of money – feeling as though the banks controlled my life – need I go on? – probably not – so I won't.

And so, as I was walking round the house and pondering the future – I began to feel that I didn't belong there any more. That night I asked Silver Cloud why I was feeling this way?

Silver Cloud:
"It is proof that the visualisation that John has been doing – is working."

NB He was referring to the gold light that John has been visualising around the photograph of the house, which was in the Estate Agents.
His team had advised him that the Universal gold light could help to sell the house.

"The house is beginning to "move" and is rejecting you both – in the nicest possible way – as you both – are rejecting it – in the nicest possible way.
Because the gold light is around the house – the house is participating and is looking for a new owner.
And so now everybody is in agreement.
Keep with the visualisation and things will move along.
We need to come to an understanding with the house – that we must all part.

A house must want to be sold - and it has hopes for its future. The house is grateful for being made into a fine house – and it looks forward to more comfort.
Now is the time to part the ways."

Heeding Silver Clouds words – I decided that I must make a concerted effort to sort through our belongings and begin to discard and pack those things that we wanted to keep.
As I went from room to room – I was telling the house that we would be leaving soon.
I chatted to the house about the new owners and my hope that they would redecorate and install the central heating radiators in the extension that John and I now couldn't afford.
I told it how I hoped that they would "finish" the kitchen and replace the worn out gates at the entrance to the driveway and – just maybe - add a conservatory like we had always wanted to do.
(The eventual new owners did that - and much more.)

Given that John and I are both hoarders – sorting through years of collected belongings, was a daunting task. I began in the spare bedrooms - sorting things into the corners of each room. Every corner was either a "Definitely Must Keep" – a "Probably Will Keep" – and a very small pile of "Maybe we can let it go" heap. That particular heap got smaller every time I revisited the room!

On the night of the 28th April – Silver Cloud was waiting for me.

Silver Cloud:
"Do your financial problems make you a different person inside?"

Me:
"Only if I let them."

Silver Cloud:
"So – who is in control of your life?"

Me:
"Me."

Silver Cloud:
"If you allow problems to pull you away from your work – who has control then?"

Me:
"Me."

Silver Cloud:
"So, who has control over your life?"

Me:
"Me."

Silver Cloud: To both John and myself.
"You must snip away the threads that pull – that create problems and once snipped – they cannot return in that form again – unless you invite them back.
By walking down your Spiritual paths you have found your true selves – your true being and your true purpose. If you do not want to be pulled in differing directions – then you must snip the tethers.
Is it your wish to rid yourselves of tethers?"

John and me:
"Yes."

Silver Cloud:
"Then you walk away from them.
By showing a lack of interest in the problems that surround you they lose their power over you.
Continue to neaten the edges of your physical life – to enable your Spirit to walk freely. Continue to do what you are doing. Focus on the future – do not look back and do not look at the problems as they drift away.
But let them fall behind – walk through them.
Walk through your physical ailments in the same manner – that is – straight and focused – as you do your Spiritual path and you will leave them behind, and they will not be drawn to you as you will be walking too speedily for them to catch hold of you again.

You walk together.
And if you both strip away the problems – you will both forget that you had the problems.
Cope with each problem as best you can – with all your effort, and then snip the cord which attaches you."

"We have discussed the parting of the ways with the house – and you have snipped that cord. Even though you cannot walk away, physically, from the house – you must continue to snip the minor threads that still keep you attached.

The new owners are looking for your house, and with the visualisation and with as much help as we can give – they will find it. As you are removed from your dwelling – you will be in a position to snip many other cords. Soon – you will be able to leave the dwelling in the hands of those who will love it and look after it.
You will walk through the sheet – the sheet, as yet invisible – but – the last break through. As you walk through the sheet – you will begin your new life.

You will end your days in comfort – but we have not allowed for you to be comfortable too soon. You have to know what it is like to be uncomfortable, before you can fully appreciate comfort – and before you can share that comfort with others.

We are all here – working on your behalf, and we know that the end is in sight, and we know you believe the end is in sight. We ask that you follow instruction and move towards us. And as you do – life in your physical path will begin to ease.
Until you walk through the sheet and all the problems of the years past fall away – only then will you be free.
But you will have gained much needed experience.
It has all been for a purpose.
The channel may go."

As I closed down, I thanked Silver Cloud for his words. In response, he added:

"Your lives are split into two distinct halves.
The one half being – struggles, battles, argument,
having and losing, sinking to depth, but in sinking –
there is rising and without sinking you could not rise.
Although you must put the past behind you – you will
not forget, but you will only remember when it is useful
to remember. That is the point of learning – you bring
the knowledge forward when it is useful for the
knowledge to be brought forward.

Your struggles have not been harsh enough to make
you reject life – the struggles have been strengthening.
Now – the tide turns and you must move freely with it.
Knowing that the tide is turning with the help of your
friends in the Spirit world.

Therefore, you can trust and move forward – as you
trust your friends in the Spirit world.

The sunny days are coming and we will share the sunny
days with you.

The channel may go."

CHAPTER TWELVE

"FORWARD - IS THE ONLY WAY TO GO"

16ᵗʰ May 1995.

Oh happy day! We have had an offer on the house.
Unfortunately – the offer is well below the asking price
and isn't enough to pay the debts and leave us with any
money for a deposit on another house. I have asked
Silver Cloud what we can do about the situation.
His reply was, *"We will walk together."*

On the night of the 17ᵗʰ of May – I asked Silver Cloud
once more – "what could we do?"
He replied:

*"I am not going to tell you what to do. An opportunity
has presented itself and it is for you two, to decide what
to do with the opportunity. I don't know why you ask
me all the time. If I was given the opportunity to have a
new tepee – when my tepee had holes in it – I would be
a fool not to accept the new tepee.*

Go away – and come back."

When I returned to "my place" – my uncle Armon was
waiting to speak.

Armon:
*"You are embarking on a brave new start – in some
respects – you are jumping into the unknown – but an
unknown, built on a solid foundation of trust.*
*When you leave this place – you leave not knowing
quite what the future will be."*

*"You leave with the hope of what the future will be –
but, not knowing how the future will unfurl itself before
you. You will both jump at the same time – and together
– where you will find immediate brightness – even if
you are unsure as to where the brightness is leading.*

*We ask that you trust in the plan and the paths that are
before you, and we ask that you have faith to jump.
We trust and hope that you will endeavour to tread the
path that has been laid before you, and that in treading
the path – you will both find joy and enlightenment.*

*Your physical path will not be as comfortable as you
would wish – initially. You will be in a position – where
you will bring good things to yourselves.
The ripples will become less."*

Mr Bennet:
*"Now see here – just start walking!
We are leading the way – start moving towards the
future – the past is dead and gone. You have an
opportunity which, you must – in my opinion – grasp
with both hands. You may not be as physically
comfortable – but we must move along. We have dallied
too long. That is all I have come to say."*

Armon:
"We wish you both well. We are waiting.
We hope you trust. We are waiting."

Silver Cloud:
*"The general opinion is – we should all move forward
when given the opportunity and if you can find it within
yourselves to take an opportunity to move forward –
then take the opportunity."*

"I speak no more on the physical path.
Come back in 15 minutes."

During the 15 minute break, John and I agreed that we would accept the offer on the house even though the sale would leave us with no equity.
We trusted that having taken the step forward – our teams in Spirit would look after us.

After the 15 minute break, I went once more to "my place", I saw that Angela was eagerly waiting to speak, but my dad was also waiting – and he spoke first.

Dad:
"I've just come to say that your mother and I are watching both of you and we are excited for both of you. You deserve to get what you want out of your life – what you want for yourselves and what you want for other people."

To John – he said:
"I was talking to your mother the other day – our paths do cross sometimes. She knows that you are moving again – as she knew you were moving last time.
I am sure she will come herself – but I know that she can't come tonight."

John and I had previously moved house not long after his mum – Elsie had died. The move had been – for both of us – one of those moments when we wished that she could have physically been there with us. Like all those moments when you think – "I'll just phone mum or dad" to tell them this that or the other - and then you remember that you can't do that any more.
The space they left behind – remains.

John:
"Give her my love."

Dad:
"Oh I will – will do.
Good luck and all the best.
Cheerio."

Angela:
"Now it's my turn – I came before but they said,
"Shush". I wanted to talk to you.
There's a little girl - and its Jennifer - and she's not
very well and I wanted to ask you if you could do
something?"

John:
"I will if I can."

Angela:
"Well – she's not very well and she can't come here yet
– she's been here but she's gone back and she can't
come here to stay. I've told her, "you can't stay". So
can you keep her there? She keeps coming and I've
said, "you can't – you can't stay here."

So if you talk to her and you tell her that she can't
come here and she's to stay where she is and she's to
get better. I've told her and she just keeps coming – and
I've said – so you tell her. That's what I came to say.
She's annoying me 'cos she keeps coming and I keep
saying "You can't play with me – you're not supposed
to be here – you're supposed to be there" – and she
keeps coming – she's a pest.
So you tell her. Right.
I've said, "Your mummy wants you there."

"If they all came – there would be no sick children would there – if there was no sick children – what would you do?
They've just got to stay there.
I'm going now.
Goodbye."

Laura:
"Hi John.
She (Angela) *is getting to be quite a little madam."*

John:
"She knows her own mind doesn't she?"

Laura:
"She certainly does.

Jennifer is 11yrs old and she has been having chemotherapy. She has felt like giving up – not wanting to be in the physical world.
She has seen the children in Spirit and wishes to be with them. But it is not Jennifer's time.
If you would ask for distant healing – I will go and ask that someone be with Jennifer – to explain to her that is not yet her time – and hard as it might be – she must fight on – for she has her purpose in the physical life, and so if you could do that – I will go."

John took the time to ask for the distant healing.

When the session resumed – Silver Cloud was waiting:

"There will always be plenty of work that you can both do. Always be people to help and assist, and all we can ask – is that when the call comes – you do what you can, and this will be your path – to answer the call and

do what you can. Enjoy the work that you are doing –
in the knowledge that you are doing what you can.
We cannot ask any more. We cannot expect any more,
and if you are truly doing what you can – you cannot
do any more.

We will speak again tomorrow.
No time for questions.
The channel may go."

At 9am the next day – the 18th May - John and I rang
the Estate Agents and accepted the offer on the house.
We felt relieved. Yet the shortfall in funds which would
be left available to us (none) added a certain amount of
anxiety – certainly for me.
At 10.30am – we received a return phone call from the
Estate Agents - to tell us that the buyers had withdrawn
their offer. It was a bitter blow.

Nightime: This was a short session.
A session which began with Silver Cloud saying:
"An Indian has to have courage."
A session, which was ended by Wolf, who - whilst
sitting on some sturdy cardboard boxes – held up a
piece of card with the hand written words on it.
The words read:
"The channel may go."

I laughed at Wolf and his cardboard boxes.

You see – Wolf knew that I was becoming obsessed
with collecting them. He and I had been on foraging
missions many times.

Although John and I were continuing to sort out our possessions – we still had a lot of things that we wanted to keep, (if we didn't need to sell them) – and they needed to be packed away. That meant many trips to supermarkets to obtain cardboard boxes. I was very selective in the size and sturdiness of each box and would triumphantly return home with my chosen selection.

These days – as we now all live under a deluge of plastic bags – supermarkets no longer offer them to customers. However, I discovered that our local garden centre – here in North Wales where we now live – has a lovely selection – and they are only too happy to rid themselves of a few! My obsession and attachment to useful sturdy boxes has remained with me over the years and even today – our garage contains a few "useful" boxes that I find too difficult to dispose of.

So take note – if you are short of a cardboard box – I just might have the right one for you!

19th May 1995:

Today we received another offer on the house from a different couple. This offer was even lower than the first one. With the words of two of our friends, (who both - knowing our circumstances, independently advised us to reject the offer, in the expectation that a better one would surly come along) – running through our minds- John and I were eager to hear what our teams would advise.

Nightime:

Alexander the boat builder was waiting to speak.

His vibrations and mine remained at a distance - which meant that he didn't speak through me - but I was able to repeat his words to John.

Alexander said that:

"When he made boats, he knew the cost of the materials that went into the boat – and the time that it took him to make the boat. He would put a fair price on the cost of the boat, and the buyer would recognise – having looked at the boat – that a fair price was being asked – both for the quality of the materials and the craftsmanship. So – if the buyer was, a fair man – he would pay a fair price.

That is not to say that – being the builder of the boat – *"I could not reduce my profit - if I recognised that the buyer needed the boat – but had not the funds.*
But a fair buyer, will buy at a fair price."

Silver Cloud:
"An Indian must always portray a dignified manner – even in the heat of battle. In the battles of old – it was those Indian who were slain, who died with the utmost dignity, and those who returned from battle – although wounded – knew that their dignity was intact – that the physical scars would not scar their whole being."

Kato: To John.
"The heights that you have risen to – have been achieved by much work from within. You are not the Indian – but you are linked to the Japanese – the Samurai – honourable in battle – you are above the taunts of those who do not know."

"You will not fall because an ant crosses your path. Neither will you step on it. You will surely let it go in its way – unhindered, and in looking down to the ground – you will find the flower. You have fought battles – but you would not fight an ant.

Remain focused on your purpose. Ask for what you want and you will attain it. I cannot say what you must do – I can only say how I find and recognise your inner being. I report to you – how I see you – so that you should not lose the knowledge of who you are and why you are who you are.

I remind you to look up and forward.
The ant has his own path and the ant must carry on with his work and his ambition. You have your own ambition to fulfil and to achieve.

The Samurai – like the Indian – have died for their honour, but without their honour – they would not have been the Samurai. Without the dignity of the Indian – the Indian race would not have survived – as the dignity is passed from generation to generation.
Do not lose sight of your goal – you are committed to achieve what you want. This is acceptable. You are permitted.

I hope this has helped.
I remind you of who you are – the inner you – not the battered. I am pleased to have been able to come.
I feel the air has lightened.
We all have a purpose in the physical world.
We are permitted hopes and dreams and realities.
It is permitted.
Good day."

Silver Cloud:
"Continue to do what you have been doing.
We will wait.
It has only been seconds since we last spoke.
The channel may go."

The next day – the 20th May - and after much deliberating – John and I decided to reject the very low offer for the house. We both felt that the gentleman concerned was just – not, *"a fair man"* and as the money offered wouldn't free us financially – we decided to let the *"ant"*, *"go on its way – unhindered."*

That night, Silver Cloud was, I felt, very non-committal in his response to our decision.

He said:

"You must do what is right for you.
You must not drag the past with you."

However, my spirit lifted when Alexander said:

"Do not sell yourself short.
You must be healthy when you get to the cottage – and when you get there – you will be glad that you waited."

My feeling was - that we would have sold ourselves short - had we agreed the latest offer – I was heartened by Alexander's words of encouragement.

The nightly sessions continued.
In the main, the subject of the communication related to various patients of Johns.

However – I would like to share with you – some thoughts on Monks as delivered by a visiting Monk, who gave his name as Michaela.

If you remember, I have previously mentioned that John had been asked to dowse at a nearby "Abbey" which had been bought by some developers.

Johns Guide Kato had given various recommendations regarding the visit to appease the "resident" monks. Recommendations such as

"Do not disturb the energy – just record it." – *"Do not leave any markers – lay the sticks on the ground – do not insert them."* And *"Do not stand in one place for too long – the negative energies are very strong."* Finally – *"Ground and protect yourself."*

On the 17th June 1995, Michaela shared his thoughts with us.

Michaela:

"The monks followed the Druids way of life. But the monk's way of life attracted ordinary men – criminals – who retreated into the monk's way of life, but they did not have the "calling".

The way of life attracted them because they could hide away. They had power – as seen through other people's eyes because of their way of life – and they wielded that power. They used their way of life, and the power that they held over others – in a selfish – destructive – murderous way.

But those that followed the Druids – felt they had a calling and as their numbers grew – their way of life was seen as a means by which one could gain riches and power."

"The very first monks that followed the Druids had a calling – but were weak to the minds of others – the others that joined their ranks. They turned to God for deliverance – not just for themselves – but for those that swelled their ranks. They believed that Gods way, would persuade the rogues and malingerers to change their way of life and turn to him.
But greed is the enemy."

When I "raised my vibrations" on the night of the 18th June I was immediately aware that Wolf was very close to me. Not only Wolf – but also Mr Bennet was in attendance. The seriousness of their attitude made me realise that something was slightly amiss and it was with some irritation – I discovered that Banjou had returned.

I really disliked this character – sorry, but I did – and so I braced myself as he stepped forward to speak.

Banjou:
"You mistake what you call negative energies – they are not negative – they are positive. You must use the positive energies to gain power for yourself. A negative is a positive – to be used to get what you want – you are frightened of the negative energy."

He paused to laugh at me in his unique, mocking way. Then he continued:

"You are misguided – you have an opening before you – use it you fool.
I told you, you were misguided –
I told you they are no use to you –
And now I laugh in your face."

Silver Cloud spoke to Banjou:
"You have passed your message – you waste your energy."

Banjou left.

Silver cloud continued:
"It is only right, that having made contact with Banjou – we allow his message to be passed. It is only right that you, as channels – be given different views ....."

White Cloud:
"Good evening.
It is not our place to protect you from others peoples points of view. It is our place to protect you as you work with us, but we have to allow both sides – both views – to be passed to you. As Silver Cloud says – the link has been made with Banjou and he felt strongly that he wanted to come and speak.

As a channel – with a free spirit – it is not our place to forbid such communication and this is why the communication has been permitted. We can only guide.
It is not our place to impress our own views and beliefs on you – but merely to work with, and pass information as we see it, and it is the right of others to pass information as they see it. The channel has been given the information from the other side. The channel is free to follow whatever path the channel chooses.
I bid you farewell."

Mr Bennet:
"I concur with White Cloud.
It is only right that you should have views from all sides, but, my own belief is that you do not wish to be

bombarded with such outmoded thought such as we have all just borne witness to."

Silver Cloud:
"The channel may return."

I have to agree with the essence of part of Banjou's communication – the part that says that a negative can be a positive. How often have I said, "Every cloud has a silver lining". "When one door closes – another one opens." Yes – I agree that a negative event can have a positive outcome - and it is up to me to find the positive, but – the negative energy has to be CHANGED into positive energy before it can be utilised. There must be a positive intent. Merely "changing" its name and using the energy, as Banjou was suggesting, will never bring good to anyone - it will bring only harm. Negative energy is harmful and must be converted into positive energy. This is achieved with the help of our Spirit guides or through crystals and ALWAYS with good intent. Just as we can never predict the consequences of our good actions – so – the consequences of our negative actions are totally and utterly, unpredictable.

The Universe works in mysterious ways.

26th June 1995.

Following the instructions of our teams – John and I had been visualising gold light around the photograph of the house that was in the Estate Agents window. I had been sorting and packing boxes and I continued to

tell the house that new owners were coming soon – thus
- I felt - breaking my links with the house.
John and I were more than ready to move on and
looking forward to whatever our future held.

At the end of the nightime session of the 26th – Silver
Cloud gave us one more piece of advice:

*"Let the land that this house is stood on – call to the
new owners. Let the land call"*

Immediately after this advice – John and I took a few
minutes each and asked the land to call to the new
owners.

Khylifah:
*"The visualisation that you have been experimenting
with – to do with the sale of your house and land – is
also a good experience for those that you may meet –
who need to share the same experience. I would suggest
that you remember each visualisation – so that in the
future you may suggest such efforts to others.
The land is now ready – let it call."*

Silver Cloud:
*"As the homelands of the Indian communicate with the
Indian and unite the Indian with his homeland – so
your land has the ability to call for its' new owner.*

*The white man does not understand the ability of the
land – but the Indian land and the white land – are the
same land. The Indian land is understood – the white
mans land is not.*

*Allow the land to call and the owner will come – as the
land called to you – so the land is released to call to*

another. We are all the same people – just a different race. Each race, having different understandings – different knowledge."

Silver Cloud continued to speak in his familiar "tongue in cheek" manner:

"The Indian race is a privileged race - as the Indian understands these things. The Indian – being most gracious – passes the knowledge to the white man.
The white man has a lot to learn.
The white woman has a lot to learn.
The white race, definitely has a lot to learn.

The Indian is signing off.
The channel may go."

Sundays were good days – there was no post!
No letters from the bank informing us of another bounced cheque – which only bounced because the bank had taken more extortionate charges out of the account – with no warning, may I add!

I remember one occasion when we had invoices amounting to over £2.000 to send out to clients – and no money for the stamps. A friend came to our rescue and gave us some stamps so that we could post the invoices off. There was the time when our goldfish had run out of food – and so had we. To raise some money, we sold a dilapidated car that John had been using, to a scrap man – for the princely sum of £5.00.
Strangely – the long forgotten air rifle – was sold for £25.00! Can't the world be a mad place?!!

I found it difficult to have – in the words of my great grandfather - "Positive Energy At All Times."

My notebook reminds me that the 29th of June had been a particularly difficult and frustrating day. My notebook doesn't tell me why that was – but that night, White Cloud and Silver Cloud combined their energies and communicated this rather long communication – which I now relay to you in its' entirety.

White Cloud and Silver Cloud:

"Keep calm.
Keep doing what you are doing.
Keep moving towards the exit.
The exit is well sign posted.

With each day – with each step – you move nearer to the exit. When the steps are hard – step out of yourself – and then step back in, with fresh eyes and a new strength. We are all doing what we can. You are doing what you can – but you must keep the momentum – and so must we.

Each new day is a step further towards the exit – as long as you keep walking – and don't look back.
Look forward – look forward each day – and know that you have done a little more - taken another pace – towards the exit. This is twofold – it moves you nearer towards the door and it keeps your mind in a positive frame – however small the step may be.

Your endeavours must be – to take that small step each day. It is only through staying calm and being light of heart – can you gain new strength.

The door is open a little bit – but with each step – you are becoming within arms length – forcing the door wide open."

"Sort each problem as it comes along – as you have been doing. Do not give up. You have the ability to take more steps of your own accord.

These are things within your power.
You have a grasp on your own momentum – maintain the grasp on your momentum – however hard and painful the steps may be.

You will get to the door using your own momentum – you will not be placed at the door.
Do a little thing each day – that you know – moves you closer to the doorway – however insignificant.
You will sort problems yourself – they will not be taken out of your hands.

The property is a stumbling block – but you are following our guidance. The guidance is given for a reason – the guidance is there to be followed. You have allowed the land to call – the house wants rid of you – the house is ready to move on – you are ready to move on – so how can you not move on?

We shall all meet at the cottage – where life will become easier over a period of time – if a little cramped, by your own standards, and you will not look back. You will have no need to look back – as forward is the only way to go – up is the only way to go.

The experiences that you have had – have not just been for yourselves. The knowledge that you have gained from the experiences is the important thing - and it is the knowledge that can be passed to others.

There will be those – guided - who through no fault of their own – do not know which way to turn."

"Do not know how to disentangle themselves from physical restraint. Because you have learnt momentum and forward looking – and because you have experienced that momentum and forward looking works and gains results – you will be able to advise others on a practical level.

There are many of you who surround yourselves with the past, and the burden becomes heavy as you carry all your belongings and memories with you. With each passing year – you gain more weight. It is not until you turn your back on the heavy load and decide to leave it in the past – where it belongs – that you can move forward. And you have learnt this lesson.
And you may not believe that each small thing that you leave behind – helps to unburden yourself – the tiniest of possessions – the smallest backward glance – left behind – gives momentum towards the future.

Continue to do what you have been doing with a new heart – a new vigour – and you will be surprised – or maybe not?

You must remember that you will feel held back and restrained, until the last time that you walk from the property, but as you move forward – the restraints lose their power – lose their hold. Know that your restraints are being weakened with every step forward that you take. Even though you cannot feel it – you must trust and believe that this is so. We wish you – we urge you – forward. We know that it is difficult at times – it is easy for us to say "continue to move forward" – as we – through seeking further knowledge without restraint – can move forward at a faster pace – at an easier pace – because we have no restraint."

"We here – have all had restraints in our physical life, and although memory fades with time – we can still help you.

And so what a wonderful opportunity that is.

You are correct when you say you are on a learning curve. The learning curve – the lessons learnt – to be stored in the memory, but only to be triggered by somebody in want or need.

And so we urge you forward.
We are moving along with you.
There are those ahead who are trying to smooth the path. There are those who – with their efforts – are beginning to weaken restraints.
We are beside you.
We are in front of you.
We are above – watching.
You are surrounded.
But only you can provide the momentum.

White Cloud and Silver Cloud are one.
The channel may go."

As I was "returning to my chair", Wolf said:

"Play more music.
Move the energy around.
This will help to give you momentum.
Play something lively that will move the energy.
And within that swirling energy – you will move easier.
Goodnight."

11ᵗʰ July 1995.

At the end of the evening session, during which I had sat for a healer friend – Silver Cloud shared with us, his insight and thoughts, on the subject of – "walking on your path."

Silver Cloud:

"Each channel who walks the path, must discover the path for themselves – as only they can experience what it is like to walk along that path. You must all discover for yourselves. You cannot be told that your starting point was here – and that the end result is there – and that in between you experienced many different problems – joys and sadness, because you would not have experienced them.

The penalty for living in the physical world, and at the same time, walking down the spiritual path – is that – one has to walk physically – but travel spiritually, and this action – hurts the feet. It is the walking – not the experience – that gives you the pain, because through the walking – you have the feeling – and it is the feeling that gives the pain – when the road is hard.

If you travelled purely on the spiritual level – you would not feel the pain because you would not have the physical, to feel the pain.

Be thankful that your paths are mapped out for you – it is easier on the feet."

22ⁿᵈ July 1995.

During that evenings session, I suddenly saw a pair of hands appear before me. At first glance, I thought that the hands had been badly burnt, as they appeared to be

knarled and also, I noticed, that the ends of some of the fingers were missing. Then, I realised, I was looking at the hands of someone who suffered from leprosy.
I heard a voice say:

Anon:
"Healing would work well on leprosy.
If you ever get the chance – work amongst the lepers.
Leprosy is the crumbling of the spirit – find the spirit and you will straighten the limbs, and what has been eaten away – will heal."

Me:
"It is a missionary doctor speaking."

Anon:
"This is my message – my hope for the future – that healers will work with the lepers."

John:
"I will pass your message on."

Anon:
"Please do

The Austrian – Goodbye."

Silver Cloud:
"Why have healers not joined the voluntary services to work in other lands?"

John:
"One problem is – it's illegal."

Silver Cloud:
"What law is there in some distant village? – only the law of the people.
Laws are made by governments."

John:
"There must be healers who have tried – and those who do go out – although they are not classed as healers."

Silver Cloud:
"Is it not time that healers offered their services?"

John:
"Yes."

Silver Cloud:
"I pose the question – What would be the response of the Federation?"

Silver Cloud was referring to the National Federation of Spiritual Healers.

John:
"I will find out."

Anon:
"On a voluntary basis, for a short period of time – for those who can afford to spend the time. Ask them the question, and if they question your question – tell them that they have been asked by the Spirit World.
Suggest that they ask their own guides and helpers.
The Spirit world has come to ask the question why – why not?"

To my knowledge – no healing organisation from the U.K – is as yet - funding or assisting in any such trips.

About two weeks later – on the 8th of August – John had the opportunity to ask his guide Kato – a question that had arisen from the communication from the Austrian visitor.

John:
"A question about Leprosy and the crumbling spirit –I don't understand."

Kato:
"The crumbling of the spirit occurs when that spirit is trapped within a physical body – a life style that does not allow the spirit to continue on its' true path.
It could be said that the spirit has decided that it cannot proceed within the physical body.

There are many spirits who crumble.
There are those spirits who are so tormented by the weight of physical life, that they decide to return home – you call this suicide.

These spirits are maybe new spirits to the earth, who find themselves in an intolerable situation – and they fear for their own existence, and so they create a physical situation wherein the physical body cannot be maintained and the spirit returns home.

Leprosy is one of the most – in my opinion – negative physical ailments that can befall – because the ailment comes from within and the spirit within, does not want to remain in the physical world – the spirit wishes to return home. And who can say that if one was born into those countries where there is dictatorship, hardship, starvation and cruelty – that one would not wish to return home oneself."

"When Spirit decides to visit or re-visit the Earth – although the choice is made openly – the path is not fully understood. The reasoning for "Why" is not understood, and so the spirit finds itself in a situation it may feel it does not need – it does not need the experience of – it cannot cope with the experience of.
There are many cases throughout the World – where spirit prematurely returns home and one of the reasons – is that the spirit is not strong enough to carry on its life's work in the physical, and it may be – that the spirit has to return to a similar pattern in the physical world – until the spirit has fully experienced the path."

Me:
"Why are there so many in one area?"

Kato:
"Tradition.
A life of a spirit not fully expended – when it returns – has to continue that same path."

John:
"A continuous cycle."

Kato:
"Correct.
In the Western countries – suicide is a tradition among spirit – by way of self-destruct.
Suicide is not a tradition in the African countries – suicide is a disgrace. But – illness and perishing – is understood."

John:
"The reason healers can help with leprosy – is that healers can help the spirit understand more – so that

they can fulfil their time – not cut it short – and so break the cycle?"

Kato:
"Correct.
The healers will hopefully be able to extend the life of that spirit. The life becoming more meaningful – so that there is not the rush to return home.

Tradition is the root cause of many a premature death – a lesson not learnt in a previous life. The reward for those spirits who fight on, is in our view, the view of the Spirit world – the biggest reward is to be able to choose not to come back to the physical world. Those spirits who submit – have not learnt the lesson. Those spirits who fight – are perhaps aware that the more lessons there are to be learnt, and the harder the lesson to be learnt – the less need there is to return. Which – from our World is seen as the biggest reward - to live life in the Spirit World and beyond, assisting those in the physical world, assisting each other in the Spiritual World. But – the biggest reward – is not to have to return to the physical world."

My problems paled into insignificance when compared to the plight of Jennifer and all those who have suffered, and are suffering from devastating illnesses. My life was and is comfortable – when compared to those thousands of human beings who live under the rule of dictatorship, starvation and cruelty - and I thank my spirit guides for drawing my attention to that fact.

But whatever the cause of anxiety – pain is still felt – the spirit can become weakened. There is no shame in admitting that you feel defeated by any given situation.

But - you owe your spirit the chance to become lighter.

You have the right and the power to lighten your load. And therefore the advice and instruction related within this chapter are valid for all people and all situations.

Know that we all have a purpose in life - and remain focused on that.

Physical scars need not scar your whole being.

It is only through staying calm and being light of heart – can you gain new strength.

Do a little thing each day.

Endeavour to take a small step each day and continue to feed that forward momentum.

Have the faith to jump.

Remember – *"There are those ahead, who are trying to smooth the path."*

And finally – in the words of Mr Bennet:

"Now see here – just start walking!"

CHAPTER THIRTEEN

ESSENCE OF LIFE.

Acting on the advice of Silver Cloud and Kato, John and I continued with our visualisations, i.e. gold light around the house and photographs in the Estate Agents window, and we periodically reminded the land on which the house stood – to call to the new owners. We continued to sort through our possessions – not only those things we had collected over a period of 21years together – but also the contents of the two, fully equipped, photographic business premises which we had closed down. The house and double garage were bulging at the seams.

On those rare days – usually at the end of a month – when we had done all we could do to get money in and pay what bills we needed to pay – we would escape (petrol permitting) for a few hours.
Our escape was to drive to Llandudno – a seaside resort in North Wales. There we would sit on the promenade and say to each other – "Well we have done everything we can do at the moment." and then we would fall silent and watch people walk by.
We both found that the few hours we spent there by the sea, allowed us to refresh and replenish our energy.
We would return home – ready to battle on.

On one such trip, we spotted a cow in a shop window.
She is a square bodied cow with a happy face - she is made out of paper mache and painted brown.
Both of us noticed her at the same time - stopping us in our tracks. We stood looking at her smiling face and said in unison - "Angela's cow".

We entered the shop and looked at the price tag which was dangling from her neck. Relieved to find that we had enough money to buy her - we left the shop with our present for Angela in a plastic bag. There was only one name that we could give her – and that was - "Angela's Cow".

30th August 1995. Nightime.

When I arrived in "my place" I found Silver Cloud standing near a well. "Lets go over to the well", he suggested. We walked over to it and I peered over its stone wall, down into its' vast depth.
"Did you know, that if you wish into a well that holds stagnant water – your wish will not come true.
This is clear water. You have got one wish."

I thought carefully and made my wish.

The well disappeared and suddenly, a man walked towards us – he was an African native with very dark skin.

"Who is this?" I asked Silver Cloud.

"Oh – that is Walnut." He replied – in a tone that expressed no surprise, either at his arrival, or (as I thought) his rather odd name.

Walnut spoke to me in a deep low tone. Although I felt he was speaking in English, his accent was very strong, plus he was quietly spoken. I didn't understand a word.
I've always been rubbish at understanding accents, as of course, Silver Cloud knew, so I was very grateful to Silver Cloud and Walnut – in their pre-arranged agreement to use the name Walnut.

Silver Cloud:
"He is a Guardian Angel."

Me:
"I don't understand."

Silver Cloud:
"Particularly for the children.
He is a guardian for those in Spirit who will come to communicate. He is part of your team – he will help to protect. Walnut will now escort his first child."

Walnut turned to the rear of "my place" to collect someone. That someone was a very indignant Angela.

I heard that now familiar cry – *"I come on my own!"*

Angela was wriggling to remove herself from the close proximity of Walnut – protesting as she did so.

"I don't need him" and turning to Walnut, who was wearing an expression of patient resignation, she said – *"Go away – I can come on my own and I go on my own."*

Angela freed herself from Walnut, who in turn, allowed her to walk forward.
She began to speak:

"I've come to say - I like the cow.
It's not as nice as my cow – can I have the cow?

Can I come to look at the cow when I want to look at the cow? – pleeeease.
I like the cow."

John and I said that she could come and look at the cow at any time, and with this is mind – we had placed "Cow" on a low shelf near the fire.

Angela:
"I'll send you another picture.
It is a flower – and when I've drawn it, I shall give it to Jim and Jim will give it to you.
I'll draw that flower – a sunflower.

I'm going now.
Bye.
I'll go on my own Silver Cloud."

As Angela had been speaking, Walnut had been moving towards her – aware of this – Angela would occasionally turn to him and say, *"Leave me alone."*
But now, as she turned to leave, Walnut turned to watch, but did not escort her.

Silver Cloud:
"Good evening John.

Not all our visitors will be as independent as the child Angela. There will be those who reach out to a guiding hand – to bring them to communicate – both child and adult spirit alike. I am sure you will learn more of our friend Walnut and you will have some understanding of the reason as to why he has chosen the work, that is his path."

Silver Cloud then passed communication to John regarding an acquaintance of ours.
Both John and I felt that this person who, like us, had no medical knowledge, was avoiding the opportunity to ask the advice of Spirit when "healing".

He had also admitted that he had been attempting to "visit" (send out his Spirit) other healing channels - without their knowledge or agreement – adding that he was waiting for one of them to telephone him to ask, "Did you visit me last night?"

Following further conversations with him, and in reference to a patient he had seen – during which he said – "I just asked for blue or white or green energy because I think that is what they need" – John had asked Spirit what they thought of this approach.

I will now share part of that communication.

Silver Cloud:

"They (Spirit*) are attempting to keep him on his rightful path, but they are finding it difficult to maintain his level of vibration – this cannot be done from the Spirit World. It can be aided from the Spirit World, but the channel himself must lift his vibrations towards his true path. The experiments are misguided and unwanted and unwarranted.*

The ideas that he is experimenting with can be used to bring good to others – but only when the channel is connected to their spirit guide.

The haphazard experimentation is ill thought out – unwanted and potentially harmful. Thankfully, it (the experimentation to "visit*")* is directed to those channels who are in touch with their spirit guides and who obviously have Doorkeepers to protect them.*

If the channel directed thought form to a patient without asking permission – as you have indicated to him – that thought form will return to himself – adding greater confusion."

"The spirit of the physical being, must be prepared to accept the thought form.

He is not, at this moment in time – endangering any ones well being – except his own."

8th September 1995.

John had been invited to dowse at someone's recently built house to see if there were any negative or harmful lines and if so – what – if any - changes to the house or land needed to be made. It was a family of four that lived in the house – two adults and two young girls.

John had been aware that Angela had accompanied him on the visit, and sure enough - that night as I arrived at "my place" - Angela was waiting to speak as Walnut stayed near the entrance.

Angela:
"Those two little girls see fairies.
Well – they' re not fairies – but they call them fairies.
Well – they're people - not fairies – they're silly."

Suspecting that John and I were maybe not taking her too seriously, Angela continued:

"This is a serious message.
I've come on my own – he (Walnut) *has been told.*
I haven't drawn my picture yet – I've not had time, I've been busy."

John:
"What have you been doing?"

Angela:
"I've been to hospital to see the children."

"I'm not a fairy – I'm a person – silly.
This is a serious message."

John:
"Thankyou very much."

Angela:
"I'm going now.
Bye."
To Walnut - as she swept past him – *"Bye you."*

As Angela and Walnut left – a man, who I did not recognise, entered. He introduced himself as the father of the man who owned the house that John had visited.
I relayed this information to John.

The father came and stood in front of me and told me that he was concerned that an electrical storm could hit the house. When I relayed this to John, he said that he had already warned the owners about a possible lightening strike and he had advised them to take some preventative measures. I turned my attention back to the father who, being a plain speaking man, said:
"Tell him to earth the bloody thing!"

15ᵗʰ September 1995.

Today, I had been repeating to John a conversation I had had with our next door neighbour.
She had been telling me about the different illnesses suffered by some of the people living on the opposite side of the road. These illnesses ranged from migraine to a heart condition.
John had dowsed on the subject and received the answer – which was that there was a negative energy line emanating from the Abbey about two miles away.

The same Abbey that John had visited at the request of the developers, and of course – the Abbey where he had been prohibited from doing any energy work.

That evening Silver Cloud gave us both, some more information.

Silver Cloud:
"It is the bell – it is vibrating."

I must explain here, that there was no bell visible at the Abbey, but legend was, that the Abbey bell had been thrown into the pond, which was in the Abbey grounds.

Silver Cloud continued:

"The bell is tolling as it did when the Abbey was inhabited."

Me:
"How can we stop that?"

Silver Cloud:
"Tell the bell it can no longer be heard.
The bell means no harm – it is the puller of the bell that calls the tune. Tell the bell, that if it is pulled – it must play a merry tune."

John:
"Like distant healing?
But we agreed not to change the energies of the Abbey."

Silver Cloud:
"You would not be changing the energy of the Abbey – you are changing the effect of the energy."

Immediately after this, another of John's helpers came to say that she would go and speak to the bell if he so wished – John said that he did indeed wish it.

Later that night, John, his helper (Kuru) and his doorkeeper (Jim) - worked with the bell.

16th September 1995. Daytime.

Today, I received a telephone call from a friend that I had "sat" for a short time ago.

"They" had told her that she would buy some land in a "hot" country and she would heal the land and people. This had come as news to her – she had not been planning anything like that.

She had telephoned to say that she was flying to Australia to look at some land that she had been told about – with the possibility of buying it. I was surprised at her news and she also seemed a little surprised – she hadn't contemplated living in Australia – but had decided to "go with the flow" and was excitedly making travel plans.

She did buy several hundred acres of Rainforest in Australia and lived happily, in very humble surroundings amid her Rainforest, and as suddenly as she had bought the land – she sold it – but still resides in Australia. Some time after this phone call – when I was "sitting" for a client – imagine my surprise when the client was told he would go to Peru. I began to wonder if my Team had shares in a Travel Agency!

After the sitting, the client told me that his dearest wish was to visit Peru, as he was a practising Buddhist, and yearned to study in Peru.

I never heard whether he made his trip. I hope he did.

16th September. Nightime.

After lengthy communication with John about another of John's patients – Mr Bennet, (a healing guide of John's), ended by saying, in that sarcastic – yet gentle way that is - Mr Bennet:

*"The cow (*Angela's cow*), has been shown to all your guides and helpers and of course – we are very much appreciative. We think it is a wonderful object and we are most grateful that we have been brought – individually – to view the said object.*

The cow in India, is a sacred animal.
*The cow in School Road (*our road name*) – is also a sacred animal as it is the only cow in School Road.*
This has to be looked upon as an Icon – and we are most grateful. Thankyou for placing us in such a position – as to view, said Icon.
We are grateful.
I will leave you now – there will be no more questions.
Goodnight cow.
Good day."

Following the departure of Mr Bennet, I began to receive communication from an unknown male – I did however get the word, Father as he began to speak.
His communication related to the work that John and his guide and Doorkeeper had done, with the Abbey bell. The communication began:

Anon:
"I have come to say that you have served a great service to the community in which, I believe, you are temporarily dwelling."

*"Nothing has altered at the Abbey, from the monks point of view (*the monks in Spirit who still inhabited the Abbey and its grounds*) but you have lessened the effect of the negative energy from the Abbey – to the community. You have not interfered with the energy, as they (*the monks*) understand it, but you have asked – and it has been done – that the energy be converted into a positive energy – as it reaches the community – and we are grateful. This has long been a concern and we have needed a channel – to ask – to recognise and to ask, and so we thank you.*

*Rest assured – there will be no retribution – you have not broken the unwritten understanding that was made between the spirit guardians (*the monks at the Abbey*) and your own spirit guides.*
*They (*the spirit guardians*) are free to – unfortunately – continue on their path – but this is not a matter for you – it is a matter for the Spirit World, but you have lessened the effect.*

You have also made the bell happy, as it now has a new purpose and will rejoice when its' rope is pulled – as it knows of the message it now has to send.
It is a happy bell.

We thank you
We thank the spirit guides – particularly the communicator to the bell."

Silver Cloud:
"The channels have worked well.
That is all I have come to say.
There is no more communication.
Goodnight."

On the 18th September (my dads birthday) 1994 – Silver Cloud had taken the opportunity to remind me that I would write a book. That book is my first book – "More Friends Than You Know."

Exactly 12 months later – the 18th September 1995 – Silver Cloud was once again suggesting (this time to John) that he could produce a book - not of words – but of paintings. John had studied and enjoyed Art, and - working as a photographer - had channelled his artistry into photographs. Silver Cloud was suggesting that John produce paintings – using his airbrush – as healing pictures. Bespoke pictures - for an individual patient – and as general healing visions, and so given that Silver Cloud was witnessing the selling of many of our possessions – he advised: *"Don't sell your airbrush."*

John has produced some individual chakra paintings but has not put them into book form.

As I write this piece – I can hear John in the next room – he is busy working on a new Meditation CD of his. So I will not interrupt his train of thought now. But - when he very kindly edits, "Spirits In The Sky" for me in a few weeks time, and reaches this page – he will be reminded about the book again, and maybe the time will be right and available to him, to do the book.

SURPRISE!!   "Get the airbrush out, John!!"

19th September 1995.

John had been to visit his sister today – and Angela had accompanied him.

That night – Angela was waiting to speak.

Angela:
"That lady's you're sister."

"I've got a brother – not a sister – a baby brother.
He's not here – but I've got a brother.

I've looked round her (Johns sister) house. She's got a
lot of toys – I went and had a look when it got boring.
She's got animals but not a cow – I've got a cow.

My brother – he doesn't know he's got a sister – but
one day he will know he's got a sister - and it will be
me. I'll go "Boo – I'm your sister."
Why do we have brothers?

I've got a brother 'cos they haven't got me.
Mummy and daddy wanted me – but they haven't got
me so they had a brother 'cos they can't look after me –
so they had a brother so they could look after him.
I like her house. I sat on the chair with my feet on.
Can I go again?

I'm going now.
Bye"

28th September 1995. Nightime.

As I "raised my vibrations" my memory turned to the
early days of my channelling. I remembered how Spirit
had, had to lower their vibrations in order to
communicate with me. I remembered the effort I had
employed – to enable me to raise my vibration in order
for us to meet at a higher level. I remember the days
when I had struggled to reach those levels, and I
remembered the patience and practical help that my
doorkeeper – Buffalo – had extended to me.

It was with these thought in my head – that I arrived in
"my place" – to find Silver Cloud waiting to speak.

Silver Cloud:
"A channel raises vibrations through it's own energy field, then – at some point – you work within the energy field of the spirit with whom you are communicating."

Me:
"When you astral travel – you are linked with the physical body.
Who breaks the link when you pass over?"

Silver Cloud:
"You do."

Me:
"How?"

Silver Cloud:
"That is something that you are only told once in the life that you are living."

Me:
"I forget our conversations when I come back.
What can I do?"

(I have had many many conversations with Silver Cloud and others – during a meditative state. These conversations can last anything from five minutes to half an hour – in my time. But how annoying I find it to be - that on my return to "my chair" – I sometimes find it impossible to recall all that was said. This also happens after I have passed communication.)

Silver Cloud:
"Ask your Soul to give it back to you."

Me:
"I don't know how I lift my vibrations and people ask me "How?"

Silver Cloud:
"Every Soul knows how to do it because every Soul does it. It is a trigger to switch the memory on – every Soul has the memory – it is just waiting for the trigger. It is a natural thing to do."

At this point in the communication – I felt the need to ground myself again. I felt that my vibrations would be ascending higher and that the communication would be lengthy. I grounded myself.
The communication continued:

John:
"What is the difference between the Soul and the Spirit?"

Silver Cloud:
"The Soul is part of the whole essence of life – it is the link with the individual – to the whole essence of life. The Spirit goes from the Soul to live within the physical."

John:
"Is there one Soul to one individual – or a group Soul for a number of individuals?"

Silver Cloud:
"One Soul to one individual – linked to a group – linked within the Spirit world. The Souls of the individuals – linked as described – come from one. The one, is made up of Souls going back in time – eons."

"The Soul regenerates after many, many years – to become the Soul of an individual again. The Soul is precious – the Soul is unique to the individual – but has previously been unique to other individuals.

The Soul brings learning from previous lives – stored in the memory of the Soul, not necessarily the memory of the individual being. The individual being is the caretaker of the Soul – the individual beings add experience and knowledge to the Soul.
It is unique to the individual – but has previously been unique to others."

John:
"Those others being linked in some way to the physical being that the Soul is now linked to?"

Silver Cloud
"We are all connected in the Spirit World and those of us who know and work together, are connected by unique and individual – yet grouped – Souls, and we pass the learning and the memory through the Soul of the individual being – which was once ours.

Since the beginning of recorded time – man has lived physically – and so too, the animals and plants, and man has passed back, homeward bound, and takes with him – the knowledge, fears, understanding and problems. The Soul is then regenerated and passed to another caretaker – and so it continues.

The Soul remains within the protection of the Spirit World, and yet – through the Spirit of an individual physical being – the Soul is a library, a library that absorbs the feeling, understanding, abuse, knowledge, fear – the very being – of a physical being."

"The Soul will return to the Whole – to give understanding – and then the Soul will be reborn perhaps – after a period of time – to be the library for another physical being. That physical being – being the caretaker of the Soul at that time.

The Spirit hops between the two – the Spirit is the link. The Spirit is the energy of the physical being and the energy of the Soul. The Spirit is the communicator – the communicator to the Soul – the Soul – when returned home – gives it's information.

As the world progresses – although memory has been stored in the Soul – some memory is no longer used – it is replaced, and thus – the human race develops with new thinking. It is the responsibility of the individual to return the Soul to the Whole – with wholesome knowledge and understanding.
In this way – the human race moves on.

Obviously – if the individual understands their responsibility – the Soul will be happy. Those individuals who do not recognise their responsibility – who do not wish to think of the future or of others – only themselves – their Souls return to the Whole, and have to stay awhile in order for their library to be brought up to date.

It has been recognised, that throughout the world – the numbers of those who understand their responsibility to their own Soul and to the Souls of Souls who came before – are greater in numbers. Thus – it is possible – that slowly – with much hardship for some individuals – the destruction of the worlds surface and oceans and air – will be halted – initially slowed."

"There is a greater hope for the future than there is dread. We in the Spirit World see this when the Souls return. There are a greater number of those returning – who wish to help to stop the destruction of the world – who wish the Universe to continue for the benefit of ALL it's inhabitants.

The lost Soul, is the Soul that has not been given all the information from the Spirit. You have been told previously – that it is important that the Soul and Spirit pass together. The Spirit is continually passing information to the Soul for storage – but after the final passing of the physical being and Spirit – there is more information that the Spirit can pass to the Soul. Time is allowed for this process.

The Spirit returns to the Soul – the Soul returns to the Whole. The Spirit is then a free Spirit – to live and develop within the Spirit World.
The learning of the Spirit, when within the Spirit World, begins to fulfil the potential of that Spirit.
In due course – that Spirit may chose to communicate to the physical world – as a bridge – the bridge between the physical being and the understanding.

The Soul – after the passing of the physical being – is free to return to the Whole.

The physical being is freed into the Spirit World – that Spirit being free to live unencumbered and happy – reunited once more with those who were seen to be as loved ones in the physical world - and also – with those spirits – unconnected in the physical world, all free to associate and learn and rejoice in their continued progression through life – unencumbered."

"The Soul returns to the Whole, with the information it has received – and eventually – the Soul will, yet again – send a Spirit to a physical being – to learn again.

No more communication."

Wolf:
"The channel may go."

29th September 1995. Nightime.

That evening, Armon, my uncle was waiting to speak.

Armon:
"Hi kid."

He then announced the subject of his communication:

"The Soul and Spirit. The Soul sends out the Spirit – unique to the individual. If that individual questions a previous life – the Spirit goes back to the Soul to find its family tree. It says to the Soul – "What was the Spirit that went before me?" You are born with access to that information – of a life previously gone – so that is your family tree. Those people who have come before you – have made you who you are today – but they are not always relations – the understanding, knowledge and experiences is the essence of those people.
Their information has been used by the Soul and created the Spirit – which is your Spirit."

John:
"So even being reincarnated – that person has a new Spirit, but with information from a previous Spirit?"

Armon:

"Yes, and this is how things progress and this is why you are not born as a "cave" man – with the mentality and with the understanding of life as a cave man.
Man has been brought "up to date" and that is why it is important that the Spirit gives all it's information back to the Soul, so that the information can be catalogued and used to reform another Spirit."

John:

"Is Lynn's Soul – family tree – containing information from parents – yourself and maybe Silver Cloud?"

Armon:

"Yes. The family tree, as understood in the physical world – is an anchor. You would not send a spirit out into the physical world without the anchor and the security of those who had gone before. But the true family tree – the reasons as to why we think as we do and believe what we do – comes from the Spirit World and beyond.
Why does Lynn feel an affinity to the Indian – prior to working with the Indian? Why did you, as the healing channel – feel afffinity with the Japanese art – the Chinese art? This is not something new to you. You have had an affinity with those who have used their minds to overcome illness – used their minds to overcome struggles – why, from an early age?"

Kato; Johns Guide. Speaking to John.

"We are brothers.
We are brothers and shall continue to be brothers.
Was I once and Englishman?
Were you once the Japanese?
Or were we once both Hindu – African Spirit?"

"Does it matter? As a brother – on another occasion,
you may ask for more information.
That is all I have come to say.
Goodnight brother."

John:
"Goodnight brother."

Kato:
"I am the eldest.
Thankyou Silver Cloud."

9th October 1995.

When I arrived at "my place", I was met by a Native
American Indian who introduced himself as Running
Bear.

Running Bear:
"Do you agree that a stone plays a tune?
If you put that stone in a river, and the river ran over
and around – would the stone play the same tune?"

Me:
"I think its vibrations would be changed."

Running Bear:
"If you brought the stone out of the river and put it on
the river bank – would the stone play it's own tune?"

John:
"Would the water have changed the stone for ever?

Me:
"I thought the stone would revert to it's own tune
because it wouldn't want anything interfering with it."

Running Bear:

"But if the stone preferred the tune that it played when the water was running over and around it – could it not then play that tune?"

John:

"I suppose it could – but would it? It's a stone – so you would expect it to play a stones tune."

RunningBear:

"But who is to say that a stone has to play a stones tune. The only thing which can say which tune a stone must play – is the stone, so – if you held the stone and heard the tune – how would you know that you were hearing the tune of the stone – or that you were hearing the tune that the stone chose to play."

John:

"There would have to be an underlying tune that was the stone."

Running Bear.

"But you would first have to know what that underlying tune was, and the only way that you could do that - would be to hold many stones and recognise the familiar in all stones. The essence of a stone."

John:

"That which makes it a stone."

Running Bear:

"Each and every human being has the basic responses – the basic tune, but because each and every human being has experienced different things – in different ways – in different times during their life – during their growth – they sing a variation of the tune."

344

To John:
"In your job of work (counselling) *you need to know the essence of the human being, but you need to recognise the individual tunes which are not sung by all human beings."*

John:
"No two people are the same."

Running Bear:
"Everything has an essence.
Remember the stone.
In the centre of the stone is the Spirit of the stone.
In the centre of the physical being is the Spirit.
The Spirit is the essence of the physical being."

CHAPTER FOURTEEN

"WALK IN THE LIGHT AND FEAR NOT"

20th October 1995. Nightime.

Tonight, Angela came to speak.
She was visibly, very upset and I was upset to see this
normally ebullient child – in distress.

Angela:
"Why do you kill babies?
Why do you kill children?

There's enough children coming back who are ill – so
why do you kill children?

You shouldn't do it.
The children have not been naughty.
You shouldn't kill children.

They are alright when they get here – but it's not fair.
Silver Cloud says you don't know.
Silver Cloud says the person that killed the baby knows.
But there's so many children here now. They couldn't
help it – they had to come back, but you're sending
them back and we don't think its fair."

John:
"I wish we could say something to give you an
answer."

Me:
"I've asked her to ask Laura."

Angela:

"We can look after them when they get here – but its' not fair is it? – Its' not fair. If you talk to somebody and they're going to kill their baby – you tell them not to – it's not fair."

Silver Cloud escorted a tearful Angela out of "my place".

Laura:

"Good evening.
One of the penalties of growing up in the Spirit World – is coming face to face with the harsh realities of life and death, and although Angela is young in years – she has an understanding of what happens in your world – as she visits your world. She will have the understanding at a much earlier age than she would – she becomes aware of the various sins of the world at a younger age than if she where in the physical world.

She also has the ability to see injustice at first hand and this – she cannot be totally protected from.
She is on a learning path and as you have been told before – the children grow to a certain age – and then it is deemed that they mature earlier than they would in the physical world.

The understanding that Angela has – as the 4yr old – is comparable to the understanding of a young girl of 10 or 11yrs in the physical world – at that age – maturity begins to come to the fore. It is at that age – when the child begins to be, no longer a child – but is forced into becoming an adult. Although Angela is herself merely a baby you can see for yourself that her understanding – her thinking – her experiences – are far in advance of that of a child growing in the physical world."

"Although – we have noted that childhood in the physical world is lessening in years – due to the pressure from adults – both those with good intent, who wish to protect – but – due largely - to those with bad intent – who wish to inflict.

It is only right, that Angela be allowed to ask the physical world the question. Having asked the question – she does understand that you do not have the answer. Now that she has returned to the spirit dimension – she will be given counselling and care. She will – at least – understand that there are those children who are - at the hand of perpetrators – killed, deliberately and wantonly, but she will also understand and experience – that those children – just like herself – will grow within the Spirit World."

John:
"I wish we had been able to give her an answer."

Laura:
"There is not one answer that can be given – especially to a child. The reasons as to why a child's life is tken are many – varied and complicated – and originate within the physical world. There is not one answer. We do not expect you to be able to answer her, but she feels she has played her part, in asking the question. She will soon bounce back. She will be drawing trees tomorrow.

There is not a thing we can ask of you. We cannot ask of you – to attempt to eliminate wanton destruction of a child's life – or indeed the wanton destruction of any life through murderous activity."

"This is a question that has been asked between Spirit and Spirit, and in asking – and then reincarnation upon reincarnation and with the general healing of the physical world in exultation – then hopefully – the world will not be such a murderous place.
But this will not be achieved in your lifetime.

Thankyou for listening to Angela.
You have performed healing in the listening – and that is comparable, both in the physical and the Spirit World."

The communication continued that evening with a visit from another helper of John's called Mr McDonald.
Mr McDonald had been with John that day – to an exhibition entitled "Mind Body Spirit," An exhibition where John and others had been giving healing to members of the adult public.
It had been a hectic - and initially - a disorganised day, and Mr McDonald – in his own straight talking way – had given this advice:

Mr McDonald:
"When one is surrounded by naughty children – it is difficult to concentrate – and if you can picture them as naughty school children – it may make your task a little easier. Your walk around the Arena brought your concentration back. You have done a good job today – you did all that was asked of you."

Silver Cloud:
"Well – I think that is all for this evening. We shall take care of Angela – but she did need to ask the Question of the physical world – as she is no longer part of the

physical world and therefore will not be able to grow up within the physical world – to ask the question.

Tonight was for Angela.
She will now go back and receive a suitable answer.
So we thank you for your attention.
The channel may go.
Goodnight."

I continued with my routine of "raising my vibrations" twice a day and I continued to receive communication.
I shall now continue the story some three weeks later.

10th November 1995.

John had been discussing – with Mr White – the guide who works with John, mostly during his sleeping hours – the subject of Spirit Release.
If you remember – John and Mr White worked together during the night to aid those people who passed suddenly as a result of trauma. John felt that on some occasions – he returned to his body sooner than he maybe should have done, i.e. before the work was completed, also – on his return – John would have partial memory and feelings – of the person who had passed over. Which could be quite disturbing.

Mr White:
"You will always return to your body because your thread is holding you. It is some of the things that you see and experience – that bring you back.
In a morning – if you feel you have a memory of something that has not been very pleasant – it would be advantageous to centre yourself – this will allow you to function throughout the day."

"You are reasonably well centred – which is why they have chosen you to do this work – but as an added precaution – centre yourself.

You are not in any danger, and here are 1000's of releases that need to be done."

John:
"What can you tell me about Earth Bound Spirits?"

Mr White:
"They cling on and won't let go – they don't want anyone else to have what was once theirs.
They don't want people to have their property.
They don't want people to live in their dwelling.
They don't want people to live a physical life, as they lived a physical life. They are drawn back to the Earth.
They want to hold on – they can turn on the physical being. They try to destroy and disrupt to the best of their ability.

There are those Spirits that have feelings of jealousy and lust – they do not realise what is waiting for them, and even if they do – they are always turning back to the physical. There is a lot of work to be done."

NB: Obviously – not all Earth Bound Spirits are motivated by jealousy and lust. Many Earth Bound Spirits are simply lost, sad, or wish to pass a message – before they return Home. At the end of Mr White's communication – Silver Cloud spoke:

"We Indians take things at a slower pace – both life and death."

To me he said:

*"You haven't thrown enough out yet! You are still clinging! You would need a whole village of tepees.
Just imagine if you only had a saddlebag.
What would you put in it?"*

"My tapes, notebook and music" I replied.

White Cloud:
*"What you possess is inside you – that is what you are.
What Silver Cloud is trying to teach you – the message
– if you had no ornaments – no decoration – you would
still be you – doing what you are doing - your life's
work. Keep those things that bring back a happy
memory – if you must – but do not take those things that
will never see the light of day – things that will never be
of use to you in your everyday life.*

*Silver Cloud is envious of the walls on which you place
your objects – as the tepee has not walls of this nature,
but - heed Silver Clouds words. We do not ask that you
lose all your possessions, but we remind you that it is
you that is important and not those objects.*

*We wish you both Goodnight.
The channel may go."*

It was at times like this, that I was reminded that
whatever I did or did not do – Silver Cloud and others
were always watching.
A comforting thought – but on the other hand!!!

11th November 1995: Nightime:

When I "raised my vibrations" – I was to be greeted by
Silver Cloud, who was sitting on a dustbin.

As I walked over to him – I realised that we were both standing in our back garden.

Silver Cloud:
"What does this land mean to you?"

Me:
"Nothing now.
I feel as though I have learnt all I can here.
I want to move on – to learn again and use what I have learnt already."

As I spoke I saw a light ascending from the ground and disappearing through the clouds in the night sky.

Silver Cloud:
"In buying land – you hold yourself to it – you commit to it. It is better to borrow the land - so that you are free to move when you have learnt what you are supposed to learn."

Looking towards the disappearing light I asked,
"Under Universal law – let me be free to move on."

I then asked Silver Cloud if he thought They would agree?

"You have every good reason to ask." He replied.

14th November. Nightime.

Tonight, when I found Silver Cloud – he was vigorously shaking the dust from out of a rug. The dust cloud that surrounded him made me squint and meant that I stayed some distance away from him. Thinking that he hadn't heard me arrive, (how stupid is that!) –

I called: "Hello – will there be any communication tonight?"

You know – I can be such an idiot at times!

Silver Cloud replied:
"Communication? I am too busy."

Me:
"What are you doing?" (I bet you know what comes next.)

Silver Cloud:
"I'm shaking this mat."

Me:
"Is there anything I can do?"

Silver Cloud:
"I don't think there is."

And that was the extent of that night's communication.

This encounter with Silver Cloud where I asked a silly question – reminded me of my first days and weeks in Senior School. Our English teacher – Miss Hughes – had an uncanny knack of totally confusing us girls.
In her efforts to teach us correct Grammar – and in response to the question, "Miss – can I go to the toilet?" She would answer the request with: - "I don't know – you may have a medical problem which prevents it." She would then proceed with the lesson, leaving us, sitting with our arm waving in the air and wearing a very puzzled expression on our faces. She would then say – usually with her back turned to us – "When you have learnt to say, "May I" - I may consider it."

17th November 1995.

Throughout the day I had been feeling nervous about the future. I have always been a person who likes to know that I have some control I over my life – and I felt that that control was rapidly slipping out of me grasp. That night, Silver Cloud said to me:
"You cannot let go.
I understand why – but - Trust me."

Me:
"I Trust you."

As I spoke the words – my heart chakra opened wide and my heart left my body – touched Silver Cloud – and then returned to me. It was an awesome feeling.

Running Bear, who had passed communication before – returned to add this.

Running Bear:
"You Trust all the communication – Trust us now."

Silver Cloud smiled and said *"Goodnight."*

19th November 1995 Nightime.
Entry from notebook:

I felt my vibrations going high and fast – saw white light. I said, "Guiding Light – lead me to safer pastures.

The reply:

"Walk in the Light – and fear not."

23rd November 1995.

Our healer friend joined us for this evening's session, which was a very long question and answer session.
I would like to share two pieces from Silver Cloud – which I will combine as one piece.

Silver Cloud:

*"The Spirit World is a mediator being developed to assist those who walk on the planet earth, but – developed also – to ensure that the planet earth exists not merely for those who live and walk its surface – but because of it's importance – as every other planet is important – it's importance to the Whole Universe.
The spirit World is Home – where you will return.
There are Worlds beyond which, you are not part of – in as much as you do not work for them.
You do not belong to those Worlds – you belong to the World in which you walk – and you know where Home is. But we are all connected. We all have a duty to look beyond ourselves and that, that we know, and to give a thought to that, that we do not know."*

And finally – in response to the question from our friend: - "Should we try to emulate our guides? or – should we avoid that?"
He replied:

*"You have your own learning to learn – at whatever level you can learn – at whatever depth you can learn.
The status of a guide – such as myself – does not add status to my channel."*

After this last piece – Silver Cloud told me to *"Break"*
.

When I returned I announced to John and our friend:
"I have an Inca here who has come to say that we have
been given a false picture of the Spirit World. He says
that we cannot – in returning to the Spirit World as has
been described – we cannot hope to reach the realm and
status of the Inca."

Banjou had returned to share his particular version of
wisdom with us.
He moved closer to me.

Banjou:
"I have a right to speak - in order to save your souls.
The Inca is the highest race and it is the thinking – the
way of life – the behaviour – the very being of the Inca
to which you should aim yourselves, but – as mere
channels of the spirit world – you are not worthy, and I
come to tell you that what you have been told is a lie.

Those who believe in the so called God – will be
deceived, as the Inca was deceived – the Aztec was
deceived – as all great races have been deceived, and
you in your little world will never attain the great
heights. So I leave you to your little world and to your
guides – so called – your protectors.
The channel has no choice but to speak my words."

Kato:
"We allow the roving Inca to speak his words – which
he means well – but lacks understanding.
We allow his words to show the visitor that there are
two sides – two views to every picture."

Our friend:
"I am grateful for that."

Kato:

"And it is up to those working channels to view the picture that they wish to view. The guide of the communication channel allows the communication – in order to help the sitter, and were it not for that – I feel that the communication channel would not speak the words of the Inca again.

I hope you understand our reason for allowing the communication.

Everyone in the Spirit World and indeed – he is occasionally in the Spirit World – has a view – that is not everyone's view – it is not everyone's understanding, but then – we have not experienced the experiences that he and his race experienced.

I am allowed to tell the channel –
The channel may go."

This was the last time that Banjou entered my world.

Although I never enjoyed his visits – I am however – glad to have helped the lady with whom he first came to communicate. I am also pleased to have had this opportunity of sharing his words with you.
As Kato said – he *"has a view."*

I continued to visit "my place" twice a day but Silver Cloud had gone away again. There was little communication passed to me.

On the 4th December 1995 – my birthday – Silver Cloud was waiting for me. He gave me a bunch of flowers, which appeared from inside his sleeve.

Wolf handed me a twig and said –

"This represents the growth that will come in the future."

Over the next few days both Wolf and Silver Cloud were nowhere to be seen – which I found very confusing – although I did recognise that it was yet another opportunity for me to practice PATIENCE.

Mr Bennet and another helper of Johns' came on the 7th December and I spoke to Silver Cloud on the 10th.

On the 18th December I saw Silver Cloud and asked him why there had been no communication for over a week. He only reply was – *"Shut down."*

The next few days continued in the same vein, adding to the frustration that I was already feeling. We still hadn't received another offer on the house and we felt that it was – only a matter of time before the Banks called in their loans. It was difficult to remain positive. Christmas was looming and I only had a £5.00 note in my purse to buy five presents for the family. There was no New Years Eve party to organise as in previous years, and with every batch of Christmas cards – came another letter from a bank.

On the bright side – the puppies – Jack and Jill – were now 1yr old. They had both grown into happy healthy dogs and provided hours of entertainment and joy.

On the night of the 21st of December, Silver Cloud spoke to me.

He said:

"Spirit hear the laughter and they hear the crying.
The laughter comes readily – but so does the crying.
Make the best of what you have got – while you have
got it. "

23rd December 1995.

I "raised my vibrations" and was very happy to find
Silver Cloud waiting for me. He was sitting in a
rocking chair. He asked:
"What do you want for Christmas? "

Me:

"To be happy and healthy and to have a contract for the
sale of the house."

Silver Cloud:

"Do you think we don't hear you?
Happy New Year. "

24th December 1995. Christmas Eve morning.

My vibrations were really lifting fast.
As my vibrations lifted and quickened I asked for help
with my grounding. Into view came Silver Cloud,
White Cloud and two other men. They were sitting
behind a large table in a room that I had visited before.
I had named the room, "my wise man's room."
It was - and is still – a room that I visit – sometimes at
my request and sometimes at their request. A room that
is always occupied by at least one male - sometimes I
know him and sometimes I don't – but the advice that I
need to hear – is always forthcoming and forthright.

As was my practice when entering this room – I waited for a signal, which told me I could approach the table.

This signal is usually a slight nod of a head or an outstretched hand – bidding me forward.

White Cloud signalled me forward and I knew that I was allowed to speak.

It's strange how – as soon as I stand in front of the table – I know the question that I have come to ask – even though I often - consciously - have no question in my mind, which just proves that they know me far far better than I know myself.

I stood in front of the four of them and asked:
"What can I do to make your work with me easier?"

One man said: *"Be True."*
Another: *"Be Strong."*
White Cloud: *"Be Honourable."*

I admitted that I found it difficult to tread the line between trusting, expecting and knowing that they would help me – whilst taking responsibility for myself. In essence – I believe that I was finding it very difficult to let go of the control of my life. Although – looking back – dispassionately – I was not in control, and anyway – look where it had got me!

White Cloud responded:
"You will be useful to us. You have our blessing and with that blessing – is our protection."

I thanked them and as I did so – I looked round the room.

White Cloud:
"Who are you looking for?"

Me:
"Armon." My uncle was very often in my "wise man's room." – but not today.

Silver Cloud:
"We shall be very busy next year."
Wolf appeared and escorted me back "to my chair."

Christmas Eve. Nightime.

I arrived at "my place" and in the middle of the floor stood a huge parcel. It was wrapped in red paper with a red ribbon, which had been tied into a bow, on the top of it. Silver Cloud said that I wasn't allowed to open the parcel.

Including Wolf – there were six of our combined "Team" members and as I relayed the information to John – they formed a line in front of the parcel. The sight of them all - was indeed - a great gift.

Jim – Johns doorkeeper spoke first – *"Merry Christmas – get one down for me."* he said. Given that John didn't drink alcohol, we suspected that this statement was a reflection of Jim's past life. Mr Bennet – true to character, said: *"Seasons felicitations."*

They stood in silence – then - they all held their arms outstretched towards John and I.

The unconditional love that they extended towards us was so tangible that it filled our living room. – leaving John and I overwhelmed.

Silver Cloud:
"We wish you a merry Christmas.

There is no need for further communication tonight.
We too – are having a celebration and hope that once more – the good will that is amongst you all on the Earth – will stretch into the New Year to come – and will not disintegrate – with every season.

This is an occasion for those who have been estranged – to meet again. For old wounds to be healed, and we in the Spirit World welcome such an occasion and give energy to the goodwill and intent that is spread from one of you to another.

At this time each year – there are those who heal old wounds through the festivities of the Christmas and New Year period, and we send energy to such occasion. So – we will go ourselves and meet with others we have not perhaps been in contact with for some time – and we too – shall have a celebration.

Silver Cloud bids you Goodnight.
The channel may go."

31st December 1995. New years Eve.

As I arrived in "my place", I was greeted by an angel.
Instantly – I knew his name – it was the Angel Gabriel.
A bright white light emitted from him – so strong a light, that it hurt my eyes. Slowly, and from the doorway at the rear of "my place", a man approached. He introduced himself as *"The teacher Matthew."*

Matthew spoke to both John and I:

"Go forth – speak and heal.
You have been given a God given duty and you must go
forth and do it – like all the disciples.

All disciples all over the World have been and will be
given this message this night."

Kato:

"Forget the past. Carve the future from that, that you
have around you in the present. The present is the
mould for the future – therefore – use what you have in
the present to create the future."

Silver Cloud:

"Forget the past – the future is now – therefore – you
build the future with what you have to hand in the now.
You have everything in the now – or – have access to
those things that you need – to create the future –
which is one and the same thing.

Use the skills that you have learnt. Use those around
you who can advise. Build the future which has begun.
Also - Trust in those above who will give you the
materials that you will need for the building.

The future is bright. The bright light is already shining
and will shine brighter as the light is nourished.

Do not condemn the past – but use the skills learnt.
For the past is always necessary for ones future.
For without the past – we have no future.
Without the future – we have no place to go – we have
no aim. Continue to dedicate yourself to the future and
the future beyond and the future beyond that. In other
words – always set your eyes on the far distant horizon
and move towards it."

"Keeping your eyes fixed on the far distant horizon and moving towards it – you will find that the horizon continues to move away – but this is the plan.

Work together for the good of others.

As the old year passes and the new begins – move forward to the Light. Burn the old year away – and as it dies in the ashes – the phoenix will rise.

Your friend – Silver Cloud."

Kato moved forward – he was brandishing a sabre.

Kato:
"I cut through the ties to the old year – as is my way. The Indian burns.

We bid the old year away and bring in the new. Our message to you both.. The channel may go."

Once more – John and I were very grateful (to say the least) to Silver Cloud and Kato. We spent several minutes sitting the in silence - both - absorbing what they had said - and enjoying their energy which had enveloped, and still lingered, in the room.

1996.

For the first three days of January I had no communication to pass. Instead – everytime I "raised my vibrations" I was taken on a different journey.

On each journey – I was either near water – on water – or could see water. The 3rd of January's journey was a particularly happy one, as it was spent with a group of happy relaxed people in the garden of the "cottage" - where we sat, on a beautiful summers day – watching boats sailing down a river.

We stayed until the sun sunk on the horizon.

4th January 1996. Nightime.

As I "raised my vibrations" I heard a voice calling: *"Silver Stick."*
Believing that he meant me – although I had never been called that name before – I said, "Hello."
The voice continued:

"I am the one who speaks Wisdom.
I am White Eagle.
You have my blessing."

And that said – he left.

Silver Cloud came over to me and I said – "I know someone who has been trying to reach White Eagle."

Silver Cloud:
"You like working with guides. Do you want to work with guides? Is that your forte?"

At that moment I noticed some movement behind Silver Cloud. There was a group of Spirits, who appeared as glowing lights. From the back of the group and rising high into the air was a man. He was wearing a long flowing garment with wide sleeves and he had long grey hair and beard.

I knew this to be the Joseph whom I had previously met. (Described in Ch 3.)

I quickly told John what I was seeing and John said: "That is Joseph of Arimathaea."
"Yes it is." I replied.
I can't explain how it is – "when you know" something – but when you "know" – you don't just "know", you "feel". I was standing transfixed on this sight of Joseph – when – directly in my face – Silver Cloud said *"BOO!"*

I jumped and focused my attention on him:
"I knew that would make you jump" he laughed.
"If I told you what you were going to do – it would shock you in the same way."

Ignoring his invitation to ask what he meant by that last comment – I asked: "Will it be useful to work with guides when John is tutoring his courses?"

Silver Cloud:
"Yes.
The channel may go."

13th January 1996.

Early this morning while I was asleep, Jill, one of the dogs, woke me up. I was irritated at being woken, because I had been having an interesting conversation with a man who was dressed in a grey cloak, and in his hand, he was holding a white glowing ball.
As so often happens in life – the interruption occurred just as I felt the man was coming to the really interesting part of our conversation.

Nightime.

As soon as I "raised my vibrations", I began to receive communication – I knew the speaker was the same gentleman that I had been speaking to during the night. He did not give a name:

Anon:
"The white ball is ice. It is a new World.
The ice contains minerals which will create a new World. It is not part of the Earth – it belongs to the Universe and there are, more than one. They are in different places to keep them safe."

Me:
"Has the Earth got one?"

Anon:
"Yes – but it does not have a keeper other than the planet – to keep it safe.
The ice balls are not a planet as you know it."

Me:
"Are you a guide."

Anon:
"I am too old to be a guide."

That final question and answer ended the very brief encounter.

The rest of January and the whole of February, remained quiet on the communication front.
I continued to sit at 9am and 11pm each day – as I had done for the past 2 years.

During some of these sessions I received communication which was for John and his patients – during other sessions – I would briefly speak to Wolf and Silver Cloud or, I travelled the ether – often visiting the cottage – with its now familiar fir tree in the front drive. On one such occasion I went to the cottage and unusually - it was nigh time. I stood on the driveway – looking towards the cottage – the firtree on my right hand side.

As I peered into the darkness, tiny lights began to twinkle in front of me and as my eyes became accustomed to that darkness - figures began to appear.

Those figures were Wolf, Silver Cloud, Kato,
Mr Bennet and Laura.

They were each holding a stick - which in turn – held a glowing lantern. Silently, with one voice - radiating from that glowing light – they said:
"We are waiting for you."

I was moved to tears by this vision.
I have no words to describe the power of their overwhelming, unconditional love.

March 1st 1996. Entry from notebook: I have not seen Silver Cloud to speak to for 2 weeks.

The long silence has ended.
I have stopped opening up in the morning and evening.
This is as a result of Silver Cloud telling me to stop.

"Time to move on."

CHAPTER FIFTEEN

MOVING ON.

For the last two years of my life – the majority of my day had been spent opening up to receive Spirit communication and transcribing the resulting audiotapes into my notebooks. Being told to stop – was a bitter blow, not just for myself – but for John – who had received a great deal of communication for himself and his patients – on a daily basis.

I continued to "raise my vibrations" – daily, however – without the verbal presence of our teams and visiting Spirit – on a daily basis – we felt that there was a big space in our lives, I did, however, receive communication, as and when appropriate, for John, myself and others.

My notebook reminds me that on the 25th March – John and I had been asked to visit a farm – to search for any negative energy that may be affecting the owner and her animals. The farm belonged to a lovely elderly lady – who still kept some chickens and two elderly ewes.
On our arrival – I detected that the mother of the lady – long since passed over - still kept a very cautious and watchful eye over her daughter. Her watchful presence was tangible. We discovered some negative energy which was a result of the slaughtering of pigs on the land – over a period of many years – and also - the noise of a battle that had taken place many years ago – in the fields away from the house - was also adversely affecting the property. It had been a battle that had involved "Roundheads".

After we had completed the work, and with the permission of - "The watchful one" – John and I enjoyed a cup of tea in the farmhouse before we left.

8th May 1996. Entries from notebook.

"Today – we had some people 'round to view the house."

They were a group of four Chinese people, who explained that they were part of a religious order - looking for a house in which they could practice their teachings. They asked if their "Master" could come and view the house if necessary.
We agreed. (John and I never got to meet the "Master")

"Today – we have got a court date for the repossession of the house – 10th June."

9th May 1996. Entry from notebook. Morning.

Silver Cloud told me that my mum and dad sent their best wishes and he advised:
"Tread with light steps and walk toward the future - which is now."

Evening:
I asked Silver Cloud what I needed to take tomorrow when I went to visit a pub – to do a Spirit release.
His advice was very clear. He recommended that I took a green crystal, attached to a short stick, and as he spoke – I could "see" exactly, the tool that he was describing and whatsmore – I "saw and heard" that the crystal was in a container, which gave it freedom to rattle!

Unfortunately – I didn't have in my possession – a short stick with a rattling green crystal attached to it.

I wrote - "I'll have to ponder on this!"

I'll tell you about that Spirit Release in the next chapter.

As the title indicates – this chapter is about "moving on" - both spiritually and physically, and as John and I were about to step out into an unknown future and leave School Road, I began to reflect on the homes I (and we) had lived in previously.

Being born - and living - for the first six years of my life - in a 1930s semi detached house - has given me - I believe - an inbred "love" of older houses.
To me – they feel, "solid" and comforting.
I like their wonky walls and skirting boards that don't, in places - touch the floor. They add character.
I don't like draughty windows – but have always lived with them. In fact, like many others of my generation and before – I can remember waking up on a winters morning, opening the curtains - and using my finger to draw patterns on the ice that had formed on the inside of the windows overnight.

When I was 6yrs old we moved from our 30's semi detached – to a larger semi. The "new" house was a large "back to back" semi detached and had once been a rectory. It had a big garden and was beside a Parish Church. This house had both character, and draughty windows – and still – to this day – I love it.

I remember the black iron latch that opened the wooden slatted, kitchen door. The latch not only secured the door with a clunking noise - it was also useful for hanging your coat on. I remember the back door knob, which was made of brass and was round in shape.

For the entire 17 years that I lived in the house, that knob was loose. So loose - that if you weren't paying attention, when you turned it – it would trap the skin between your thumb and first finger – between the door itself and its sharp edges – occasionally drawing blood. Don't ask me why it was never fixed – I don't know – but then – if it had been – I wouldn't have had the memory would I?

The house had a cellar – into which the coal man – through a grill outside in the garden - would empty his sacks, sending the coal tumbling and rumbling, down a wooden board and landing in a heap on the cellar floor. I can remember taking the shovel down into the cellar to fetch the coal, and being surprised to see a piece of coal jump off the shovel. Further investigation would reveal a tiny frog – hopping back to its dusty hideout.

The kitchen in the house contained a range cooker, which burnt Anthracite. The range was always warm – even in summer, as it heated the hot water. Above the range - hung a clothes dryer. The dryer was constructed of wooden slats that were held in place at each end by two pieces of ironwork. The whole thing was hoisted to the ceiling by means of a rope and secured to a hook on the wall by means of a knot in the rope. I well remember the day I was pulling the dryer up – when I accidentally let go of the rope – sending the dryer plunging to the ground – only for it to be stopped in its tracks - by my mothers head. How I laughed – after I discovered that mum was herself laughing – at the sight of mum with her head trapped between the poles and washing – her glasses hanging askew - off the side of her face. It took some effort to disengage her, I can tell you!

The house had large rooms with large windows, which let light, as well as draughts, in. I remember how – at least for my fist two Christmases in that house – I would spend ages on Christmas Eve - peering out into the darkness – in the hope of seeing Father Christmas and his sleigh galloping across the sky, and I believe – that one particular starry night - I did catch a glimpse of him.

My allotted bedroom was situated over the kitchen – but as the house had four bedrooms – and only three in use – I decided that I would periodically, change rooms. The first mum or dad knew about my decision would be the noise they heard, as I dragged my chest of drawers across the landing. "What are you doing!?" one of them would shout up the stairs. "Just moving my bedroom." I would reply. You see – it made sense to me that in winter – the bedroom over the kitchen range was a good idea. But - the light summer nights drew me to the smaller bedroom at the front of the house – with its view over the garden.

In September 1960, when I was 8yrs old, I contracted Scarlet fever. I had spent the long summer, school holidays in the front bedroom and just as the new school term began – I found myself feeling very unwell and covered in a rash. With the diagnosis of Scarlet fever – I was confined to quarters.
Apparently in 1960 – the thinking surrounding the quarantine of Scarlet Fever patients had changed. No longer were they taken to an Isolation Hospital – but it was thought that they could now, safely, be treated at home. This was very good news for me – but meant

that my mother – who was at home all day – did the majority of the caring. Along with supplying drinks and food in an effort to entice me to eat, came the dose of pink medicine every four hours – day and night.

She must have been worn out running up and down stairs each day and she must have got very weary of offering that spoonful of medicine to a complaining child – particularly at 4am.

My dad had the joy of delivering a comic to me every day, on his return from work – which was far better received than that medicine.

Question: "Why do doctors and adults repeatedly tell children that "the medicine tastes nice" - when you know that they haven't tried it?"

Apparently, I was supposed to be kept in my room for four weeks – but the Scarlet Fever attacked my kidneys – which laid me low for a further two weeks. With this added affliction came another bottle, of even nastier tasting medicine! After six weeks of confinement - and when I was back on my feet – it didn't take me long to scurry, with my chest of drawers, back to my winter quarters, with its view of the outhouses.

Not only were the rooms large – but as I have already said – this house had a large garden. It was like an adventure playground, and at the bottom of the garden, by the big apple tree – there was an "air raid" shelter. Built during the Second World War to house the children from the village school, in the event of an air raid – it now stood intact and untouched by any bombs.

It was of brick construction and covered in earth and grass and the previous owners of the house, had fixed a wrought iron gate across the entrance.

It was a wonderful place to play and a cool place to rest on hot summer days. Also in the garden was a large compost heap which had been started by the previous owners - who were keen gardeners. This large area had been fenced off with a small wooden fence and was surrounded on two sides by overhanging trees and a tall hedge. The first time dad saw it, he said that it reminded him of a "Bandstand" in a park.

I'm sure some of you will remember how many municipal parks had a designated area where - usually on a Summer Sunday afternoon – a local brass or silver band would play for a few hours to entertain the visitors. So it was, that all our garden rubbish and the Christmas tree was put on the Bandstand. Occasionally, dad would set fire to the heap, using paraffin to get the fire started. This became a favourite activity of mine – especially in the late autumn when the fallen leaves had been raked up off the ground. I found it very satisfying as I watched the heap grow smaller in size – making room for the coming years rubbish.

In fact – I must tell you – John and I have recently bought ourselves an incinerator. It's not exactly of bandstand proportions – more a bass drum – being the size and shape of an "antique" galvanised dustbin. However – it is a very efficient burner and allows us to dispose of all the paper and cartons etc that cannot be recycled. So on Christmas morning 2007 – we braved the cold wind and "christened" our incinerator with Christmas wrapping. It was brilliant.

John and I got married in 1974, and for two years, we lived with my mum and dad in that house. The house was spacious enough for us to have our own living room and as mum had difficulty climbing the stairs she and dad slept downstairs – this meant that John and I used the main, large bedroom.

One day, as John and I were in our living room watching television – dad knocked on the door – and said he wanted a word with us.

He shocked us by announcing that he and mum had decided to sell the house – they wanted to move to a bungalow. We had no inkling that they had been discussing this and the news came as a bitter blow.

John had grown to love this house and garden and we were both very happy in our surroundings.

Suddenly – we had to turn our thoughts to buying a house for ourselves – think about a deposit and what mortgage we could get, and I had to face the fact that - I had to sort and dispose of lots of childhood possessions that were still in my playroom – as they had been for seventeen years.

Even though I could understand mum and dads need to move to a more convenient home – and realised that the move would be a wrench for them - I was shocked and angry by the suddenness of it all. But it was obviously time to move on – so move on we all did.

The land, on which the first house that John and I bought, stood, - had recorded history going way back beyond the build date (circa 1900s) of the house itself.

In fact – shortly before we bought the house, an archaeological society had been very busy digging up the garden in order to produce an accurate survey. The land had formed part of a Roman Fort and apparently we had the only washing line pole – in the area – which was sited in a Roman posthole!

This house was a sturdy detached house, quite narrow in appearance - with a good sized garden to the front and back. One outstanding feature was a square bay window, which had been set on an angle to the rest of the house. Legend was - that the gentleman who commissioned the building of the house – had business premises along the road and with the window set at an angle – he could view his premises outside business hours – thus reassuring himself that all was well.

John and I also had business premises along the road and although we couldn't quite see them – we too would periodically look out in that direction.

When we first moved to this house, the Building Society insisted that the damp course be replaced. That entailed removing the plaster off the inside walls to a height of about four feet - exposing the brickwork underneath. It amazed me just how dusty a house becomes without its protective inner skin.

Cups of tea with a crusty surface became "normal". The food was similarly coated. As the nights drew in, and our only source of heat was a portable Calour gas heater – I realised that John's car – a Jaguar – (he was paid expenses!) – was a far more comfortable place to sit in in the evenings, than the house was.

So with dark nights and chilly evenings – my choice was to accompany John as he drove around Cheshire taking photographs, at various locations, for the local paper. I sat - ensconced in the warmth of the car – reading a magazine - on many a chilly night.

The installation of central heating – for the first time in both our lives - was a wonder to behold, but I noticed from that time on – I felt the cold quicker and more intensely than I had done before – and the thought of waking up with ice on the inside of the bedroom window – well – it just doesn't bear thinking about! I don't know how we all survived it!

We were happy in this house and our "family" now numbered four. We had bought an Old English Sheepdog, who we called Trampus and 18 months after that - a Bearded Collie called Muppet who was in fact a present from John's mum – Elsie.
The park across the road was ideal for dog walking and we were regular visitors. Trampas in particular – loved the freedom that its open spaces allowed.

We made this house a home. The purple hessian wallpaper on the bedroom wall, (well it was all the rage in the 70s!) was a particular dream of mine - and was expertly hung, by John's dad. The mushroom coloured bathroom suite – was very modern at the time. The fake (but very well done) "old oak beam" which John had hacked at with an axe and then burnt with a gas torch – was fixed across the kitchen ceiling and was the perfect place for me to hang my collection of "horse brasses".
Yes – we had made this place our own. It had taken us nearly 11yrs to put our unique mark on it – we were comfortable – that is until one day - someone broke in.
I came home from work to find the back door wide open. For a split second I couldn't comprehend why this was. Then I saw the broken glass in the window that looked into the dining room. In an instant, I realised that we had been burgled. With the back door left wide open – I realised that the dogs could have gone and I screamed out their names in panic – they didn't come. My thoughts raced in horror, at the prospect of the two of them out on the main road – or even lost.

I stepped into the house, still calling their names – and it was then that I heard scratching on the other side of the living room door. Snatching the door open – Trampas the Old English came hurtling out of the hall, through the doorway – happy to see me. Walking into the hallway, I shouted "Muppet" and looked up the stairs. His little face appeared from around the corner of the banister pole - and with some encouragement, he came, slowly down the stairs. I was so relieved to see them both, and they were very pleased to see me.

Shutting the back door over so that the dogs couldn't get out – I reached for the phone and dialled 999.
Whilst waiting for the police to come – and knowing that John would return to the photographic studio before he came home – I rang and left him a message on the ansaphone. I told him what had happened and reassured him that the dogs were safe – knowing that they would be his first concern.

The burglars stole my jewellery and other trinkets, including a very handsome silver jewelled fob watch that had belonged to my maternal grandmother, and a watch that my mother had only recently given me for safekeeping. I could hardly get the words out as I told her that it had gone – and the guilt that I felt, at losing it, was enormous. They also took the silver locket that my sister had given me as a "thankyou" for being her bridesmaid, a gold bangle that my dad had bought for me when I was seventeen, and a Tigers Eye pendant that John had presented to me on the evening of my operation to have a wisdom tooth removed (it was in the shape of a fang!) These things were totally irreplaceable and the pain of their loss was immense.

The burglars also ripped the video machine out of its sockets and took other items of sentimental value.

One very strange item that they stole was – a tinned, chocolate sponge pudding, which had been in the kitchen cupboard. They had emptied drawers of their contents and strewn them over the floor, including the bedroom, and then – when the police came - they put silver fingerprint dust over everything. I felt violated.

Thankfully – the burglars had put the dogs upstairs – after feeding them on crisps and chocolate (they left that evidence behind), but not, we surmised later - by his reaction to young people, especially boys – before they had kicked or hit the Bearded Collie.

From that day on, when out walking Muppet the Bearded Collie – he would cower whenever teenagers came near. It was a horrible distressing sight to see and I felt powerless when I couldn't help him to recover from whatever had happened to him.

The burglars where never caught, although the police did believe that they knew who had robbed us.

Our insurance company were very quick and fair in their treatment of us – and we were able to replace items – but you can never replace sentimental items.

But all that paled into insignificance when measured against the safety of our two dogs. John and I were just so grateful that the burglars had shut the dogs in the hallway.

We both felt uncomfortable after that experience and I felt that they might come back – which apparently is a common reaction – I even thought, they may telephone us. But mostly – I felt as though I had personally been attacked. I no longer felt safe and secure.

I needed to move away as soon as possible.

Shortly after this – we put our home of 11yrs – up for sale.

John and I began a search for a new home in earnest.
We both wanted an older style property and had promised Trampas and Muppet, a big garden.
Having found a buyer for our house and needing to come to a decision – in order to keep our buyer interested in our property – we decided to put an offer in on a "newish" built house. It was a nice enough house – with straight thin walls and skirting boards that touched the floors - and as it was summer – neither of us detected a draught. There was however, a very funny smell in the bathroom! Hearing no reply from the estate agent in respect of our offer – and having a rare weekend free – we decided to have another search of the areas estate agents. We drove to a town not far away, and looking in the window of an Estate Agents – we saw the picture of a lovely house – circa 1900s it was just outside our price range. The house was in School Road – the eventual home of that icon – known simply as - "Angela's Cow."

To cut a long story short – on viewing the house – we loved it – and although we knew that we were really pushing the limits of our mortgage – we offered the asking price, which was accepted.
The following Monday – I rang the other agents to withdraw our previous offer – only to discover that they hadn't passed that offer onto their clients.

The move into School Road went well – but a large cloud loomed over us.

That cloud, was the declining health of Trampas.
Two weeks after moving Trampas into his house with its large garden – Trampas was "put to sleep".

We lived well and happy in School Road. It provided us with a lot of space to fill – which as you have heard – we did, and the large garden provided plenty of "grounding " opportunities. We did some alterations and always had plans to further improve the house, and - we had two very good neighbours.

We had our share of sadness and loss whilst we lived there. John's mum died before we moved – Trampas died 2 weeks after we moved in - and within a 13-month period in 1990/91 came the deaths of both my parents and Muppet.

So – as the story returns to May 1996 – we now have a court date – to settle the repossession of the house.

Having paid all our small creditors - John and I declared ourselves bankrupt in early June - 1996.
The result of the repossession meeting was that we were given 28 days to leave our home.

During those 28 days – a couple came to view the house and John and I were delighted when they told us it was just what they had been looking for. They were a lovely family – the parents of which were retiring from farming. As they still had two sons who lived at home – they seemed more than happy with the space in the house – and they told us of their plans to keep chickens in the garden. John and I thought the sale would eventually go through – but we continued to work towards that 28-day deadline. We asked around to see if anyone knew of a cottage to rent – to no avail.

We didn't know where we were going to live.

Wayne, a good friend of ours, offered us a house that he rented out. It was a lovely house which he and his wife had just re carpeted with cream coloured carpet. They both told us that usually – they refused pets – but knowing of our circumstances they said they were happy for us to move in with Jack and Jill.
I was not keen, knowing what a mess these two young dogs could make between them. They had already made part of our garden into something resembling a Rugby pitch on a wet Saturday afternoon – and the thought of trying to keep someone's new, cream coloured carpets in pristine condition, daunted me.

A second friend Colin, also had a house that he rented out – but he had tenants occupying it.

So with ten days to the deadline – we still didn't know where we were going to live. On the night of that tenth day – there was knock on the front door. John answered it and I realised that it was Colin. I heard John invite him in, and I looked up as they both walked into the living room. Colin handed a set of house keys to John.
"Here's the keys to the house." he announced.
"What about your tenants?" we asked in unison.
"They've done a moonlight flit on me – which is bad news for me – but good news for you. Move in whenever you like."

As the deadline approached, the packing came to an end, and even some plants and York stone from the garden – had found new homes. Our sisters came to lend their support – and another good friend Dave – who himself had been forced into Bankruptcy – helped on the actual removal day.

One of the hardest farewells that John and I made, was to our very good neighbours Marjorie and Ron.

They had always welcomed us into their house – and Marjorie and I took it in turns to - "put the kettle on".
We looked after each other's houses and dogs when necessary – and we "put the World to rights" over the garden fence. Jack and Jill loved their "Auntie Marj" and whenever she came round – she always brought a doggy treat with her. Actually – the day after we brought Jack and Jill home – Marjorie called in to deliver a greetings card. When I opened the card – it said – "Congratulations! Twins." She told me that as she was queuing in the card shop, to pay for it – a friend of hers came up behind her, seeing the card her friend asked, "Who has had twins?" too embarrassed to explain that, "Twins" referred to two puppies – she quickly replied, "Oh. You don't know them."
I have still got that card.

When we were going through the bankruptcy they - and two more friends – Joe and Paul – were very supportive, lending a listening ear and offering that all-important – cup of tea.

Marjorie planned to go out on the day that we were leaving, explaining that she didn't want to witness it, so John and I went round to see them on the eve of our departure.

She had mentioned to me that they were thinking of buying a birdbath for their garden – so - as a leaving present – we gave them a small birdbath that had belonged to my mum and dad, and an umbrella for their patio table.

We all had tears in our eyes as we hugged and shook hands that evening, and we promised to stay in touch with each other.

9th February 2008.
Over the years – our friendship of some 22 years has continued. Marjorie and I have stayed in touch via the telephone, catching up on each other's news and continuing to "put the World to rights."

Yesterday, I received a telephone call from Marjories' daughter to tell me that Marjorie has died, suddenly. The sadness and shock that I am feeling, is nothing, when compared to that of Ron and her family.

Marjorie – I will miss you – Thankyou for being a friend – Thankyou for the memories.

Due to technical difficulties – there has been a delay in the editing and publishing of this book.
Although frustrating for both myself and John – we encouraged each other with that well-worn phrase – "the time mustn't be right."

Now, sadly, we understand why the delay was necessary.

27ᵗʰ June 2008.

This evening, four months after Marjories death, I received another telephone call from her daughter. She rang to say that her dad, Ron, had died, suddenly.

Once more I am shocked and saddened by this news. Once more, my thoughts go to all the members of the family.

Once more I find myself saying, "If there's anything I can do?" – knowing that really - at this moment in time – there isn't.

But - I am pleased to have been given the opportunity to write this letter and include it within this chapter.

Dear Marj and Ron,

You will both be sorely missed.
Your legacy lives on in your family - and your many friends are left with happy memories.
I know there will be a party "up there" when the time is right. Have fun.
Thankyou both, for being who you were - and are.
Hope to speak to you soon?
If there's anything I can do?

Love Lynn.

Before we left School Road, I went to visit the family who were keen on the house. I explained that they would now be dealing with the Estate Agents and the Banks. Their plans to buy the house seemed to be going ahead and I was glad that this nice couple were going to move into School Road. As I left, they were very kind and wished John and I well for the future – as I did them. We later found out that this sale, for reasons unknown – didn't go through. The house was bought by a different couple who John and I had never met.

John and I moved out of School Road, and into what can only be described as the warmest house we have ever lived in. This house was what we would describe as a "new" house, on an Estate, although the house was in fact, about 15yrs old. John and I remembered watching this estate of houses being built. A school friend of mine, and her farming family – had farmed this very land, and I had tramped through the fields and ridden her pony on several occasions.

The house was very warm, and the only draught was in the bathroom – and furthermore – our friend and his wife - now our landlords – were dog lovers. They owned several themselves, and it must have been that fact, that influenced their decision - when carpeting this house – to choose a downstairs carpet that had a black background. Perfect for dog lovers!

A couple of days after we vacated School Road, I went to see the Estate Agents. They had agreed to accept the keys to the house. This - was an act of defiance on my part. We knew that the keys should have been handed into one of the Banks - but in their infinite wisdom – neither of the Banks involved, had communicated any such arrangement with us.

In fact – since the meeting – there had been no communication from them at all.

The Agents also told me that the Banks hadn't even checked to see if we had left the house.
In the mid and late nineties – Banks and Building Societies were sinking under the weight of re-possessed homes – a trend I fear – that will return.

John began to tutor on more courses, see more patients and Dowse land and buildings.

I re-discovered my joy of listening to music - spending a lot of time in meditation and "travelling" with Wolf, Silver Cloud and others. People came to the house to ask the advice of Spirit - on subjects ranging from - their guides - to their personal and emotional matters.
Life began to settle into a routine, but always – thoughts of the cottage and its location - were never far away.

In the February of 1997 – six months after we moved into the house – John's dad, John, became ill and went into hospital. On the 6th March 1997 – he was moved into the same hospice that my dad had been in – not only the same hospice – but the same bed space.
Fourteen and a half-hours later – on the 7th March 1997 – John passed away.

Mid April came, and John had gone to the Isle of Man to attend a course – which was run by two ladies, Joy and Sandra, who had flown over from their home in Sedona, Arizona, in the U.S.
During his stay, one of the ladies asked John, to ask me, to help her deal with an issue that had arisen.

I spoke to her over the telephone and she was grateful for the help that she received.

Little did I know how important the friendship - that was established during that phone call – would become.

Jack and Jill had settled well in their new surroundings and although the back garden was small – and the front, open plan – we found some good walks.

At the back of the Estate there were some fields that had been left abandoned. Part of this land was hilly, and one day in May – as I was standing on the highest point of the land – I realised that from this vantage point, I could see two churches.

One of the churches was the Parish church that I had lived next door to for 17 years. In the opposite direction, was the Church where my maternal grandparents were buried – their grave bearing the name of their son Armon. Midway between the two churches, and further into the distance – I could see the graveyard where my paternal grandparents were buried.

Standing on that rough ground and taking in that panoramic view, I felt a sense of awe. I felt as though I was standing in the middle of my family's lives - which was, my history - my heritage. I felt very close to all of them – grandparents – parents – uncle. I had an overwhelming sense of "belonging".

It was a wonderful feeling.

I regularly visited the spot so that I could envelop myself in that sensation.

The added bonus being, that the dogs really enjoyed that land and would scurry ahead of me – stopping to sniff at any interesting smells, as they went.

On one such visit - which happened to be a chilly, yet sunny day – I stood and scanned the horizon.

Spontaneously and audibly, I announced to the World – "I'm ready to leave". "What did you say?" – I asked myself. "I'm ready to leave Cheshire." I replied – "I'm ready to leave." I continued the walk with Jack and Jill – happy at the prospect - that - after 45yrs, living happily in Cheshire – I was ready, keen and free – to move on.

John is much more "laid back" in his approach to life than I am. Spirit has never reproached him for a lack of patience. Not for him - the accusation *Why do you have to plan everything?*" So when I told John about the "earth shattering" revelation that I had had on the hill – he responded with the words – "That's great. I would be happy to go anywhere."

My revelation brought with it, a reassuring belief, that Spirit and the Universe, would lead us to the cottage when the "time was right".

Some time ago, Silver Cloud - responding to questions I had asked about the cottage before he had taken me to see it – questions such as: "Will it have a separate dining room for me to put my table in?" "What colour is the bathroom?" – had advised: "*Firstly - find your land.*" Silver Cloud knew, and was teaching me, that land and location were far more important than the dwelling itself. He was also saying that if I made the land the priority – then a suitable dwelling would be in place and I would be happy to make any compromise – or - would be greatly surprised by what I found there.

In other words Lynn – be open-minded to any possibility!

However – my new found, "laid back" approach, didn't stop me suggesting to John, that we travel to Yorkshire, (another County I "felt at home" in) - in an effort to find the cottage.

We did – and we didn't – if you catch my drift!
But it was a very welcome day out.

Travelling with Silver Cloud was an exciting experience. I never knew where – what or whom – we might see or meet.
On the 11th April 1997 – I found myself sitting alone in a hot, red, dusty desert. As I gazed out into the far horizon – I heard the cry of a bird. Looking into the sky – I saw an Eagle swooping towards me. The Eagle swept low over my head and flew away.

On the 13th of April – Silver Cloud and I both sat high in the sky – on a white fluffy cloud. The cloud felt like a huge fluffy cushion, and I hadn't realised till then – just how comfortable a cloud could be.

A month later – on the 13th May – and after some conversation between us – Silver Cloud produced a hosepipe and proceeded to spray me with cold water. After he turned the water off – I asked, in an incredulous manner, "What did you do that for!"
The reason was – apparently – *"To wash the dust off you."* As I stood before him – dripping wet – I wondered if – maybe – just sometimes – his sense of fun went a little too far!

As Silver Cloud laid the hosepipe down onto the floor – he asked:
"Are you going to ask about the cottage?"

"No – I replied – "Whatever the Universe offers will be the right place for us."

He replied:
"You and John must work in harmony and continue to push forward into the Light."

On the 4th June, I met, on my "travels", an elderly man – who advised:
"Use the month to your advantage."

5th June 1997.

I would now like to share with you, some words that were given to me whilst in a meditation.
The words are in the form of an affirmation, and we invite you to use the words yourself – if you feel that you would benefit from them.

The words were given by Joseph of Arimathaea:

"I am a child of the moon.
I am a child of the sun.

As they wax and wane –
So I allow myself to drift with them.

I use their positive energy
to my advantage.

I fly with the Eagle.
Free to fly on the
drifting currents.
Drifting - yet
with purpose."

Three days later – on the afternoon of the 8th June – Joseph spoke to me again:

Joseph:
"The purpose of the journey in the physical – is to travel the life line. Gaining information and passing information – Helping others –
Exchanging information all the time –
Exchanging energies. Work well – with love."

Later that same day – when I "raised my vibrations" I found myself - once again - in the hot, red, dusty desert. This time I was not alone – Wolf and Silver Cloud were with me. We were all standing - high on a hill.
Looking down into the valley below, I saw a "host of Indians" – both male and female - standing silently.

I was overcome by the dignified and powerful energy they emitted. I felt their energy and mine – intertwine.
The combination of our energies - making it hard for me to remain standing.

Silver Cloud and Wolf led me down into the valley to meet them. This journey took a whole day.

Once in the valley – I met with some of the Indians – the greeting being – a simple touch of hands.
Silver Cloud slowly began to walk into an open space – where he sat on the ground - Wolf and I followed him – and we too, sat down.
As we sat in silence – the Indians began to walk away in different directions. As they walked – their images became faint – and then they disappeared.
Suddenly and silently – a squaw came - bringing food and drink which she placed before us.
She too – walked away and disappeared.

Silver Cloud turned to me and said:
"You have ended a chapter."

At this point – I consciously became aware of the music that I had been playing as I had "raised my vibrations" – the song I could hear now – was, "Time to say Goodbye" – sung by Sarah Brightman.

Tears flowed down my face as I thanked Wolf and Silver Cloud for taking me on this special journey - making today - special.

I "returned to my chair".

10ᵗʰ June 1997.

John and I were both very excited.

In separate meditations, on the same day - we had both been given a road number – the A494. Remembering that Silver Cloud had said that "they" would give us a map, in order to find the cottage - I frantically went in search of the cardboard box that contained all my maps – some of which dated back to the '60s.

The big question was – in which county was the A494.

How "they" must have been laughing - at the sight of John and I searching through road maps – which we had lain out all over the floor, and how excited were we - when we found that the A494, is a road in North Wales? North Wales – the home of Llandudno – the resort that had become our refuge.

Tracing the road on the map – we noted the names of the towns that lay along its route – Mold – Ruthin – and many unpronounceable villages in-between.

Bubbling with anticipation – I "raised my vibrations" and told Silver Cloud that, "we have found it!" (as if he didn't know) and asked him what we should do next?

In a calm ordinary sort of way – Silver Cloud replied:

"Drive down the road to the nearest town.
Go to the Estate Agent and ask for Steve."

So - as soon as could be arranged – we drove to Mold –
parked the car – and set off down the main street to find
Estate Agents. There was one – so in we walked – and
asked the very helpful female assistant if they had any
properties to rent. "No - sorry" she replied "we haven't
got anything – but I can ring our other office to see if
they have."

She returned from her phone call, to say that the other
office was faxing details of a property over to her.
It was an anxious wait for those details to arrive.
The property was a several miles away and when we
went to see it we both liked it – although inside - it was
in need of some repair and decoration – and to my
dismay – there was no Firtree in a driveway. Then - we
were told that the owners would not accept dogs.

The helpful assistant said, "Really – it would be better
if you spoke to our Prestatyn Office – Steve is the man
you need to speak to – he deals with the rental
properties."

John and I wasted no time in driving to Prestatyn –
which was a few miles away and on entering the Office
– we asked to speak to Steve.

Steve was a very helpful young man – sympathising
with us over the rejection of our dogs.
Having established the type of property we were
looking for – he checked his list of properties that he
knew were coming up for rental in the near future – but

there was nothing suitable. He took our telephone number, saying that if anything did come up – he would ring us. A couple of days later – Steve rang.

"I think I've found just the right property for you – I don't believe this – the owners weren't going to rent it out yet – but they've changed their minds."

Once more – John and I travelled to North Wales to view the property. The first thing that I noticed – apart from the very narrow lane which led to it - (we later discovered that the single-track lane was a mile long) – was the Firtree, just as I had seen - it was situated on the right hand side of the driveway. As soon as I saw that – I knew we were at the right cottage.

We had lived in our friends' house for exactly 12 months, and now – just 10 days after we had agreed the rental on the cottage - John and I, Jack and Jill, and the Goldfish - Nipper - moved once more.

The cottage was named "Garth". The Welsh to English translation of the word Garth, is – hill, enclosure.

Just as I had seen, when visiting with Silver Cloud – the ground floor contained the kitchen – complete with the landlords wooden kitchen table – the table where I had sat with Silver Cloud, a small room – which was just big enough for John to use as an office.
An oak beamed living room with large inglenook fireplace (which I hadn't seen before), and three further rooms. On the first floor – just as I had been shown – there was a large room – big enough to set many chairs out. I used this room as my workroom and the acoustics were brilliant in there – just right for my music. Across the hallway was the room which - as

Silver Cloud had suggested – made a lovely healing room for John. Surrounding the house there was large garden, which Jack and Jill loved, and in the garden – there was a garden bench – ideal for sitting on, as we watched the setting sun. The Firtree on the driveway, was one of many trees, that protected us from the wind.

The panoramic view from the garden was wonderful – fields, hills and sky, and our immediate neighbours were a flock of sheep.

John was kept very busy and had the opportunity to work – not only in this country – but also in Europe.

It was in my room at Garth - I had my first attempt at writing my first book - "More Friends than You Know." Those of you who have read it – will probably remember, that the computer "Ate it!" on that occasion – and it would be a few years until I plucked up the courage to begin again.

It was while we were living at Garth that I was given the opportunity to travel abroad. For the first time in my life and at the age of 46 – I would board an aeroplane and fly with Silver Cloud to America.

15th March 2008.
My intention was to include the story of my American journey within "Spirits in the Sky". A journey, that was full of joy, magic and unexpected happenings.

However, I felt as though I couldn't do justice to the complete story within the confines of this book, and have therefore decided to produce it under the title of – "Spirits Fly High" – book three of the trilogy.

We had now been living in the Garth for two years. One day, as John and I were driving up the lane towards the cottage, and as the cottage came into view, I "saw" a For Sale sign in the garden. Arriving home – John and I were surprised to find that there was no sign - of the sign. I wondered if the owners – who lived in America - were thinking about selling the cottage. As I wandered around inside the house – I expected to meet the Spirit of the eldest daughter – who visited us periodically to check that we hadn't altered her much loved bedroom. Finding no sense of her, and drawing on my new "laid back" approach to life - I dismissed the thought from my mind. The following week I went to the Estate Agents office to pay the rent.

Steve no longer worked at this branch but John and I had formed a good relationship with the rest of the staff. A female member of staff greeted me.

"We've been looking for you – we came to the cottage but you were out – please – sit down."

I sat down at her desk.
"I'm sorry, she began – "but the owners want to come back to Wales, "Mary" (another member of staff) has

got your notice to quit – and she's been trying to deliver it to you."

Just then – "Mary" walked in through the door.
She handed me the official notice to vacate.
We had two months to find somewhere else to live.

They insisted that I stay for a cup of tea, and hastily disappeared into the rear office to put the kettle on.

As if I had been tapped on my right shoulder – I looked round towards the board displaying, "homes for rent".
Immediately my eye was drawn to a photograph of a stone built house. It was as though that particular photograph, was the only one visible.

"What's this one?" I asked, on their return.

The house looked really nice – and thinking that John would like it too – I arranged for us to go and view it the next day.

When I came out of the office I thought I would try to telephone John who was back in Cheshire for the day, working. John answered his phone and without pausing for breath – I said:
"Hi - I've just paid the rent – and guess what? We've been given notice to quit – but not to worry – I've just made an appointment to view another house tomorrow."

"Brilliant!" he replied.

One month and one day later – John, I, and Jack and Jill moved again.

CHAPTER SIXTEEN

MY WORK WITH SPIRIT.

I would like to use this chapter to describe the type of work that I do.

All the work is confidential and any notes that I need to make at the time – are destroyed soon after.
So – the following anecdotes are all written from memory and will be somewhat sketchy, in detail.

Music.

Music has been a passion of mine since I was born.
My parents both sang in a choir, and my weekly attendance at Methodist Church – from a toddler – up to 16yrs old – gave me a love of Organ music and singing. Two adult childhood friends of mine - introduced me to Opera, the Trumpet and Trombone.
My red Dansette Radio, introduced me to "pop" music.

As a child I had piano lessons - but gave them up when I was about 11 – 12 yr. old. I taught myself to strum a guitar – badly, and in my 20s and 30s, I owned a piano, electric organ, drum kit and a Karaoke machine.
Being master of none of these instruments – you can imagine the noise that I produced! Did I mention – I like to play music loudly!

I use music to reflect or alter my moods – and can spend hours, shut in a room, listening to a variety of tunes in order to achieve that. My music collection is diverse and Spirit have used that diversity to communicate with me:

Communicate through the words of a song or – through my listening to their chosen piece – helping me to move forward – "travel" with them - resolve issues and heal.

I feel so fortunate to have this avenue open to me.
Each guide and doorkeeper that I have worked with has used music, and that - combined with their unconditional love – has truly saved my sanity – on more than one occasion.

My guides sometimes guide me to play a piece of music for someone who has come for a sitting or has just come to visit, and, at their suggestion and with their guidance, I have made compilation tapes to send to people.

But – work aside – I have to say - I just love music!

From Abba to Andrea Bocelli.
And my personal favourites of the "New World Music" genre are – David Sun, Stephen Rhodes, Asha, Medwyn Goodall and Pia.

Distant Healing.

In 1994 I was watching the television, when a news story came on. The report told of a child whose mysterious illness, was baffling the medical team that were looking after him.
They were at a loss as to what treatment they could try next, and there was film showing the child in his hospital bed – he looked barely conscious

The boy's parents and family were devastated, as the child was becoming weaker by the day.

Moved by the plight of the child, his family and the medical staff – I sat and wished that "something" could be done to help them.

I knew that Spirit were around watching and caring for me – so I decided to sit and ask them for help for the boy, and that is what I did – and - knowing that there would be many other people around the country - who had also seen this report – I knew that my voice would not be a "lone" voice.

Many months later – I happened to pick up a magazine in a Newsagent. Flicking through the pages – I saw a feature about the "miraculous" recovery of a child – who had been close to death. The child that the article was referring to – was the child I had seen previously on the television I began to read the reporters words: The doctors - it said - remained confounded by his illness – and - his subsequent recovery.
Accompanying the article was a photograph of the child and his family. The photograph showed a group of happy smiling faces.

I was stunned by the boy's recovery.
I was thrilled to bits – to see their smiling faces, and I was very grateful to Spirit, for leading me to pick up that magazine which contained that article.

I continue to ask for distant healing – but unlike that first time – when I had no communication – I now receive communication.

Sometimes, I am told that my request has *"been noted"* and then I am dismissed. Sometimes, I stand and witness the healing being given by Spirit. Sometimes, I am involved myself:

I will act as a communicator to the patient – having been given facts about their illness. When communicating with the patient – I invariably find that they have a message to pass to someone, and "we" can advise them on the best way to deliver that message.

Always – I ask permission of my guides and the patient (be that physically or spiritually) – before I proceed.
Always - I listen to - respect and abide by - their answer, and – always – in the case of children – I ask permission from the parent or guardian - before I ask my guides and the child itself.

The word distant – only relates to the fact that I am not with that person physically. Remotely my spirit travels to that person - and for me to go without permission – would be unforgivable, rude and egotistical.
An uninvited and unwanted visitor – as we can all relate to – is often not welcome, and an uninvited and unwanted travelling spirit can be very distressing. These rules apply to people – animals and land.

If I am asked by a third party, to send some healing for a friend, relative or acquaintance – I cannot proceed until I have been given permission from my guides and from the persons Higher Self.
My answer to them is always – "I will ask."

Healing into death.

In 1991 – as my dad lay in a hospice a couple of miles from our house – from my vantage point in our living room - I saw the clouds in the sky – part, in the distance. The light that emitted through the clouds seemed to be descending onto the roof of the hospice.

Knowing that dad was now peaceful – and near to death, I "spoke" to him:
"Go to the Light – Go up into the Light dad."

In the early hours of the next morning – my dad died.

That was my first experience of healing into death.

From then on – and now working with my guides – I have worked, remotely - with men, women, children and animals – who are close to death. Unlike that first time - I am now given information and the opportunity to converse with the Spirit of the departing – and they with me. I work with a combination of - my own guides – the patient - guides and loved ones in Spirit connected to the patient – Angels – and those loved ones who will be left behind to grieve. As in the case of distant healing – sometimes I am directly involved and sometimes I am privileged to witness the workings of the Spirit World - as a bystander.

This work is usually done over a period of days – and Spirit guide me on that matter, but sometimes – the combined work of Spirit and the patient – is completed very quickly. Often I will play music – the title of which is chosen by my Guides or the patient.
The music, lending its healing tones and/or words – to the patient.

I remember one elderly gentleman who was clinging to life. He asked for the song "I want to know where love is?" The words of the music were his way of expressing his fear – the fear that made him cling to life, and his fear was - that once he died – there would be no one around to love him. Playing the message for him let him know that he was being listened to.

Let him know that his Spirit could be heard. It allowed him to realise that he was not alone, and as that realisation grew – I witnessed his surprise at seeing Spirit around him, and I witnessed the relief that swept through him as he saw a familiar face approach.

His face lit-up like a beacon – as his mother walked towards him – her arms outstretched in greeting.

Assisting - healing into dying - is always a privilege.

It is always moving. There can be angst, upset or anger before peace is found - and occasionally, when the work is nearly completed - there can be one or two jokes along the way.

Always – there is the unconditional love shown by all those in Spirit who come to assist.

Always – there is a Guiding Light – whose Soul purpose is to assist in that walk between the physical life and everlasting life, and always – there is a celebration to honour the returning Soul.

Several years ago, a neighbour of ours died. I didn't know her that well, and had no plans to attend the funeral, however, the day before the funeral, I was asked by Spirit to go. When I asked why – I was told that two family members were holding their loved one to them – which meant that the Spirit of the person would be held to the Earth.

That Spirit was already in shock at their death – and needed to enter the Spirit World for some rest and recuperation. As I sat at the rear of the Church – I asked for the "appropriate" guides and helpers to assist.

I could feel the presence of our neighbour as her family held her to them – and then I felt the descending presence of Spirit. The Spirit helpers gathered our neighbour into their energy and I watched, as they hovered over the family as they sat in the pews.

I was told that she was asking the two members of her family to let her go – whilst assuring them that she would return at sometime in the future.

A few seconds later, the combined Spirits left the confines of the Church, I was told – *"We have got her. Your work is over."*

I have never been asked to attend another funeral by Spirit – but I have been to several since then. I always make a point of saying to Spirit – "If there's anything I can do – just ask."

There seems to be two distinct beliefs regarding the question "Does Spirit recognise our time" – as in Greenwich Mean Time.

Some people will tell you that "Time means nothing to the Spirit World" – and others will say that they understand our GMT – and they work with us on that scale. In my experience – both beliefs are true.

In my experience – when Spirit say, *"soon"* or, *"later"* that can mean anything between, the next minute and the next few years, but - Silver Cloud taught me that if he said, *"Come back in 10 minutes."* - He meant 10 minutes - not 11. *"9am sharp!"* meant 9am – not five past. So all I can say, is that Spirit uses GMT as a time zone - Sometimes!

That is why, that on the night Silver Cloud told me that Nipper, our Goldfish would die at 2am – I knew that this would be the case. Nipper had lived with our two other fish, in a large aquarium. The other fish had bullied him – keeping him away from the food until they had their fill, but over the years – Nipper had survived his two rivals and a large cyst over one of his gills, and - having the aquarium to himself – had grown into a large sturdy Goldfish.

Nipper had been the first member of our family to move into Garth, as we had taken him over the day before we moved. Lately, he had been off his food for short periods – and now his dorsal fin was laid down on his back and his sense of balance was failing. Neither John nor I could entertain the idea of killing him – so we let "nature take its course" but nature was being very slow – and for two weeks, Nipper hovered between life and death.

Then came those words from Silver Cloud,
"He will die at 2am."

I sat up with the fish – tears of helplessness overwhelming me.
At 1.50am – he was still alive.
At 2am – he died.

Nipper had been our constant companion for 25years.
Throughout his life, we had kept the aquarium out of the sun – as it fouls the water – now - sunshine would no longer be a hazard to Nipper.
We buried him in the garden at Garth – choosing a lovely sunny spot in the grass.

As I said before – I can find myself working with Guides, patients, loved ones and Angels. I have travelled to hospital rooms were the light of Spirit is so bright - it hurts your eyes. I have witnessed Spirit doctors tending to patients. I have witnessed Angels waiting in silent serenity – waiting to lead a patient home. I have witnessed patients happily chatting to their Spirit visitors – prior to them departing this life.

But – I was not prepared for the "healing into death" that took place when Johns' dad – also named John – was in the hospice. John had told this story himself and is happy for me to tell you now.

Early morning on the 6th March 1997 – as I have already mentioned – John was taken into a hospice.
John and his sister had both been to see him – and I had planned to go the next day – although I must admit - it was with some trepidation, having being told that he was in the same bedspace as my dad had been, some six years earlier. My communication with Spirit – and healing into death experiences has not eradicated the memories that I have – seeing my dad in the hospice, both before and after he had died. But I knew that those memories would have to be left in the car park, when I went to visit John.

At 12.40 p.m. on the 6th March I was told that John was very restless. I "raised my vibrations" and asked for distant healing for John – and then I asked if there was anything I could do. I was told to hold a particular quartz crystal that I had, and went off to get it. Holding the crystal in my hand - I went with Silver Cloud to stand at John's bedside.
There were many Spirits around his bed – all glowing and radiating light – so that from my position at the end of the bed – their energy was intertwined.
Out from the energy emerged one Spirit – I knew this was John's own father. A man who I referred to as John's "Scottish granddad."
Scottish granddad approached the bed and leant over John. "You are acting like a child!" he accused.
He then leant over John and thumped him hard in the chest – just once. Not – I knew – to start his heart – but to stop it.

I was horrified.

"We can make the decision for you – if you don't make it yourself" he continued – albeit in a softer voice.

I had never witnessed anything like this – I couldn't understand these words and the action. I was shocked and looked to Silver Cloud to see his reaction.
He just smiled, and John went into a restful sleep.

I "returned to my chair" still in a state of shock.

That evening – John returned from visiting his dad and told me that his dad had become restless during the afternoon and had been sedated – adding, that whilst visiting him – John had suddenly thumped his own chest – just once. However – when John and his sister had left the hospice that evening, my father in law had been quite contented and happy and had settled down for his first night in the hospice.

Much later that night – Silver Cloud urged me to "travel" to John's bedside. I raised my vibrations and with Silver Cloud by my side I arrived at John's bedside. The small ward was dimly lit and through that dim light – John and I began to walk towards a very bright light. This was a walk that we had taken before but this time I felt a very real sense of tension and apprehension. We continued to walk side by side, down a very brightly lit tunnel, which had appeared in front of us. The tunnel expanded further into the distance as we walked, and the brightness was excruciating.

The further we walked – the brighter the light became.
Through the brightness and in the far distance, we both saw the hazy shadows of many standing figures. John

hesitated momentarily and paused. I waited, knowing that John was deciding whether to continue this walk.

John took another pace forward and together we continued our slow walk towards the brightest of white light. Emerging out of the tunnel, and standing a few yards away from us, we could clearly see figures. The figures were standing in rows, unspeaking, yet smiling as in greeting. John gasped as he recognised his parents and brothers, behind them, more spirits were standing – waiting. The bright white light created a milky haze that obscured everything – everything that is – except for those serene smiling faces.
Their energy was awesome.

Throughout my travels into the Spirit world I had seen other bright lights – I had walked towards white light – I had been surrounded in white light – but I knew that this experience was different – very, very special.

I went to step towards the waiting Spirits - Silver Cloud blocked my way.
"You cannot go any further," he commanded.

In an instant – I understood that I was at THE place of no return. I looked down onto the ground and saw, just two paces in front of me, a narrow line.
A line – invisible - yet visible.
A line - that only those who have forsaken their physical bodies can cross. A line - that marks the point of no return to life as you knew it.

THE - very fine line between life and "death".

Turning to look at John's face, I saw that he too understood the immense poignancy of this place.

413

John remained rooted to the spot where he was standing – his head moving as he surveyed each smiling face along the front line. His facial expression, telling everyone that he was not ready to cross over.

Silver Cloud broke the deafening silence. Turning to John, he told him that a bench would be placed at the end of the tunnel – a bench on which John could sit when he came to visit. The end of the tunnel, Silver Cloud explained, was a place to reflect, contemplate and make decisions – but most of all – it was a place filled with love, freedom and choice.

John acknowledged this information with a slight nod of his head. Looking towards the rows of spirit, we both bowed our heads in farewell, then John, Silver Cloud and I returned to serene comfort of the dimly lit ward.

John crossed the line a few short hours later at 3am on the 7th March.

I can tell you that John is now well, happy and pleased to be reunited with his family.

Healing into death can take many forms.
Each form – designed for the needs of the individual's higher self - at that particular moment in time.

Following the leadership of my guides, when healing into death – I have played many different roles:

I play an active role - speaking words guided to me by
Spirit.
I use music.
I use an Indian rattle.
I use crystals.
I use leaves and twigs.
Led by one guide in particular – I used prayer.
Or –
I am a silent bystander.

The common factor that I have found – is that each of
these rolls has resulted in a peaceful "death".

What all these different roles tell me about ways of
working with Spirit, and hopefully conveys to you is:
There is no hard and fast, written in stone - "right" and
"wrong" way. None of these roles is the "only" way.

For me – there is only, "Their way".
All guides are as different as each situation is – are as
individual, as we all are, and it is for each of us, to find
"the way" that works for our guides and ourselves.

Crystals.

If you remember – I told you that Silver Cloud had
asked me to hold a quartz crystal in my hand, before I
travelled to Johns' bedside. I had, in my collection – a
few tumble stones – chosen for their colour – and one
or two small pieces of quartz crystal. Quartz emits both,
positive energy and has a cleansing property.

Although I loved my tumble stones and my quartz – I
was an avid collector of rocks. If I ever walk on a
beach, it isn't long before I begin to fill my pockets –
and John's pockets – with rocks and stones that I find

"interesting". I find "interesting" rocks and stones on any land that I walk on. Some – I just stand and admire – some I find irresistible - a "must have" for my collection.

Since childhood - John has always been interested in crystals and fossils. In fact, much to his dad's annoyance - John used to dig large holes in the garden looking for hidden treasure. He once located a "lost" water pipe – the location of which turned out to be very useful information - when the erection of a Garage was planned. All useful experience for a dowser.

As I related in detail in "More Friends Than You Know." - in 1994 – both John and I had had been psychically attacked, by a person who had programmed Quartz crystals in a negative way.
This person had used crystals – which he had given to us as a "gift" – to open a portal into our home, thus allowing his negative Spirit to visit, at will.

I found that episode very scary indeed – and initially I had a negative attitude towards crystals - not wanting any more in the house.
The positive outcome - was that I became aware of how powerful a crystal can be, and once I had rationalised - that it had been the person and not the crystal that had acted in a negative way – my fears began to subside.
About 3 months after we moved into the "warmest house that we have ever lived in" – John surprised me one day, by saying that he wanted to buy a few crystals. He explained that he wished to learn more about them and believed that they would help some of his patients.
Still wary of the power of crystals and as bossy as ever – I replied "Ok – but keep them away from me."

Spirit – apparently – had a better idea.
On the day that John went to buy the crystals – Silver Cloud announced to me:
"*You - will look after them.*"
This was not a request – but an order!

When John returned home and began to unpack the few crystals that he had bought – their positive, powerful energy began to fill the whole house. The energy was so strong – I was beginning to feel dizzy.
I dashed upstairs to the spare bedroom, where I knew some of my collection of rocks was. I collected two supermarket bags full of rocks – ran downstairs – and began to place the rocks in heaps around the room.
"What are you doing?" John asked in a bewildered manner. "The roof is lifting off the house – can't you feel it! I exclaimed.
"Yes I can feel their energy – it's great isn't it?"

"Honestly!" – I silently thought – "Silver Cloud is right – I'll have to look after these crystals – otherwise we'll both be on the ceiling."

So began our joint commitment to offer a supply of clean and positive crystals to people. John eventually began to work with, and tutor - "crystal courses" – which are very popular – and I select the crystals that go on each course. I ask the selection of crystals, "Who want's to go on this course?" – and the crystals volunteer or stay silent. When the crystals return from an outing – they are all cleansed and put away till the next time.

One difference between John and I is - John knows and remembers, the names and properties of each crystal -

I don't! (a phenomenon that was also reflected in our differing exam results at school!)

But what we have in common is - a "knowing".

We "know" when a crystal is right for someone – and we "know" when it isn't, and neither of us hesitates to express that opinion. Crystals are powerful tools – they hold ancient wisdom within their form.

They have the power to open chakras at will, and – as is the case of any healing practice - be that Spiritual healing – Crystal healing - Aromatherapy or Reiki etc – the practitioner has a duty to protect the recipient.

You see – John and I believe - that not only are we responsible for people on the courses - we are also responsible for the crystals that we choose to be the caretakers of.

I use crystals in my remote work with people and land when directed to - and my collection of rocks continues to grow.

Dowsing.

This will be a very short paragraph because basically – I was told by my first guide – William - not to dowse.

"*You'll be dowsing - dowsing - dowsing!*" was his accusation.

I've narrated this story before – so I will not tell it again. Suffice to say – that William said this to me when he was beginning to teach me to communicate – therefore he quite rightly, diverted my attention away from my dabblings with dowsing.

However – with the communication that they give me – I am able to locate negative lines, for example – through dowsing through my body – and then asking for their guidance.

Actually I am so talkative at times – that I ask too many questions of the pendulum – thus confusing myself.
This affliction of mine – asking questions – has got me in hot water with Spirit before.

My previous doorkeeper – Buffalo – tiring of my constant questions, was forced to shout: *"ENOUGH – You must wait!"*

So – although I do own a couple of pendulums – and cherish my first one, which is a plastic, half chewed, apple core – that once adorned my neck in the 70s! – I prefer the communication approach.

Earth energies and land clearance.

My work with land clearance is mainly done remotely.
With the communication from my guides, and my ability to travel – I have found myself being taken on journeys through drains - and travelling underground like a worm. Drains are not my most favourite locations – but at least I don't get my Jeans dirty!

There are many diverse factors which can adversely affect land and buildings – and also - the people and animals that inhabit the land and buildings.
For example:
Ley lines.
Electricity cables and pylons.
Telephone masts.
The Earth's' own magnetic energy and gases.

Water: Streams, both on the surface and underground.
      Wells.
      Drainage water.
      Water tables – Rising or falling.
Spirit activity.
Demolition of buildings or parts thereof.
Erection of new buildings
Occupiers own negative energy and/or actions.
Earth Elementals.

So the key to a successful result, when approaching the healing of land and buildings – is definitely - to have an "open mind".

The solutions I have used and been witness to – are varied.

Always at the bequest of my Spirit guides: -
I have placed crystals in the ground to remove, or divert negative energy. I have "seen" energy barriers being erected – and have taken part in erecting them myself.
I have spoken with "earth elementals" who were angry at being disturbed by occupiers of the house.
I have grounded water courses and negative energy.
I have released Spirit from sites.

The solutions are as varied as the causes.

Spirit release and rescue.

Personally – I find this aspect of my work, one of the most rewarding. Firstly – The release of a Spirit entity which has been "trapped" in a house, building or on land – is a cause for celebration within the Spirit World. Secondly – To know and see - that the agitation, anger and distress of that entity are over – is reward in itself, and thirdly – Once the work has been completed - the relief of those people and animals in the physical world, who have been adversely affected by the presence of that entity – is almost tangible.

There are exceptions to the rule.
Not all Spirit who are attached to the Earth – wish to move on – or should be moved on, and attempts to interfere in their very existence – are futile and can result in further distress for all.

We all have free will – it is our given right.

Just as I discovered with the Monks from the Abbey: – Spirit has a right to continue their possession of the land that they inhabit. Who are we to tell them otherwise? But – as current inhabitors of the physical world – we have the right to ask for help – if we are fearful – sick – or unhappy.

Like everything in life – balance is the key to happiness.

I have spoken to Spirit – who have been frightened to leave the earth plane, frightened that the Spirit World would not welcome them because of a misdemeanour or crime they had committed. Frightened that loved ones would not "wish to know" them. Frightened to come face to face with a parent, wife, husband – or ex husband, and frightened to leave loved ones behind.

Fear and self-recrimination – is a common finding.

I have witnessed Spirit – who in their cry for help, have caused mayhem in the physical world, sob with relief as they walked into the light with a "guide" at their side.

I have also seen Spirit entities dragged back into the Spirit World – "escorted" by Angels in flowing gowns, and – in my experience - if Archangel Michael is in attendance – argument is futile!

Not everyone that requests help – realises that there is Spirit present in their house or place of work. They will just report to me, that they are unwell – or feel uncomfortable in a certain room. It is my job – to ask my Team for guidance.

Occasionally – when there is Spirit present - I am told by my team that we are not going to do the work ourselves. This is always exciting for me, because I know that the team are going ask the person who has requested the help – to perform the release or cleansing themselves. In these cases – my Team will pass precise, step by step, instructions for me to pass on – and then the team and I "watch" from a distance. This technique is used to help "nervous" or unsure budding channels – to overcome their nervousness and self doubt.

People have asked me to remove Spirit, who – I find - are only visiting, in order to give a message to that person. Invariably – I also find - during further conversation – that the message had been heard – but had been dismissed. Dismissed through self-disbelief or simply - not liking the message that was delivered.

I have been asked to remove a Spirit – only to discover that the person who has asked me – has themselves been asking for, "Spirit to come and visit me".
Having had their request answered – they have then been frightened by that very presence – or - they have unwittingly, invited a wandering pesky entity into their life that is revelling in its ability to frighten.

Asking for Spirit to visit – can be a wonderful experience – but be aware that an "open invitation" is just what it says it is.

Following a release, people report back to me:
They say how much "lighter" and "fresher" their dwelling feels and smells. How – they now feel able to walk into the back bedroom – and how their children are sleeping in their own beds – all through the night. Those people who had been suffering from ailments (which can often be an ailment that the Spirit suffered from whilst in the physical life) – no longer have those symptoms, and – the biggest relief for them can be - that doors and drawers remain shut – no one walks on the stairs in the dead of night – or stands at the bottom of their bed.

I will end this topic with the story of the short stick and the rattling green crystal.

So, there I was – the day before I was due to visit a pub to release a Spirit - looking for a stick and a green crystal. The stick I had "seen" was short, (about 5 inches long) wooden, and was "turned" – like a table leg. This stick – I recognised – was the stick which was attached to the mini "warming pan" brass ornament – that had belonged to my mum.
I unpacked the box contained the ornament and proceeded to remove the "warming pan" – apologising to mum as the two items came apart. Having got the stick and the green crystal – I had to think of a way to attach them both together. Coming to my rescue – John suggested using a small glass bottle to hold the stone – and then attaching the bottle to the stick with insulation tape. I returned in triumph – from the kitchen holding a small roll of bright blue tape.

N.B.

It is my belief that every house should have a drawer in the kitchen that contains useful things. Things like: 3 odd screws, 6 assorted screwdrivers 1 packet of washers that don't fit anything, insulation tape, a squashed box of Elastoplast, and "something" sticky – all wound together by 3 feet of unravelled string.

Anyway – I digress.

With John's help – the crystal was placed in the bottle – which in turn was attached to the stick – by the blue tape. Relieved - that I had my rattling crystal attached to the stick - yet - bothered by its' very existence. What I would use it for, was beyond me! Did they really expect me to walk round the pub with this in my hand? – I would look really stupid
The people at the pub would think I was weird!
Oh – it just wasn't fair!

Fortunately for me – because of the size of the stick – it fit into my handbag. Out of sight and hopefully – out of mind. I grasped onto the vain hope that - "They might even forget about it?"
Morning came, and John and I prepared to leave to drive to the pub, and as we stepped outside onto the gravel drive – I noticed, amongst the grey stones of the gravel – a tiny blue stone. Strangely – for me – I didn't pick it up – but thought to myself – "I'll pick that up when we come back."

John and I had been at the pub for about half an hour – and after a warm welcome from the owners – and a cup of coffee and a chat – Silver Cloud told me to walk around to the back of the bar where I knew the Spirit was standing. This Spirit was Saxon – and had lived in the village where the pub was located. He told me that he had happily chosen to live amongst the current inhabitants – but now he was sad. Sad that everything he had known - had changed. Sad that he no longer felt that same "belonging" feeling, and sad that his presence - he knew - was upsetting a member of the bar staff. Yet, he was also sad – to leave. He was uncertain that – given the length of time he had been apart from those of his era – there would be no one who he knew - waiting for him.

Silver Cloud reassured him that friends were waiting for him – and the Saxon said that he was happy to leave. I thought that my small part in this release would soon be finished.

Remaining on the floor, I listened as Silver Cloud explained that the Landlady was also sad. She had grown accustomed to his presence – and were it not for the fact that a member of staff was becoming increasingly un-nerved by the Saxon – she would not have asked for our help. I knew I needed to speak to her. To my surprise – the landlady already thought that the Spirit could be Saxon – and she had given him a name. I explained that he was now unhappy – and with a tear in her eye – she agreed that it would be best for him – to leave.

With everyone prepared – I returned to the bar.
"*You will need your rattle.*" advised Silver Cloud.
"Oh no!" I thought as I spied my handbag on a table where I had left it. The owners of the bar were standing by the table – watching – I had no choice but to walk to my handbag and retrieve the rattle – in full view! I returned to the rear of the bar, and sat on the floor – holding the rattle in my hand.

The release was very quick and peaceful.

I returned to the table to return the rattle to my handbag. Noticing the rattle – the landlord asked: "What's that?" Embarrassed – I quickly explained the story of the rattle – including the finding of the blue stone. "A blue stone?" the landlord repeated – "I had one on the mantelpiece but it's disappeared."

When we returned home – the stone was still there in the gravel. I picked it up, took it indoors, and placed it on the mantelpiece.
Not long after – the stone disappeared!

Communication.

As I have described – my work with Spirit can involve the use of crystals, stones, music and twigs. I also use a Native American drum and rattle when working with earth energies, distant healing and occasionally – Spirit release. However – the constant factor – and for me the most precious of all tools – is the communication.
The communication that has been so accurate, up lifting, moving, informative, helpful, funny, and – where applicable – "painfully" honest

I am so grateful to be a communication channel.
Grateful to all those in Spirit who have come to speak to - and through me.

Grateful to those in Spirit who continue to spend their precious time – teaching, guiding and protecting me.

Grateful and priveledged to be able to continue working for and with them.

The last words of this chapter and subsequently, the book, are the words of Joseph, who, as I typed the heading "Communication" – came to give the following piece.

I leave you with his words.

> *"Communication is the lifeblood of all living things:*
> *Animal - Vegetable – Mineral.*
>
> *What - and - How - we communicate to each other – predicts our combined destinies.*
>
> *Kind communication - combined with thoughtful action, Heralds - a World at Peace."*

Joseph of Arimathaea 6th February 2008.

Farewell

Dear reader.

When I began to write about my journey into Mediumship – I thought that I would be writing one book – "More Friends Than You Know."

Nearing the end of writing it – I was told to continue telling my story under the title of - "Spirits In The Sky."

Nearing the end of writing this book – I realised that the completed story was just too long for one volume.
Asking the advice of my "Team" - I was given a third title - "Spirits Fly High."

Therefore – for those of you who wish to read the conclusion – you will find it within the pages of "Spirits Fly High"

In producing this trilogy, I have now completed the task set before me by my Spirit team.

My hope is that individually – each book tells it's own story. Collectively – they cover some 46yrs of my life, which is more than half of my life expectancy I should think! But far more important than that: –
Collectively – they tell a story of the unconditional love and guidance that the Spirit World wishes to give to us.
A Spirit World, which is far away – and yet so near - to our everyday life.

I have shared the content my notebooks with you.
I have shared my thoughts and feelings.

I have laughed and cried as I have written.

And now – this part of my story is finished.
As I sit writing this farewell whilst listening to my favourite C.D. "Tranquillity" by David Sun I find that I cannot write any more.

My hope, is that in doing what I was asked to do - and sharing this communication - you may have found both understanding and solace – or – at least – you have simply been entertained.

Whatever the outcome, the words remain - the words of my, Spirits in the sky.

Thankyou

Love Lynn.

A Thought For the Reader

"Throughout the passage of your life
You will meet many Souls.
These Souls come as teachers – and to be taught.

Teach them well.
Treat them well.

Learn expediency in all things, and all will be well in
this great Universe of ours.

The universe is of our making.
Treat it well."

Channelled by
Lynn Quigley

Red Cloud
19th July 2007

Lynn's Photo Album

A Few Photo's relevant to the words in this book

Wolf
as drawn by Coral Polge

Mr Bennet
by Coral Polge

Jack (left) & Jill - January 1994 - 2 months old

John having a game of tug of war

All pooped out!

"Are you coming to play?"

Togetherness

Our good friend and neighbour - Marjorie

View of Northwich Parish Church Cheshire, as seen on my walks with Jack and Jill

Another view across Northwich Cheshire

John and Jack sharing a moment of
mutual admiration

In the garden at Garth

View from my workroom at Garth

The ex-rectory - my home for 17yrs with
Shep on the left - and Sally

Our first home together - built on the site of a
Roman Fort

School Road. The car in front is "Custard"

Garth Cottage

JACK

A gentle soul, who - in his relatively short life - overcame his wariness of strangers, to grow into a dog who loved people and especially children.

Jacks' healing ways facilitated many strangers to overcome their own wariness of dogs.

Thus - Jack had a large circle of friends - making new friends on practically every walk.

Much loved - and sadly missed.

Jack - 27th November 1993 - 13th November 2003.

JILL

Jill remains well, happy and playful - she was 13½
when these photographs were taken in May 2008

Other Titles
More Friends Than You Know
(Book One of the Trilogy)

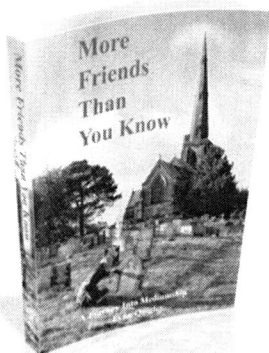

I recognise now, that all through my life, profound and poignant happenings and meetings have usually been marked with the receiving of an object, a keep-sake, the energy of the happening or meeting being held within it, in the same way as a precious crystal holds within it's form, energy, knowledge and it's own unique healing power.

(extract from Chapter Two)

Lying in bed that same night, I was suddenly aware that a man in a dark suit was standing very close to my side of the bed – just standing staring at me – saying nothing.
I dived under the bed covers and said the only thing that I knew to say – "Go to the light – Go to the light". I lay and listened. Hearing nothing – I peeped out from under the covers to see if he had gone.
No – he was still there.

(extract from Chapter Eight)

ISBN 978-0-9534946-3-7

Spirits Fly High
(Book Three of the Trilogy)

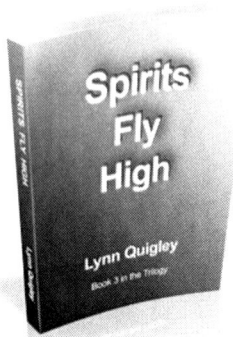

Available Christmas 2008

"What do you feel about this rock?" she asked.
"It feels like a portal – an alien portal" I replied.
"There have been many sightings of Alien spacecraft around here – maybe you will see one." She mused.
Looking down at my feet to avoid her gaze - my thoughts went to Peter, "Maybe." I muttered. "maybe I will."

(extract from Chapter Two)

I arrived at a tiny beach by a river- it was all so familiar to me. I was staggered.
I realised that this was – "our" beach – Silver Clouds' Wolf's and mine.
With tears falling down my face, I sat down.
"Silver Cloud – where are you ? – I'm here at our place."

(extract from Chapter Three)

ISBN 978-0-9534946-5-1

Up to date information about Lynn, her
other publications and contact details can
be found on her website:

www.GoldenCloud.co.uk

Printed in the United Kingdom
by Lightning Source UK Ltd.
133945UK00001BA/1-30/P